STAR WARS

DARTH VADER

DARK HEART OF THE SITH

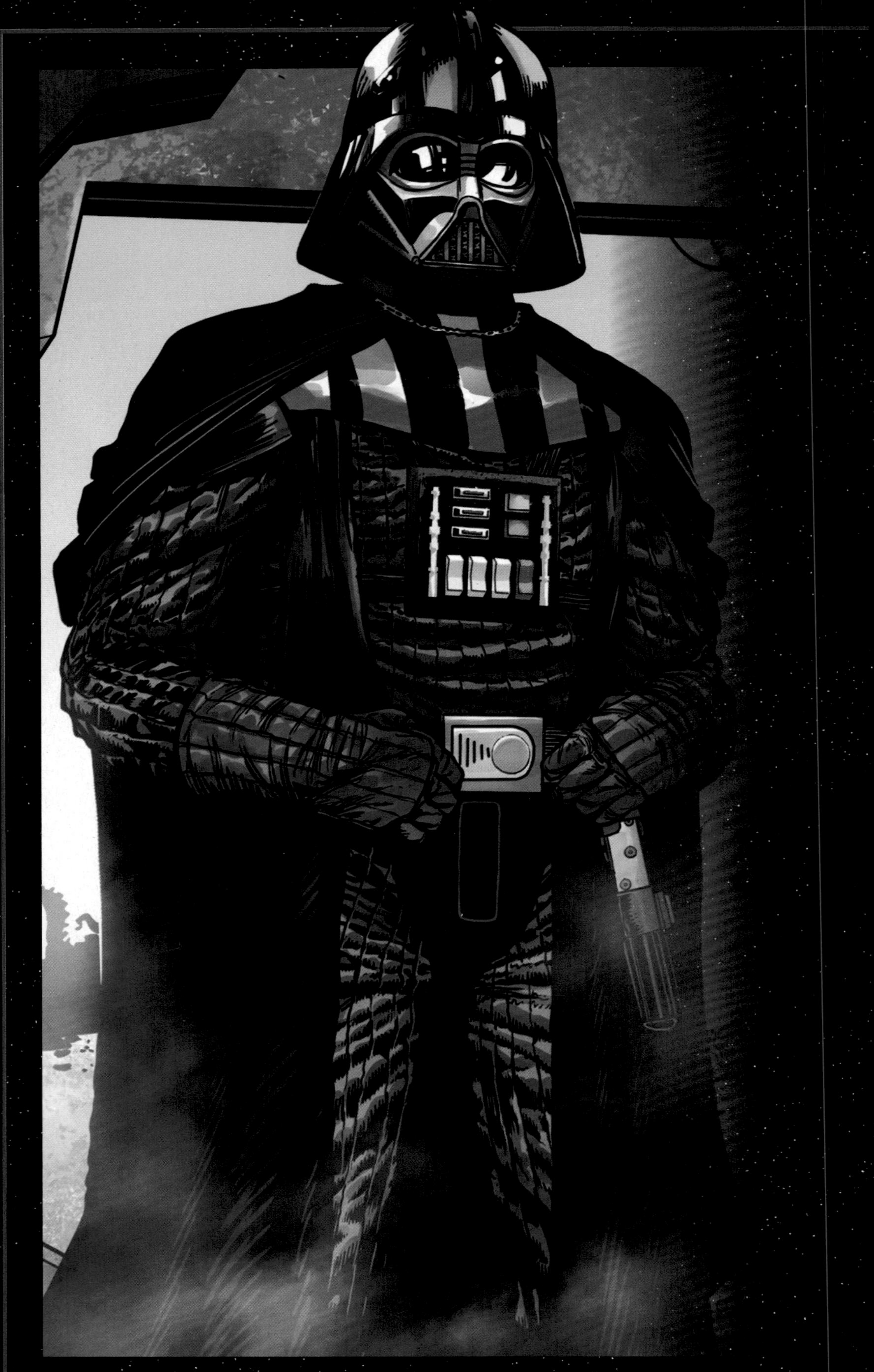

STAR WARS

DARTH VADER

DARK HEART OF THE SITH

Writer
GREG PAK

Artist
RAFFAELE IENCO

Color Artists
NEERAJ MENON

Letterer
VC's JOE CARAMAGNA

Cover Art
INHYUK LEE

Assistant Editor
TOM GRONEMAN

Editor
MARK PANICCIA

Collection Editor	JENNIFER GRÜNWALD
Assistant Editor	DANIEL KIRCHHOFFER
Assistant Managing Editor	MAIA LOY
Assistant Managing Editor	LISA MONTALBANO
VP Production & Special Projects	JEFF YOUNGQUIST
Book Designer	ADAM DEL RE
SVP Print, Sales & Marketing	DAVID GABRIEL
Editor in Chief	C.B. CEBULSKI

For Lucasfilm:

Senior Editor	ROBERT SIMPSON
Creative Director	MICHAEL SIGLAIN
Art Director	TROY ALDERS
Lucasfilm Story Group	MATT MARTIN
	PABLO HIDALGO
	EMILY SHKOUKANI
Lucasfilm Art Department	PHIL SZOSTAK

STAR WARS: DARTH VADER BY GREG PAK VOL. 1 — DARK HEART OF THE SITH. Contains material originally published in magazine form as STAR WARS: DARTH VADER (2020) #1-5. Third printing 2021. ISBN 978-1-302-92081-4. Published by MARVEL WORLDWIDE, INC., a subsidiary of MARVEL ENTERTAINMENT, LLC. OFFICE OF PUBLICATION: 1290 Avenue of the Americas, New York, NY 10104.

Printed in Canada. KEVIN FEIGE, Chief Creative Officer; DAN BUCKLEY, President, Marvel Entertainment; JOE QUESADA, EVP & Creative Director; DAVID BOGART, Associate Publisher & SVP of Talent Affairs; TOM BREVOORT, VP, Executive Editor; NICK LOWE, Executive Editor, VP of Content, Digital Publishing; DAVID GABRIEL, VP of Print & Digital Publishing; JEFF YOUNGQUIST, VP of Production & Special Projects; ALEX MORALES, Director of Publishing Operations; DAN EDINGTON, Managing Editor; RICKEY PURDIN, Director of Talent Relations; JENNIFER GRÜNWALD, Senior Editor, Special Projects; SUSAN CRESPI, Production Manager; STAN LEE, Chairman Emeritus. For information regarding advertising in Marvel Comics or on Marvel.com, please contact Vit DeBellis, Custom Solutions & Integrated Advertising Manager, at vdebellis@marvel.com. For Marvel subscription inquiries, please call 888-511-5480. **Manufactured between 7/23/2021 and 8/24/2021 by SOLISCO PRINTERS, SCOTT, QC, CANADA.**

10 9 8 7 6 5 4 3

Lee InHyuk

1

A long time ago in a galaxy far, far away....

STAR

DARTH

WARS

VADER

DARK HEART OF THE SITH

Darth Vader failed to turn Luke Skywalker to the dark side. Luke escaped but now knows the truth.

He is Darth Vader's son.

For the first time in many years, Darth Vader's path is uncertain....

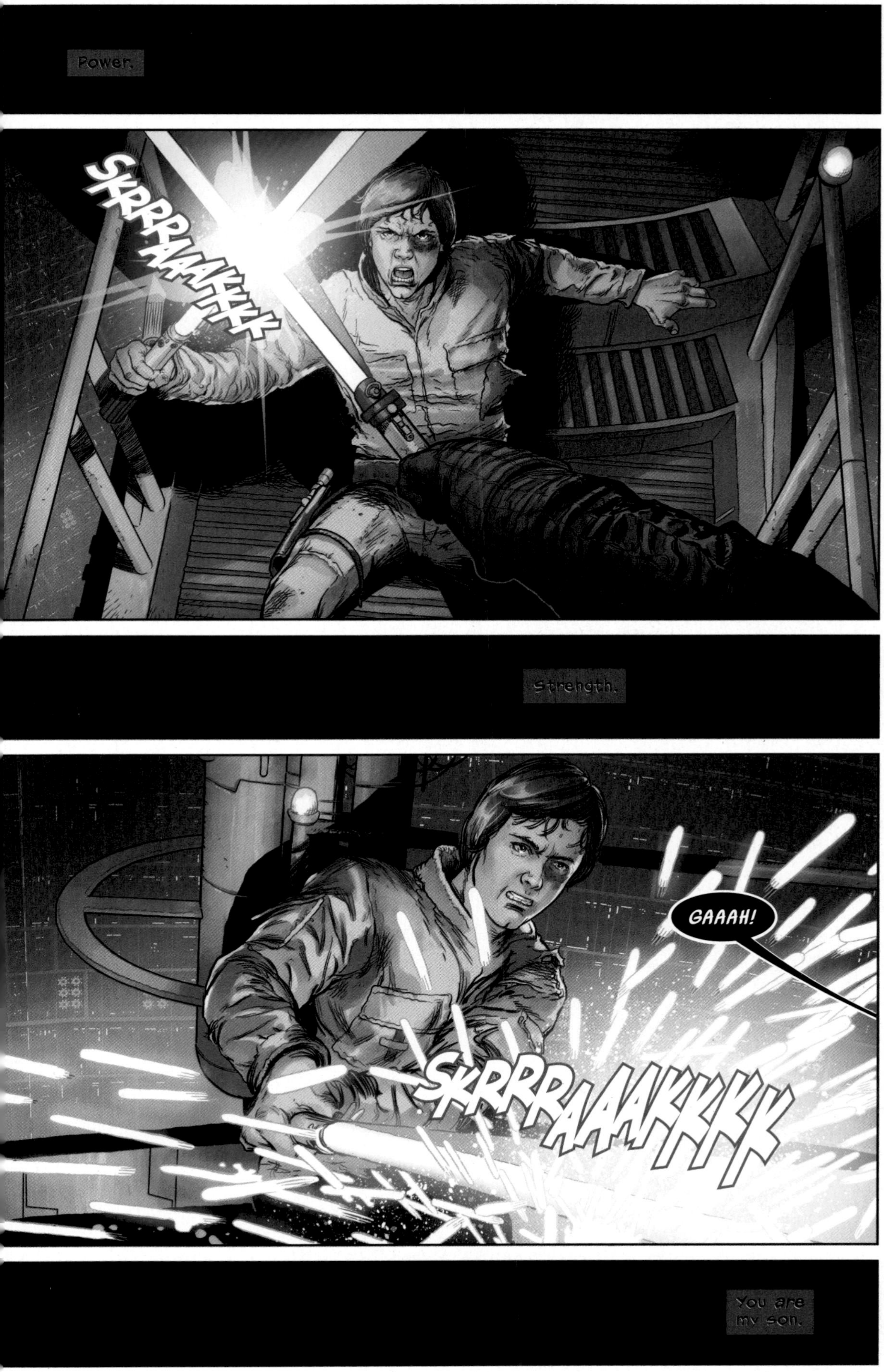
Power.
SKRRAAAKKK
Strength.
GAAAH!
SKRRRAAAKKKK
You are my son.

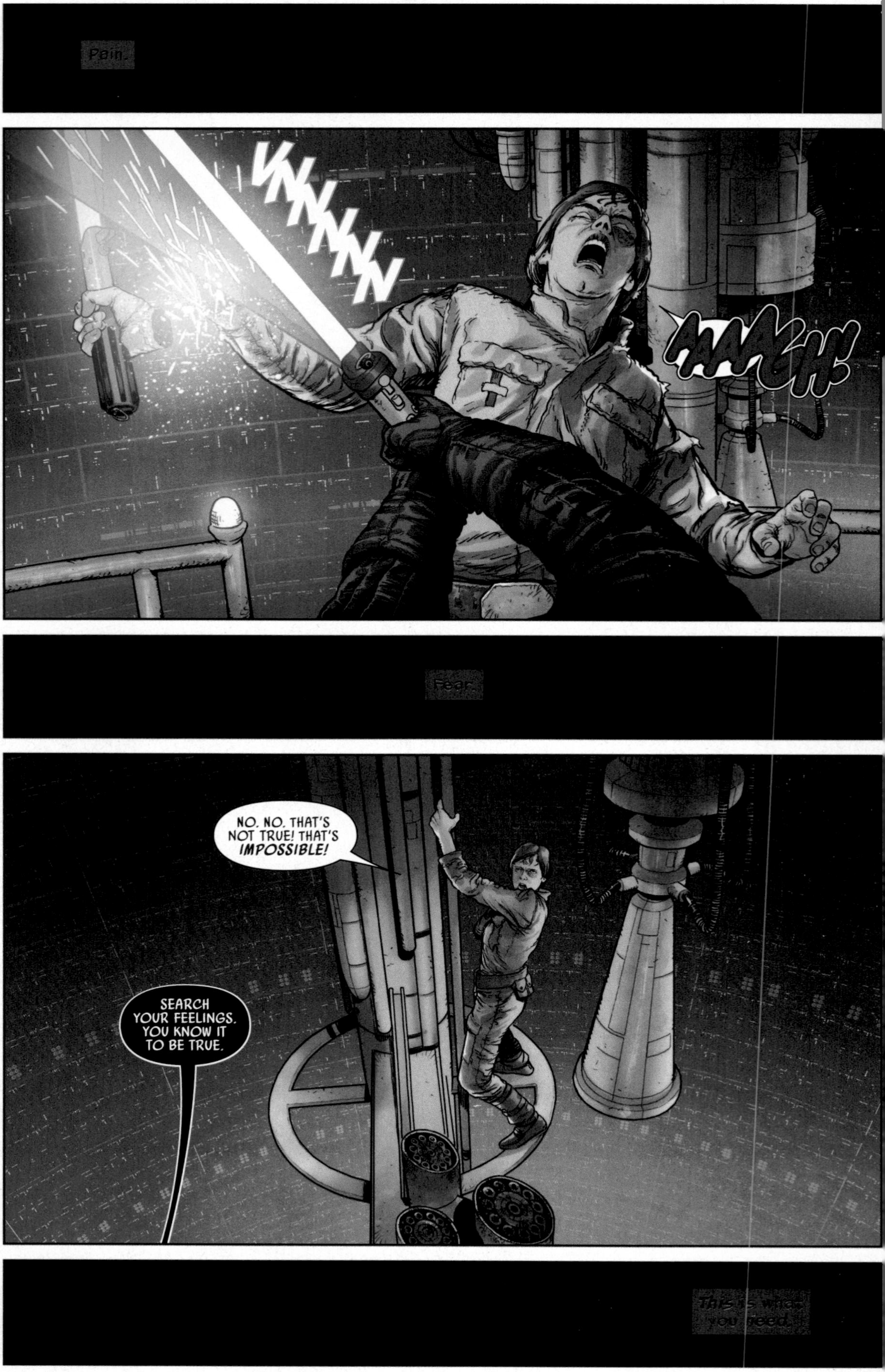
Pain.
VNNNNN
AAAAGH!
Fear.
NO. NO. THAT'S NOT TRUE! THAT'S IMPOSSIBLE!
SEARCH YOUR FEELINGS. YOU KNOW IT TO BE TRUE.
This is what you need.

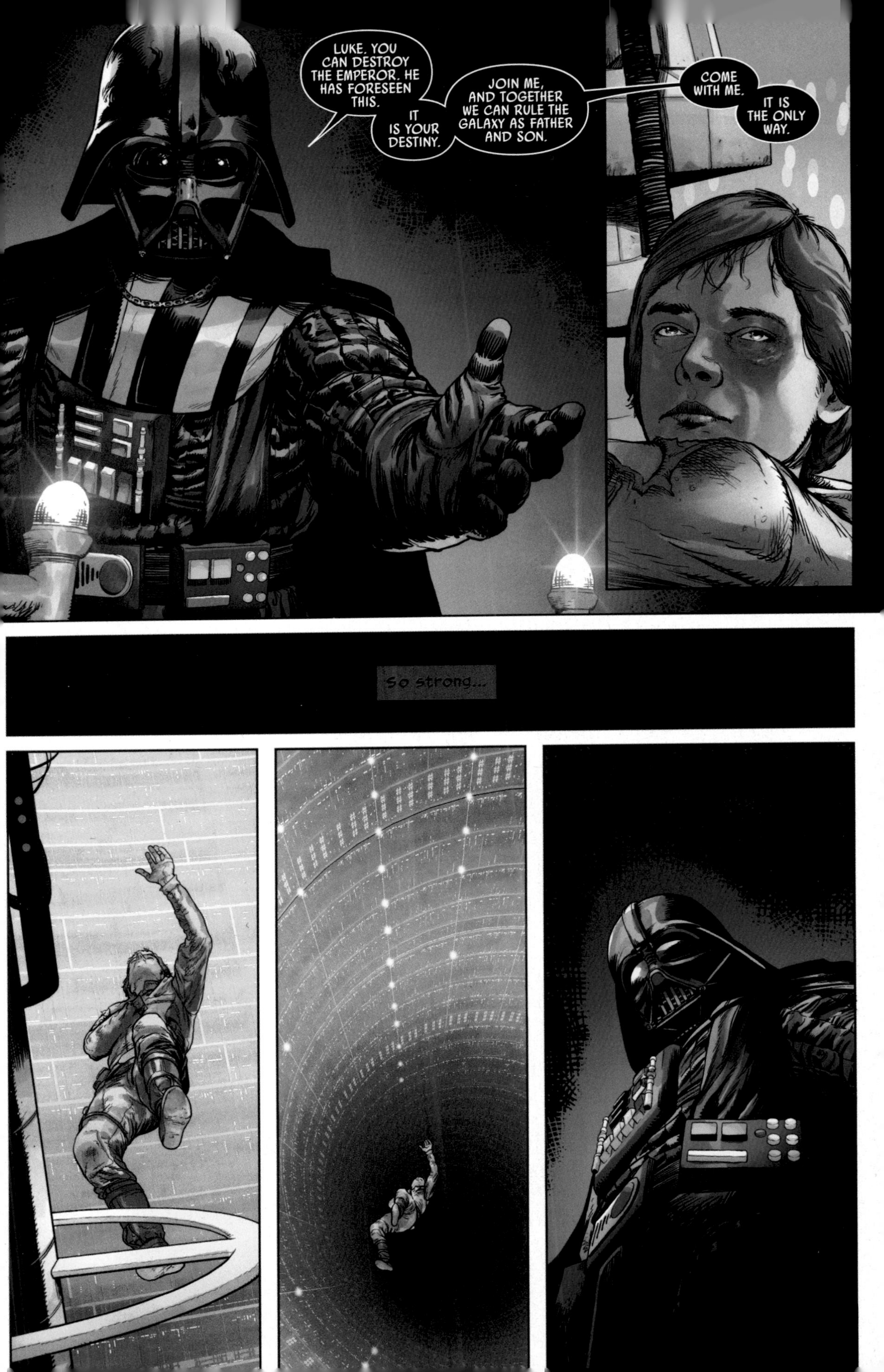
LUKE. YOU CAN DESTROY THE EMPEROR. HE HAS FORESEEN THIS.
IT IS YOUR DESTINY.
JOIN ME, AND TOGETHER WE CAN RULE THE GALAXY AS FATHER AND SON.
COME WITH ME.
IT IS THE ONLY WAY.
So strong...

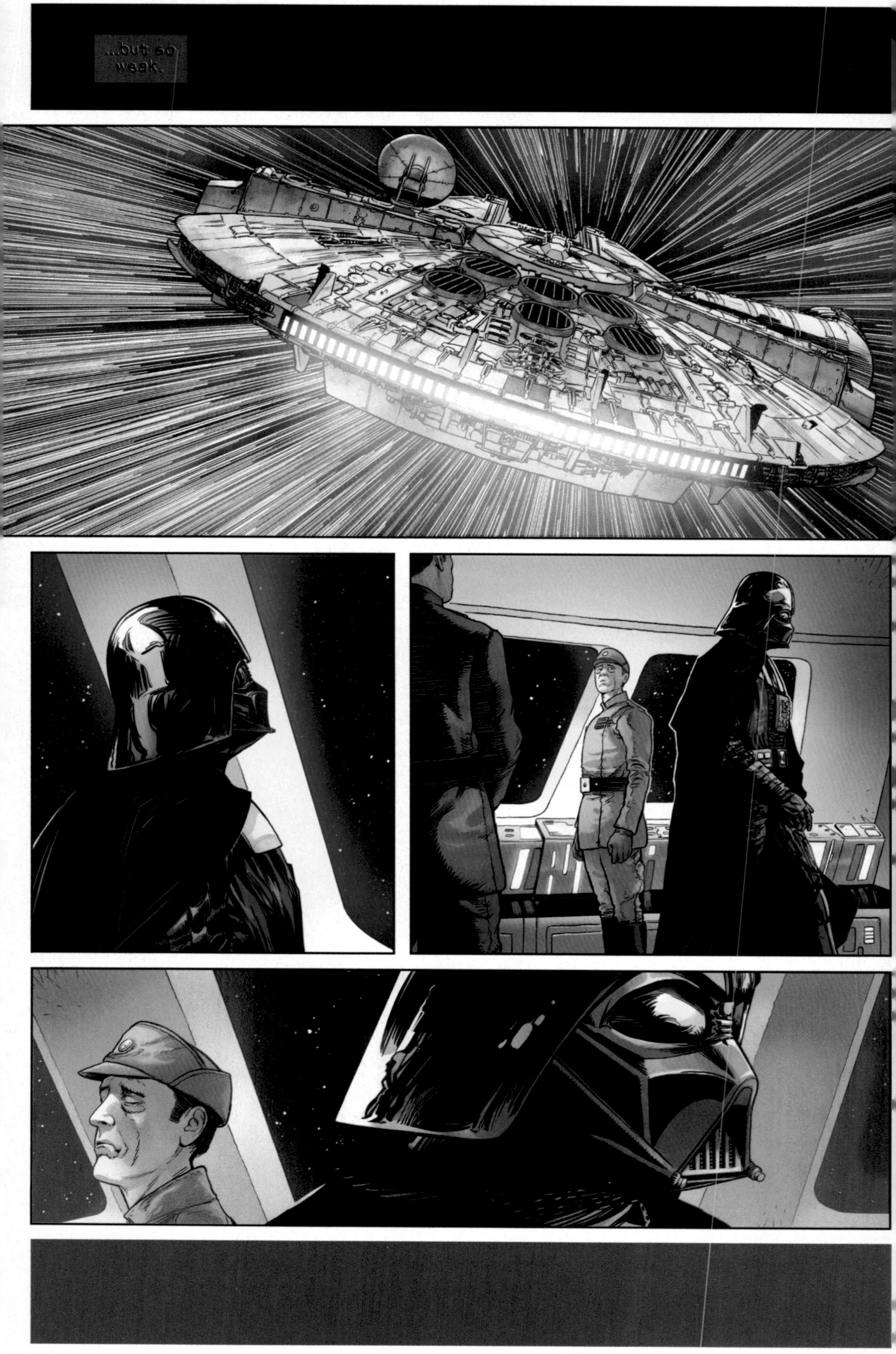
...but so weak.

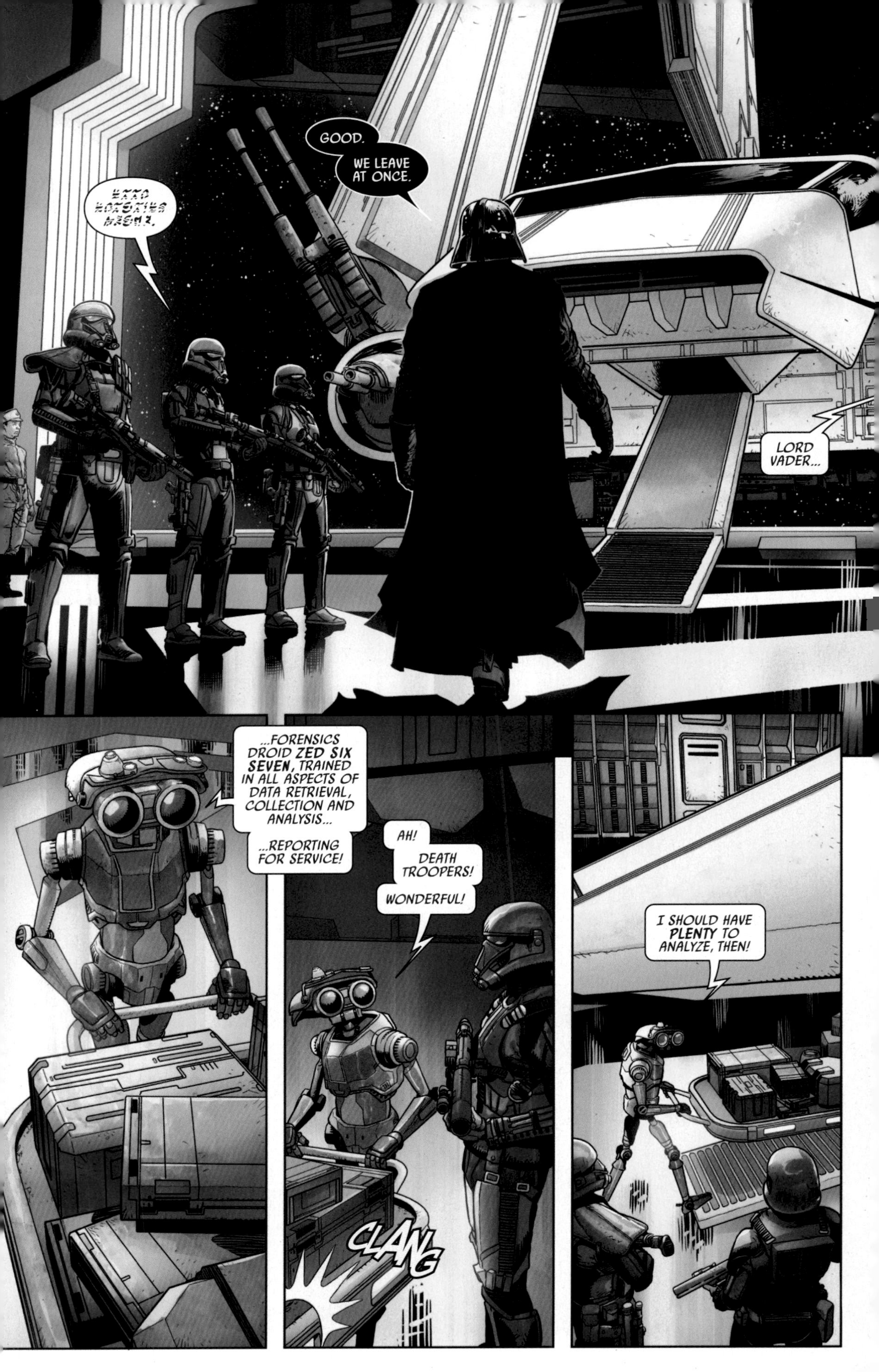
GOOD.
WE LEAVE AT ONCE.
LORD VADER...
...FORENSICS DROID ZED SIX SEVEN, TRAINED IN ALL ASPECTS OF DATA RETRIEVAL, COLLECTION AND ANALYSIS...
...REPORTING FOR SERVICE!
AH!
DEATH TROOPERS!
WONDERFUL!
CLANG
I SHOULD HAVE PLENTY TO ANALYZE, THEN!

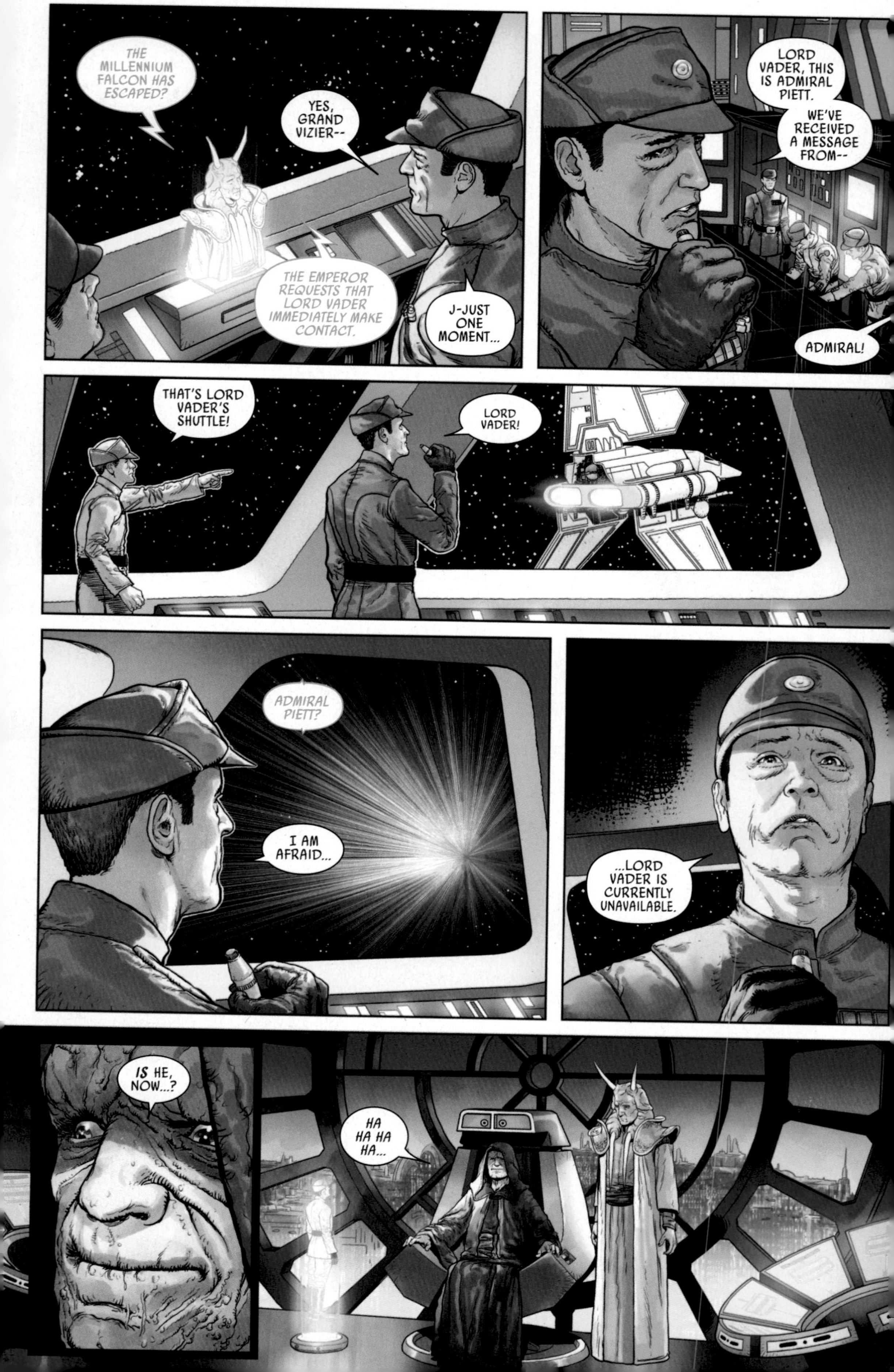
THE MILLENNIUM FALCON HAS ESCAPED?
YES, GRAND VIZIER--
THE EMPEROR REQUESTS THAT LORD VADER IMMEDIATELY MAKE CONTACT.
J-JUST ONE MOMENT...
LORD VADER, THIS IS ADMIRAL PIETT.
WE'VE RECEIVED A MESSAGE FROM--
ADMIRAL!
THAT'S LORD VADER'S SHUTTLE!
LORD VADER!
ADMIRAL PIETT?
I AM AFRAID...
...LORD VADER IS CURRENTLY UNAVAILABLE.
IS HE, NOW...?
HA HA HA HA...

LORD VADER! I WAS JUST ABOUT TO SEEK YOU OUT.

IF YOU CAN SHARE THE PARAMETERS OF OUR **MISSION**, I CAN START PREPARING ANY--

POP

AH!

WHA-- WHAT ARE YOU--

AAAH!

ADJUSTING MY MOTIVATOR?

WITH ALL DUE RESPECT, ONLY A TRAINED TECHNICIAN SHOULD--

IF YOU EVER REVEAL WHAT YOU LEARN ON THIS MISSION...

...YOU WILL **SELF-DESTRUCT.**

OH!

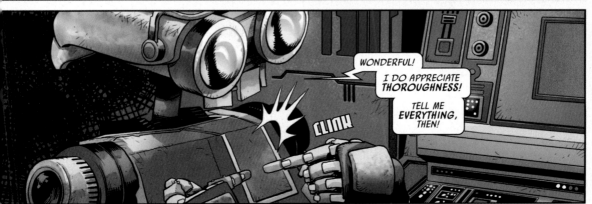

WONDERFUL! I DO APPRECIATE **THOROUGHNESS!**

TELL ME **EVERYTHING,** THEN!

CLINK

SKYWALKER.

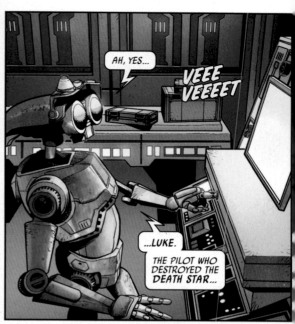

AH, YES...

VEEE VEEEET

...LUKE.
THE PILOT WHO DESTROYED THE DEATH STAR...

"...HE HAS DISAPPEARED WITHOUT A TRACE, I'M AFRAID."

I WILL FIND HIM AGAIN WHEN THE TIME IS RIGHT.

FOR NOW...

...WE WILL TRACK DOWN EVERYONE WHO HID THE BOY FROM ME...

...EVERYONE WHO MADE HIM WEAK...

...AND DESTROY THEM.

PERFECT.

THEN I IMAGINE THE BEST PLACE TO START...

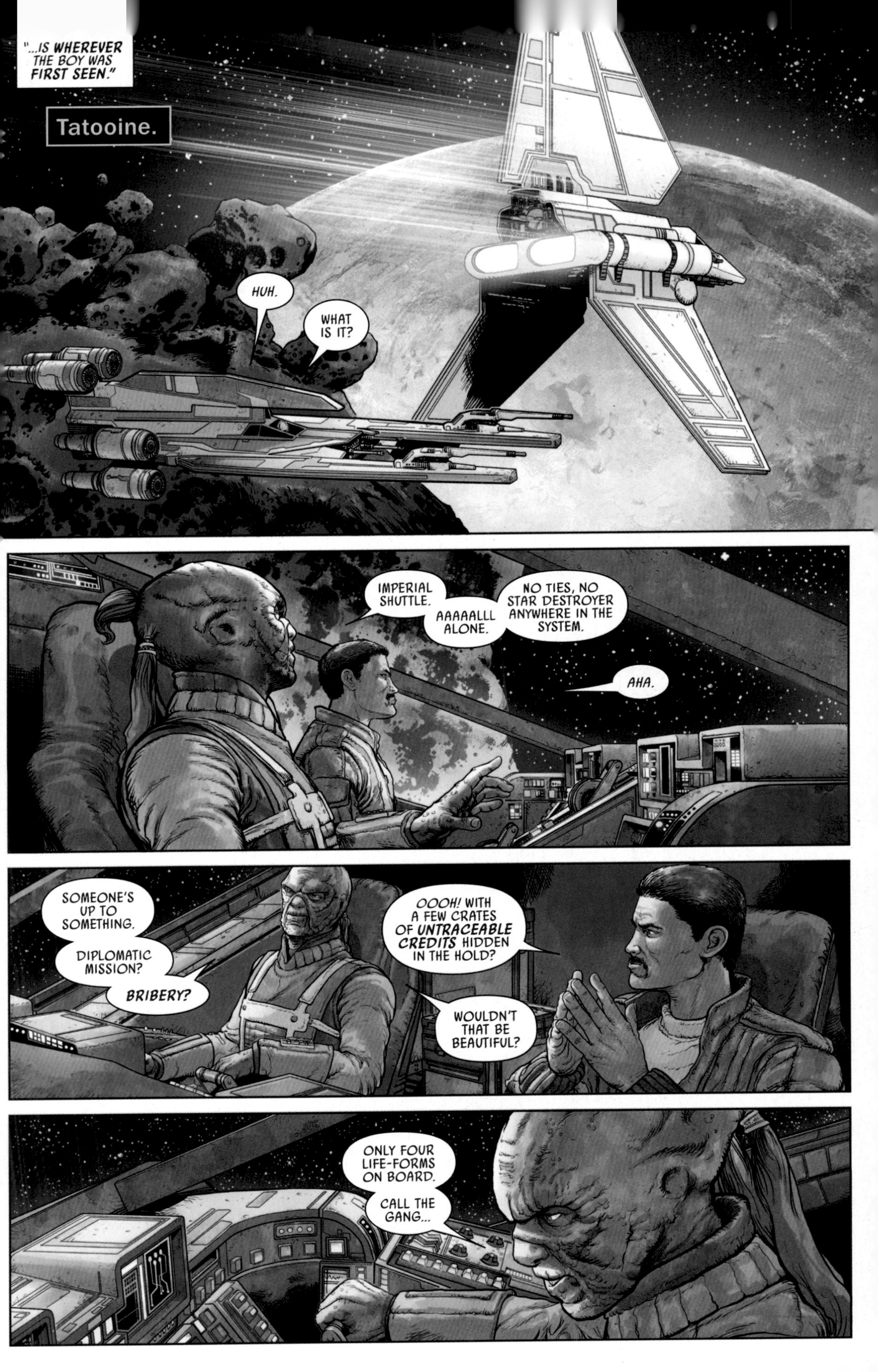
"...IS WHEREVER THE BOY WAS FIRST SEEN."
Tatooine.
HUH.
WHAT IS IT?
IMPERIAL SHUTTLE.
AAAAALLL ALONE.
NO TIES, NO STAR DESTROYER ANYWHERE IN THE SYSTEM.
AHA.
SOMEONE'S UP TO SOMETHING.
DIPLOMATIC MISSION?
BRIBERY?
OOOH! WITH A FEW CRATES OF UNTRACEABLE CREDITS HIDDEN IN THE HOLD?
WOULDN'T THAT BE BEAUTIFUL?
ONLY FOUR LIFE-FORMS ON BOARD.
CALL THE GANG...

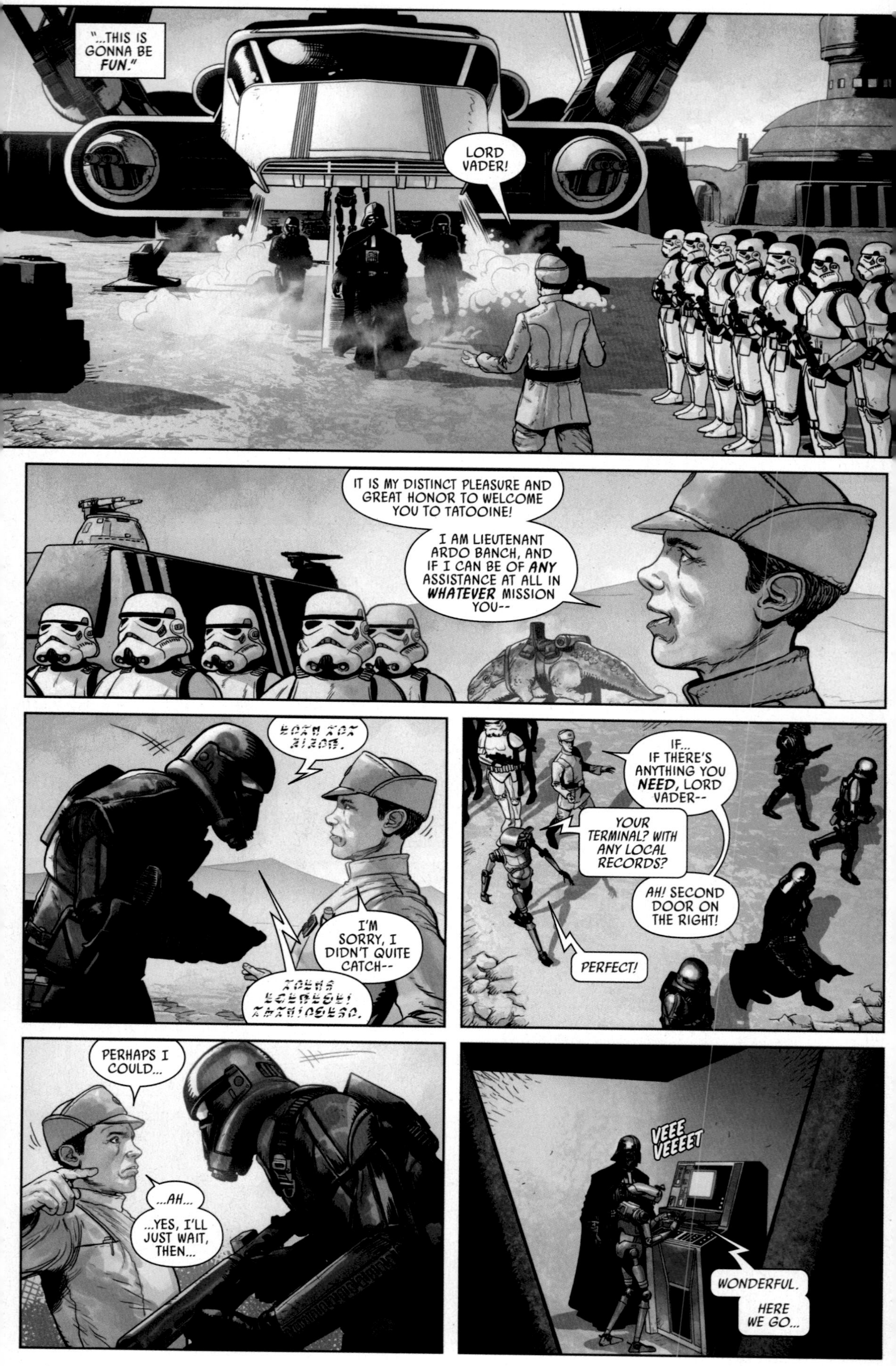

"...THIS IS GONNA BE *FUN.*"
LORD VADER!
IT IS MY DISTINCT PLEASURE AND GREAT HONOR TO WELCOME YOU TO TATOOINE!
I AM LIEUTENANT ARDO BANCH, AND IF I CAN BE OF *ANY* ASSISTANCE AT ALL IN *WHATEVER* MISSION YOU--
I'M SORRY, I DIDN'T QUITE CATCH--
IF... IF THERE'S ANYTHING YOU *NEED*, LORD VADER--
YOUR TERMINAL? WITH ANY LOCAL RECORDS?
AH! SECOND DOOR ON THE RIGHT!
PERFECT!
PERHAPS I COULD...
...AH...
...YES, I'LL JUST WAIT, THEN...
VEEE VEEEET
WONDERFUL.
HERE WE GO...

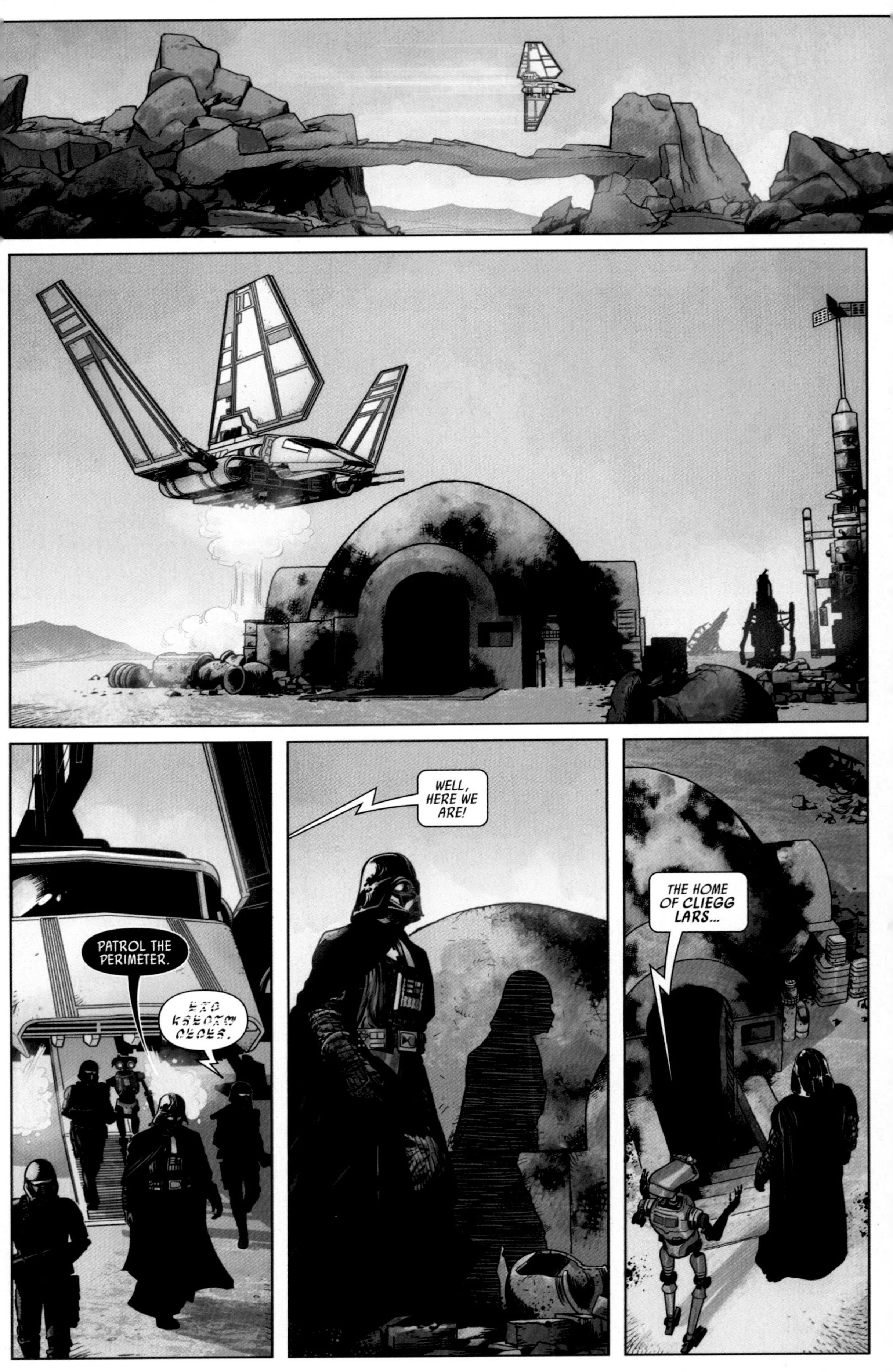
PATROL THE PERIMETER.
WELL, HERE WE ARE!
THE HOME OF CLIEGG LARS...

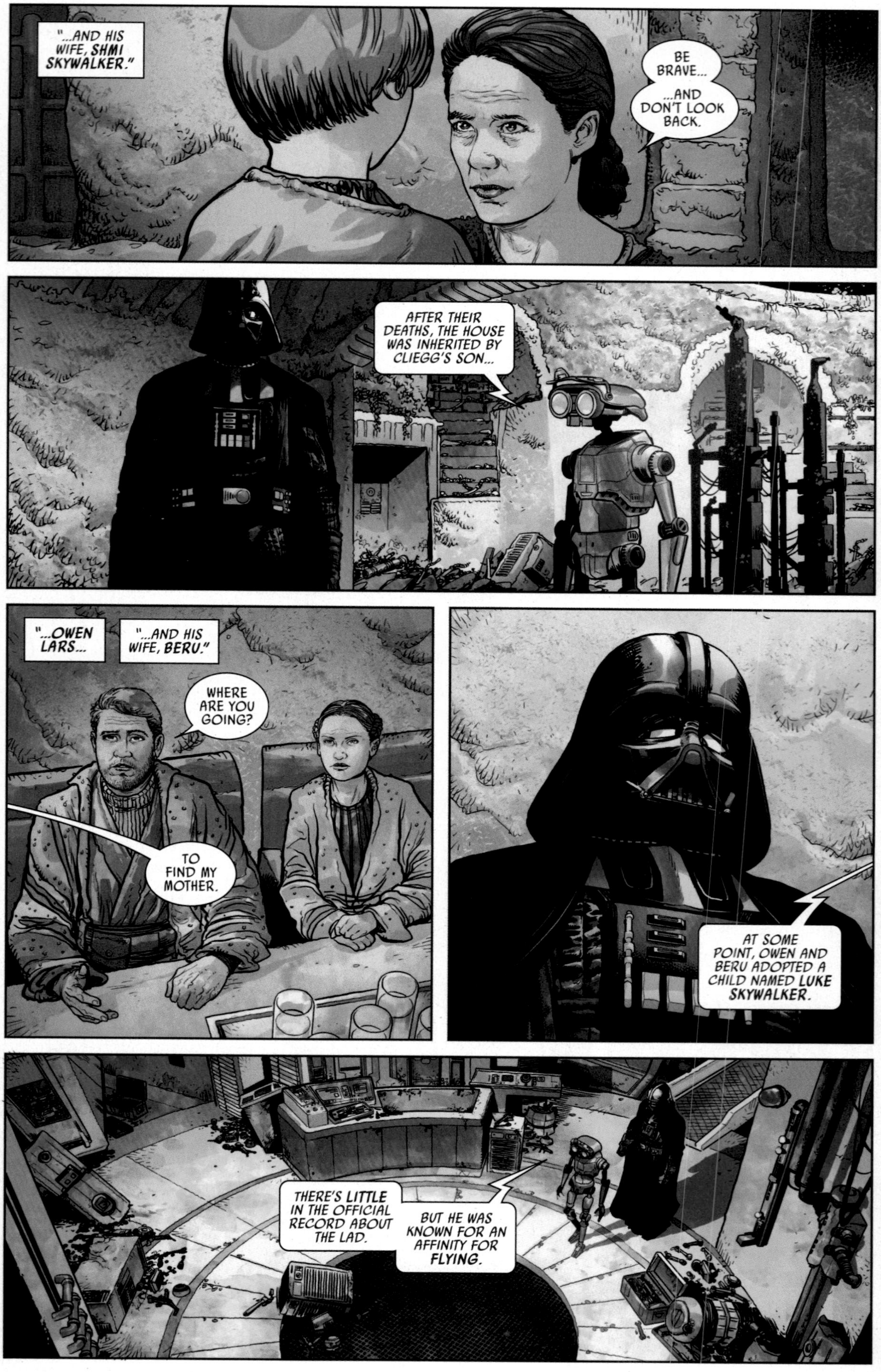
"...AND HIS WIFE, SHMI SKYWALKER."
BE BRAVE...
...AND DON'T LOOK BACK.
AFTER THEIR DEATHS, THE HOUSE WAS INHERITED BY CLIEGG'S SON...
"...OWEN LARS...
"...AND HIS WIFE, BERU."
WHERE ARE YOU GOING?
TO FIND MY MOTHER.
AT SOME POINT, OWEN AND BERU ADOPTED A CHILD NAMED LUKE SKYWALKER.
THERE'S LITTLE IN THE OFFICIAL RECORD ABOUT THE LAD.
BUT HE WAS KNOWN FOR AN AFFINITY FOR FLYING.

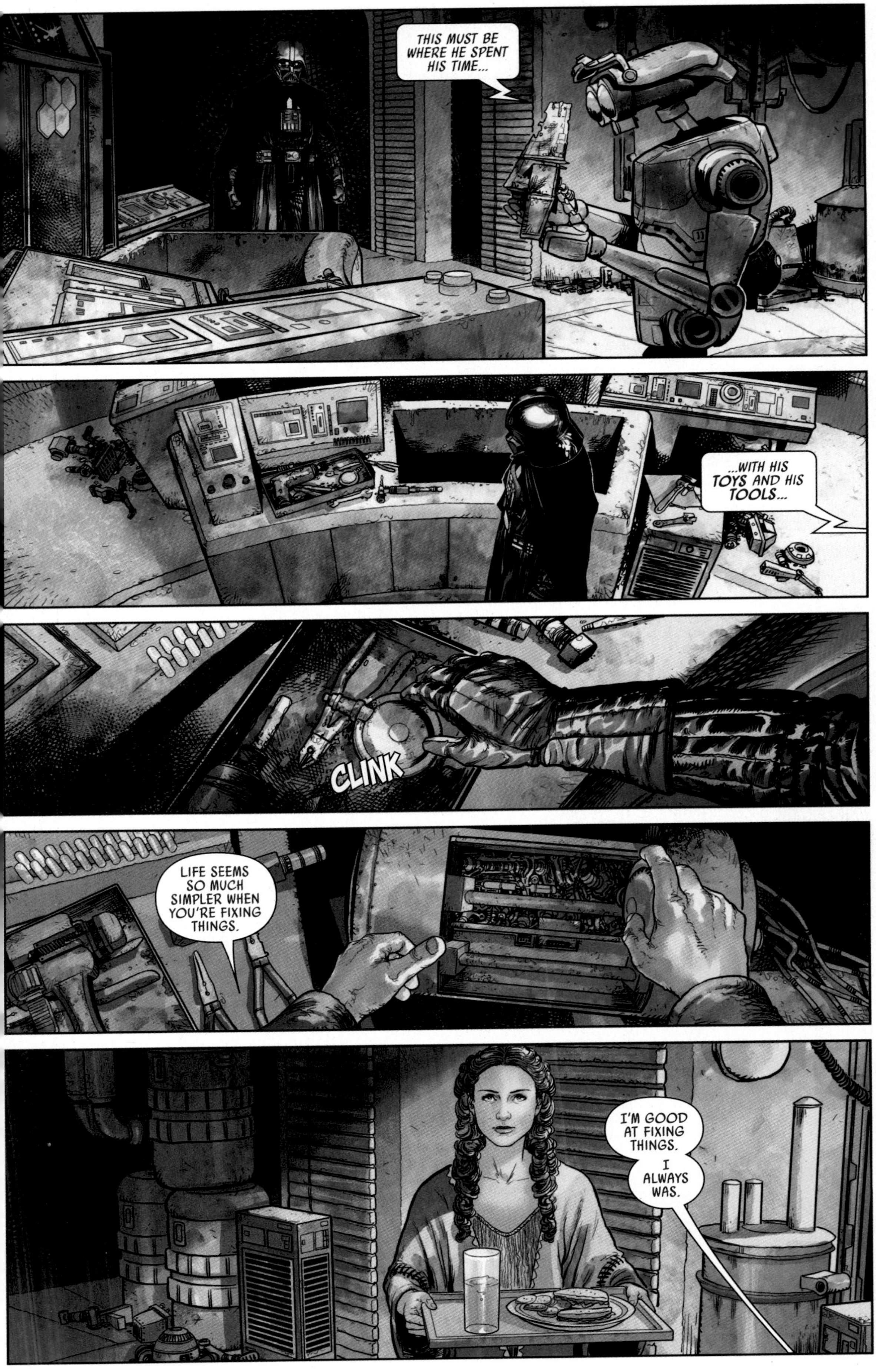

THIS MUST BE WHERE HE SPENT HIS TIME...
...WITH HIS TOYS AND HIS TOOLS...
CLINK
LIFE SEEMS SO MUCH SIMPLER WHEN YOU'RE FIXING THINGS.
I'M GOOD AT FIXING THINGS.
I ALWAYS WAS.

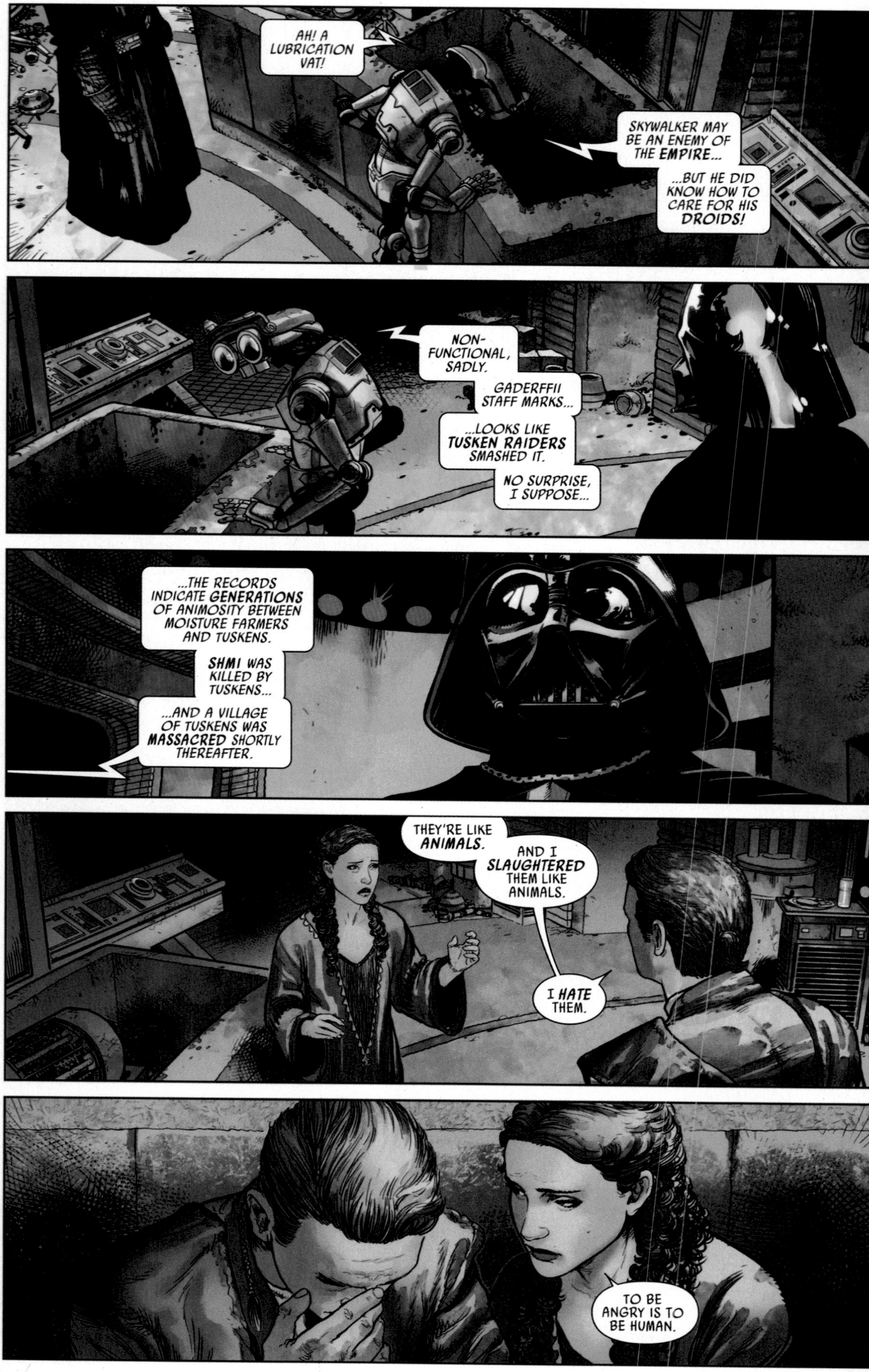
AH! A LUBRICATION VAT!
SKYWALKER MAY BE AN ENEMY OF THE EMPIRE...
...BUT HE DID KNOW HOW TO CARE FOR HIS DROIDS!
NON-FUNCTIONAL, SADLY.
GADERFFII STAFF MARKS...
...LOOKS LIKE TUSKEN RAIDERS SMASHED IT.
NO SURPRISE, I SUPPOSE...
...THE RECORDS INDICATE GENERATIONS OF ANIMOSITY BETWEEN MOISTURE FARMERS AND TUSKENS.
SHMI WAS KILLED BY TUSKENS...
...AND A VILLAGE OF TUSKENS WAS MASSACRED SHORTLY THEREAFTER.
THEY'RE LIKE ANIMALS.
AND I SLAUGHTERED THEM LIKE ANIMALS.
I HATE THEM.
TO BE ANGRY IS TO BE HUMAN.

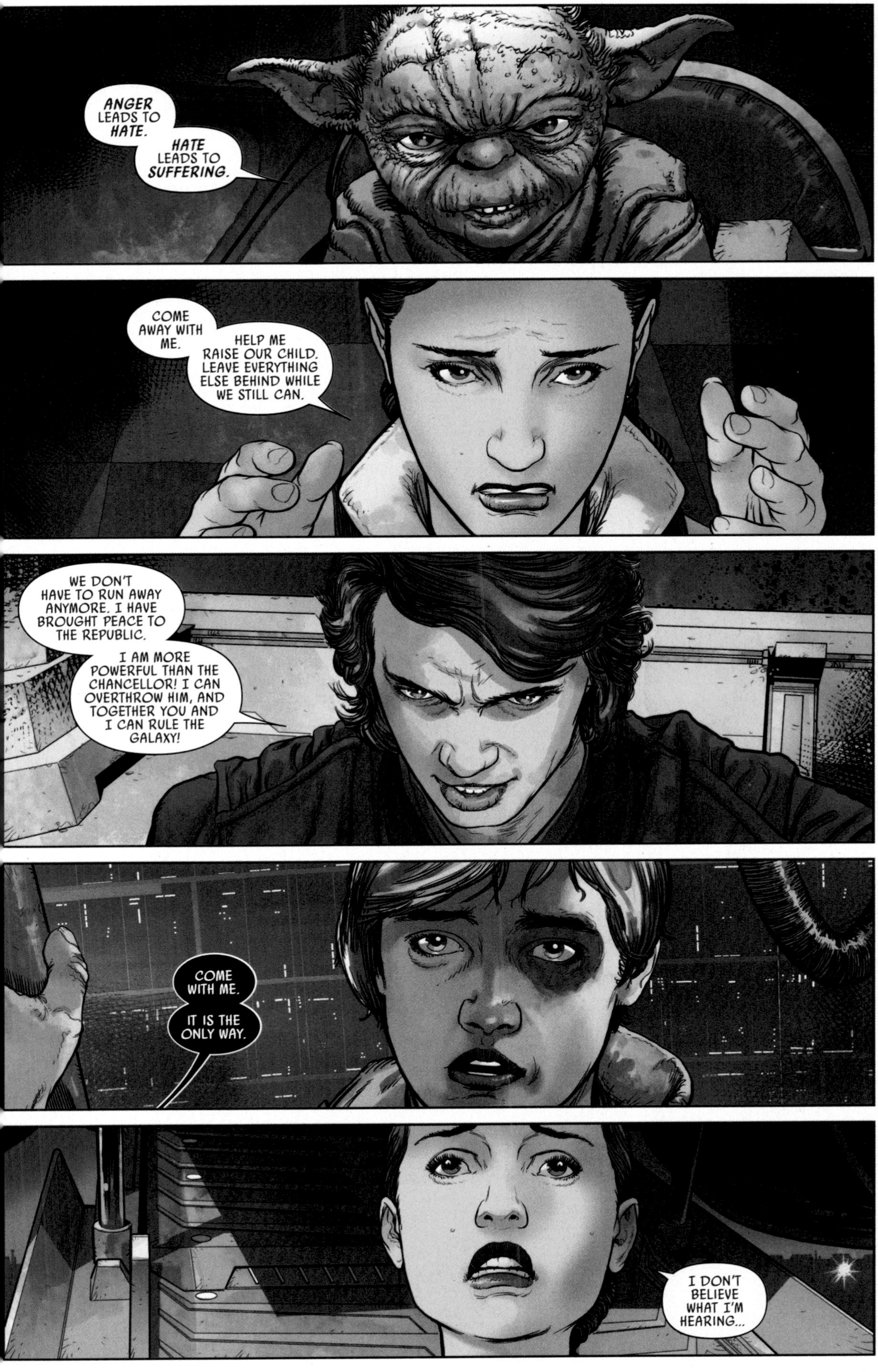
ANGER LEADS TO HATE.
HATE LEADS TO SUFFERING.
COME AWAY WITH ME.
HELP ME RAISE OUR CHILD. LEAVE EVERYTHING ELSE BEHIND WHILE WE STILL CAN.
WE DON'T HAVE TO RUN AWAY ANYMORE. I HAVE BROUGHT PEACE TO THE REPUBLIC.
I AM MORE POWERFUL THAN THE CHANCELLOR! I CAN OVERTHROW HIM, AND TOGETHER YOU AND I CAN RULE THE GALAXY!
COME WITH ME.
IT IS THE ONLY WAY.
I DON'T BELIEVE WHAT I'M HEARING...

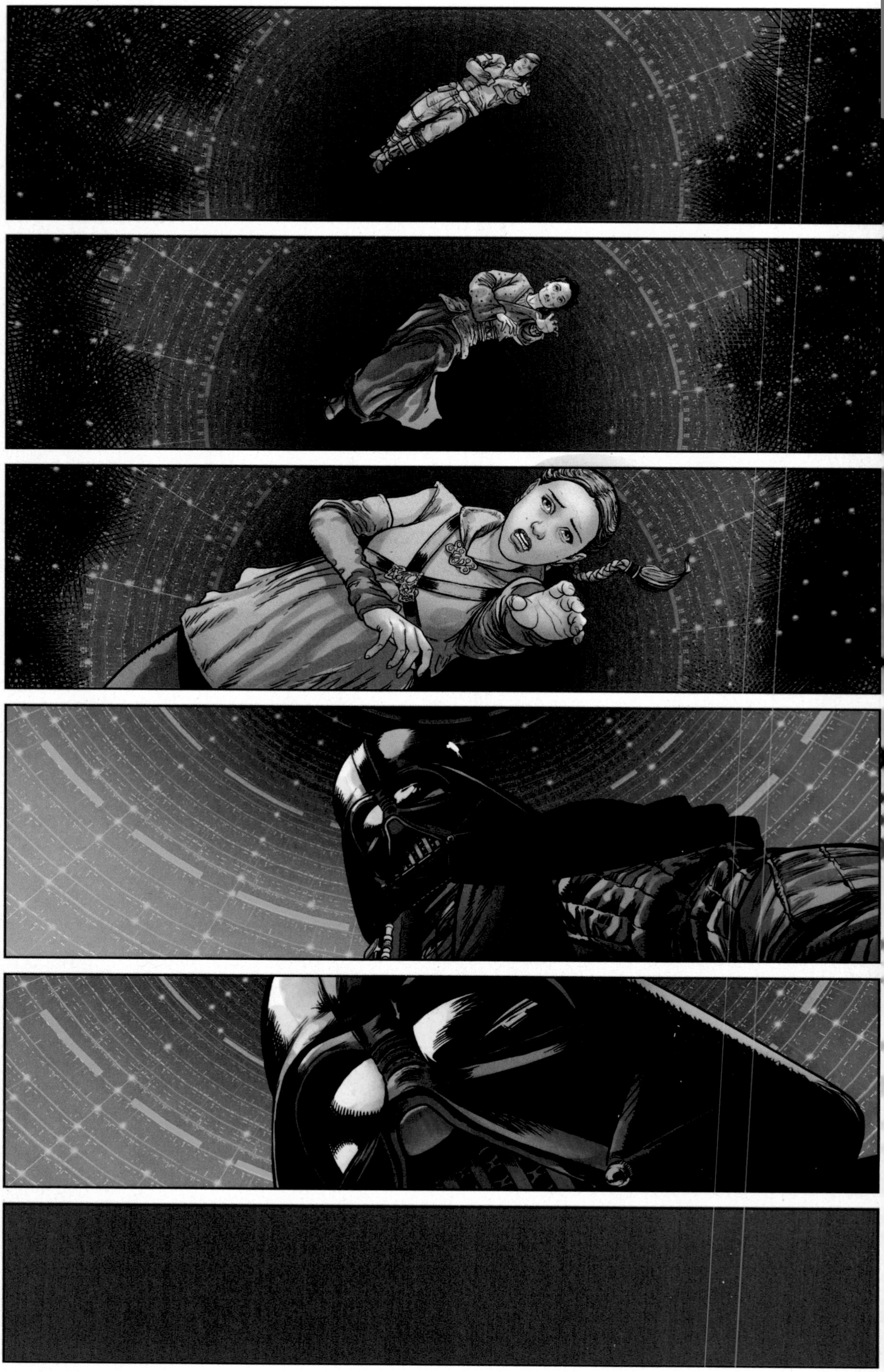

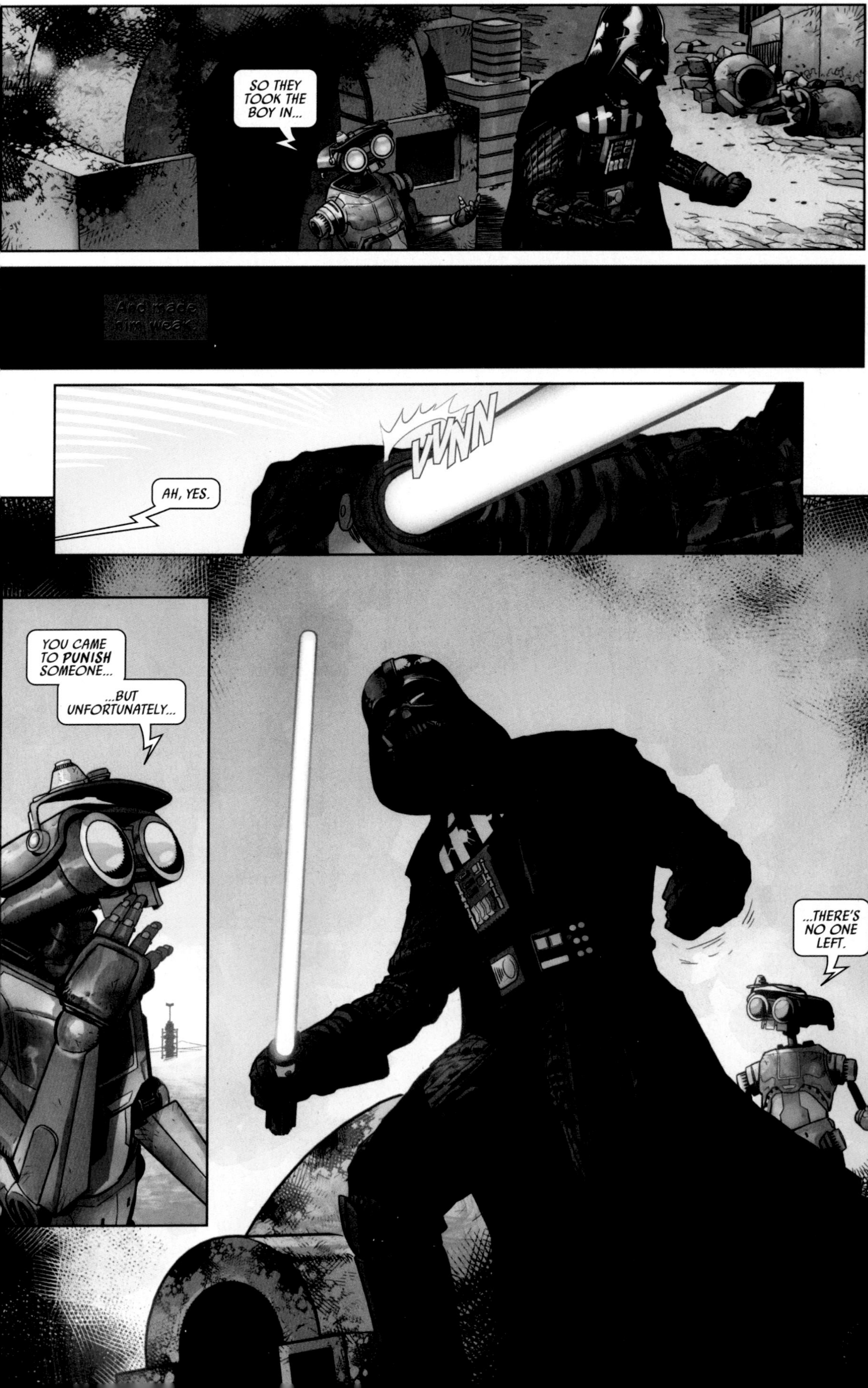
SO THEY TOOK THE BOY IN...
[redacted]
VVNN
AH, YES.
YOU CAME TO PUNISH SOMEONE...
...BUT UNFORTUNATELY...
...THERE'S NO ONE LEFT.

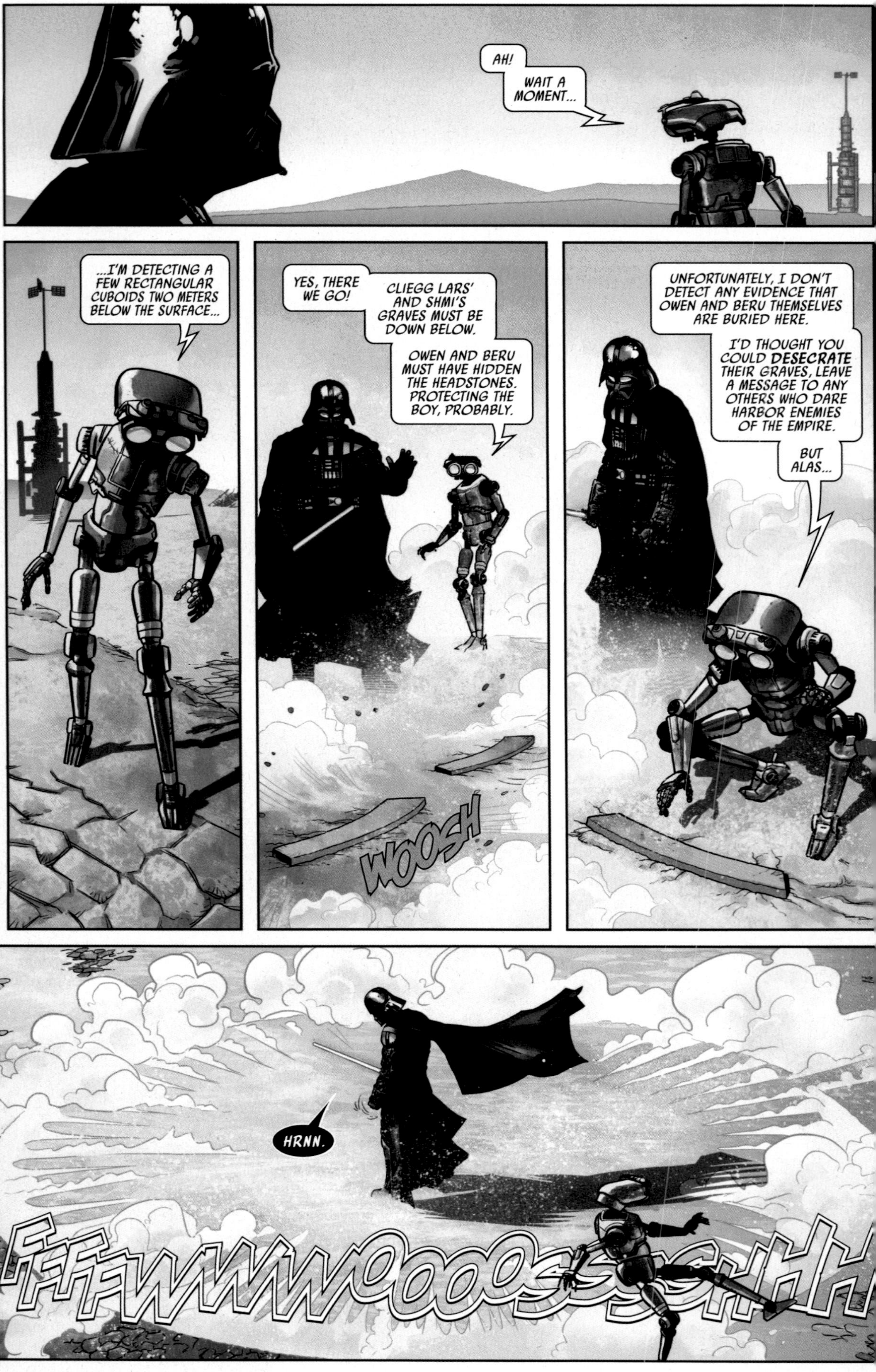
AH!
WAIT A MOMENT...
...I'M DETECTING A FEW RECTANGULAR CUBOIDS TWO METERS BELOW THE SURFACE...
YES, THERE WE GO!
CLIEGG LARS' AND SHMI'S GRAVES MUST BE DOWN BELOW.
OWEN AND BERU MUST HAVE HIDDEN THE HEADSTONES. PROTECTING THE BOY, PROBABLY.
WOOSH
UNFORTUNATELY, I DON'T DETECT ANY EVIDENCE THAT OWEN AND BERU THEMSELVES ARE BURIED HERE.
I'D THOUGHT YOU COULD DESECRATE THEIR GRAVES, LEAVE A MESSAGE TO ANY OTHERS WHO DARE HARBOR ENEMIES OF THE EMPIRE.
BUT ALAS...
HRNN.
FFFWWWWOOOOSSSCHHH

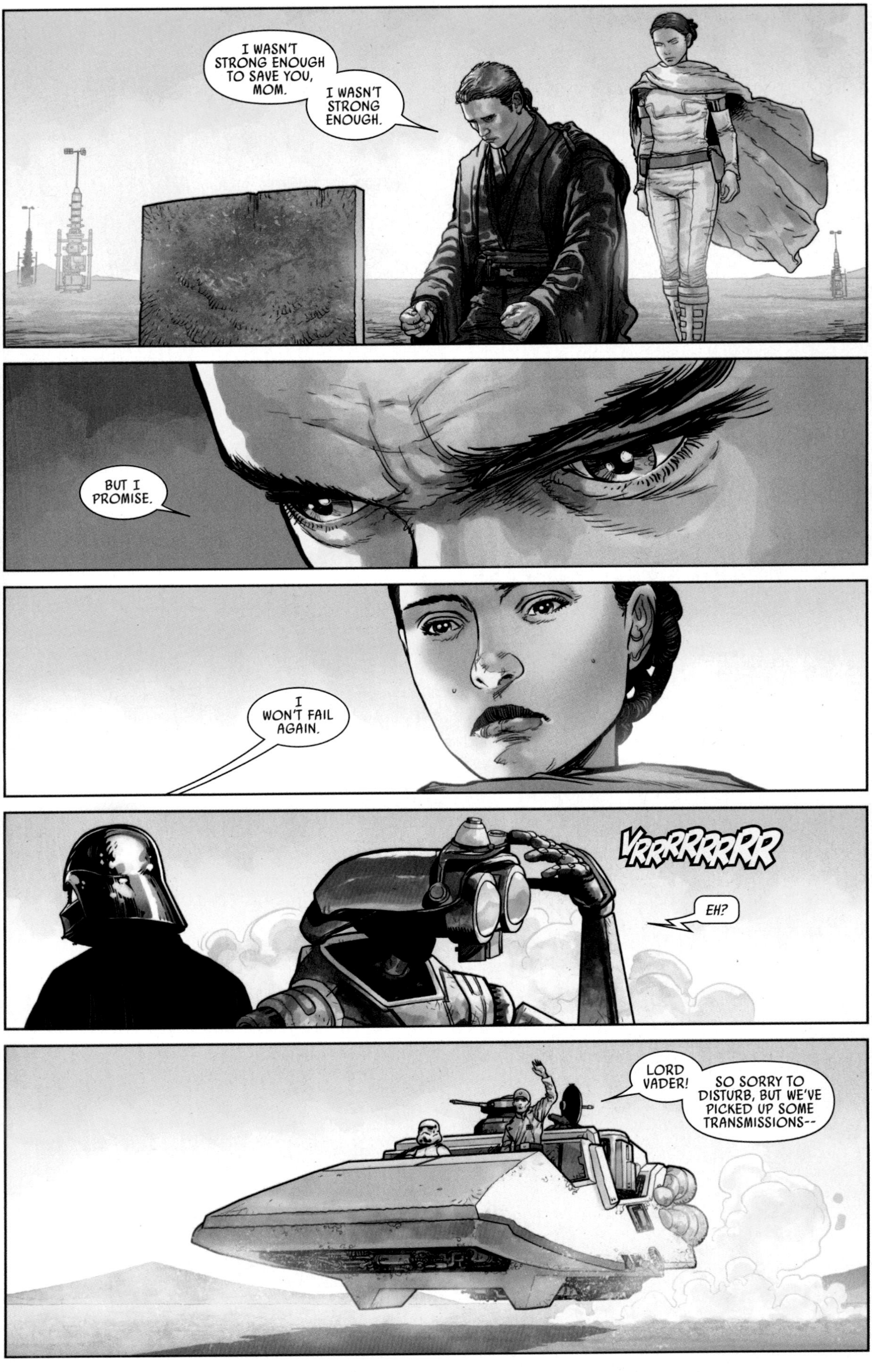
I WASN'T STRONG ENOUGH TO SAVE YOU, MOM.
I WASN'T STRONG ENOUGH.
BUT I PROMISE.
I WON'T FAIL AGAIN.
VRRRRRRRR
EH?
LORD VADER!
SO SORRY TO DISTURB, BUT WE'VE PICKED UP SOME TRANSMISSIONS--

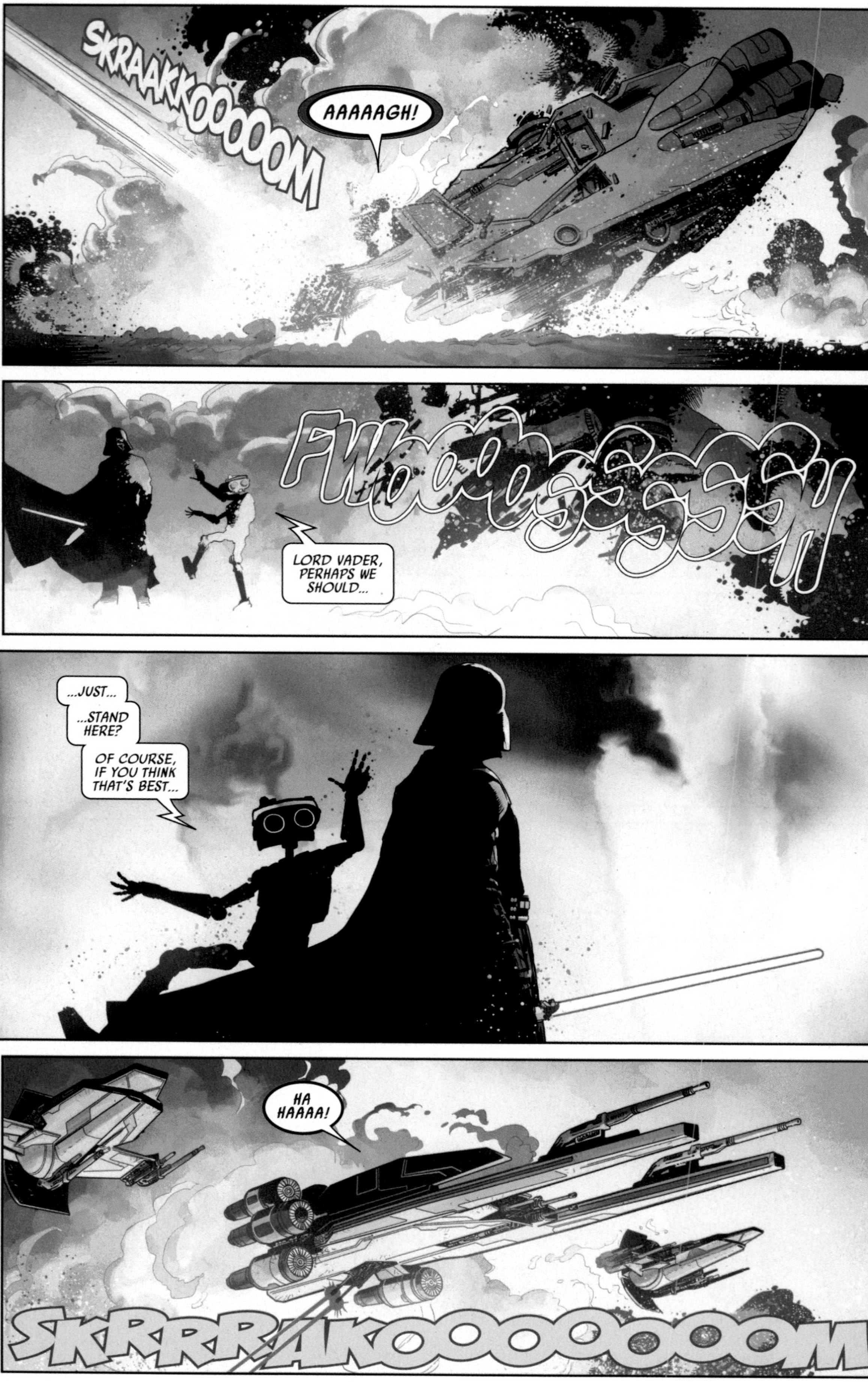
SKRAAKKOOOOOM
AAAAAGH!
FWOOOOSSSSSH
LORD VADER, PERHAPS WE SHOULD...
...JUST...
...STAND HERE?
OF COURSE, IF YOU THINK THAT'S BEST...
HA HAAAA!
SKRRRAKOOOOOOOM

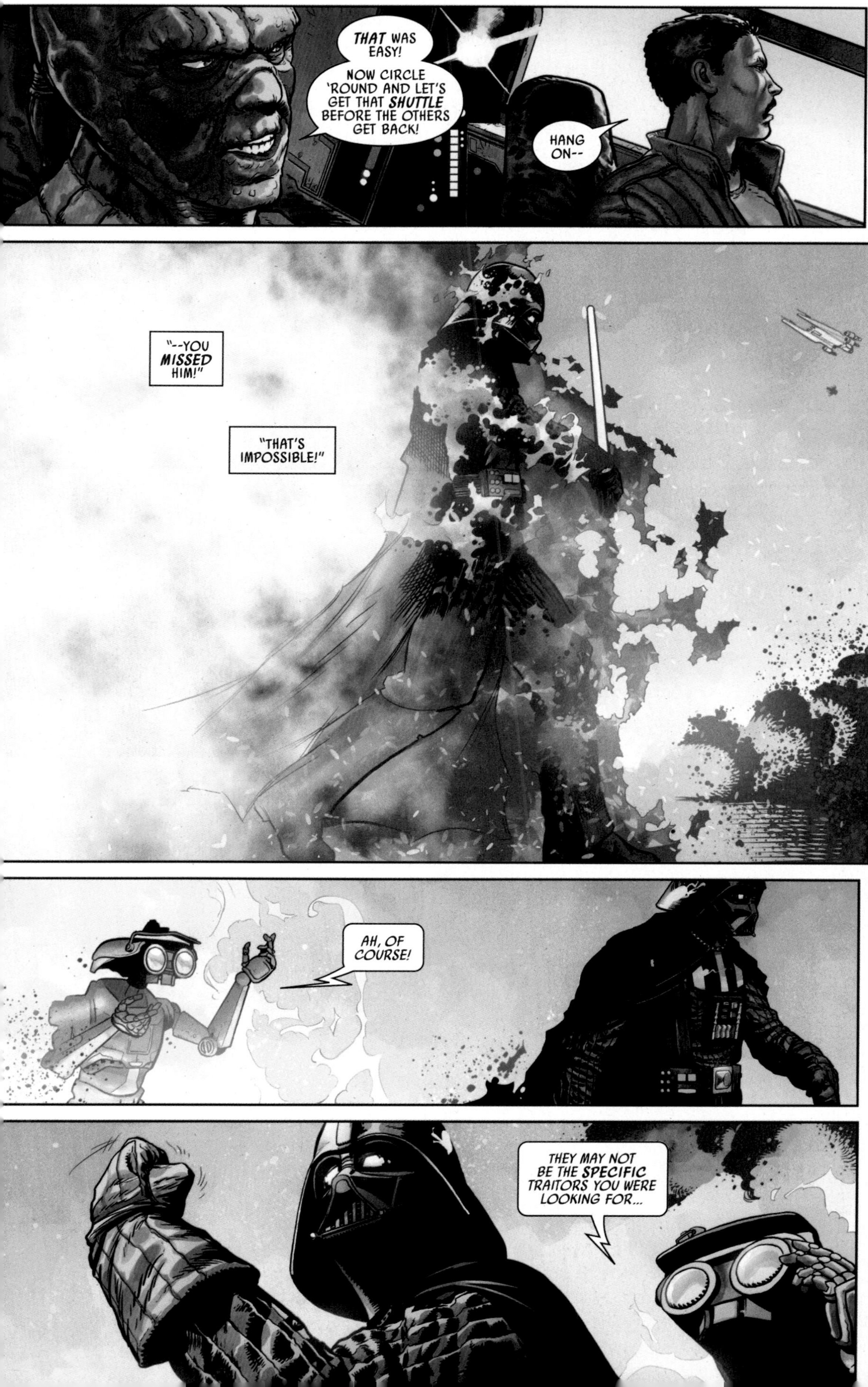

THAT WAS EASY!
NOW CIRCLE 'ROUND AND LET'S GET THAT SHUTTLE BEFORE THE OTHERS GET BACK!
HANG ON--
"--YOU MISSED HIM!"
"THAT'S IMPOSSIBLE!"
AH, OF COURSE!
THEY MAY NOT BE THE SPECIFIC TRAITORS YOU WERE LOOKING FOR...

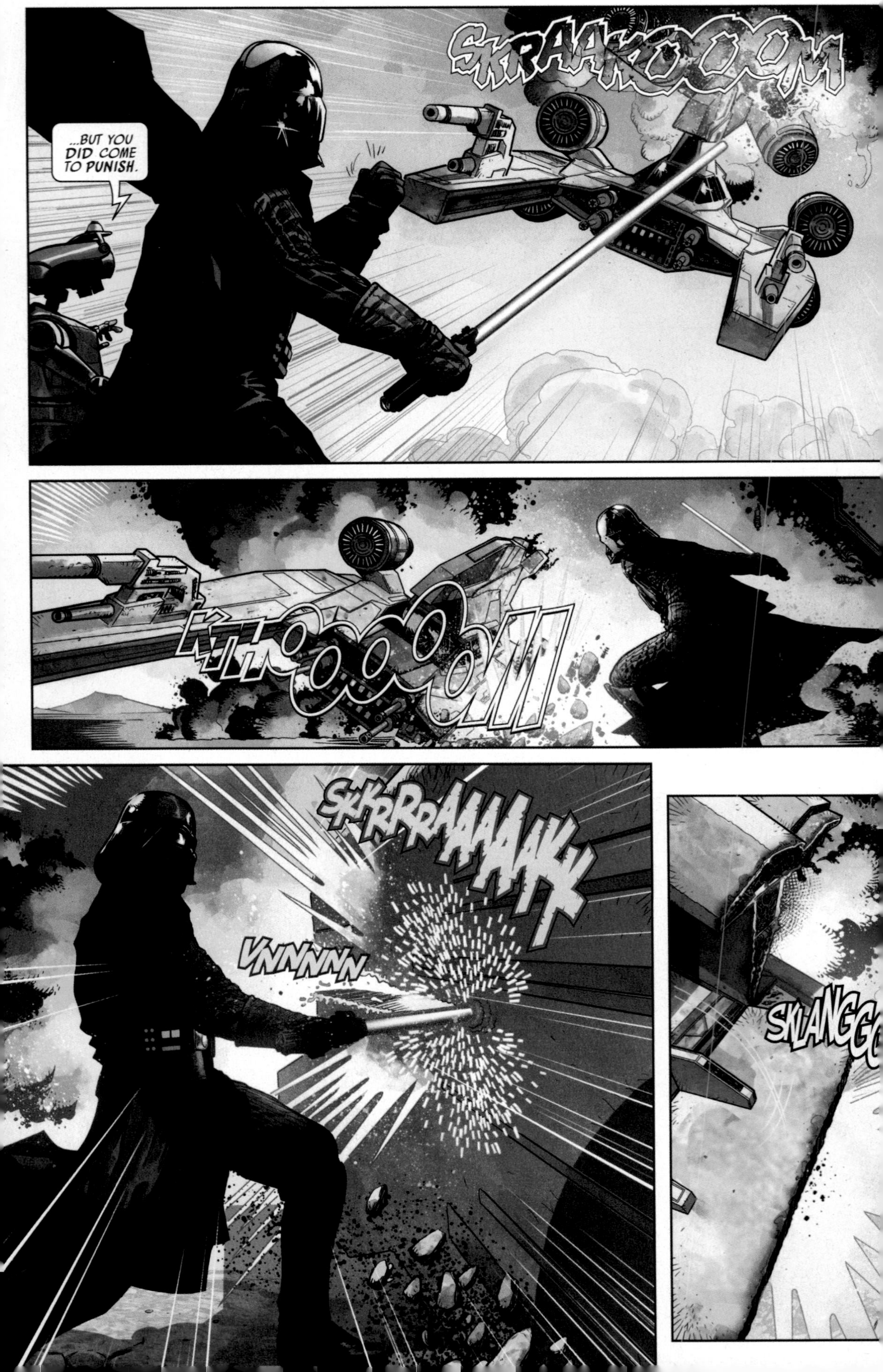
SKRAAKOOOM
...BUT YOU DID COME TO PUNISH.
KTHOOOOOOM
SKKRRRAAAAAAKK
VNNNNN
SKLANGG

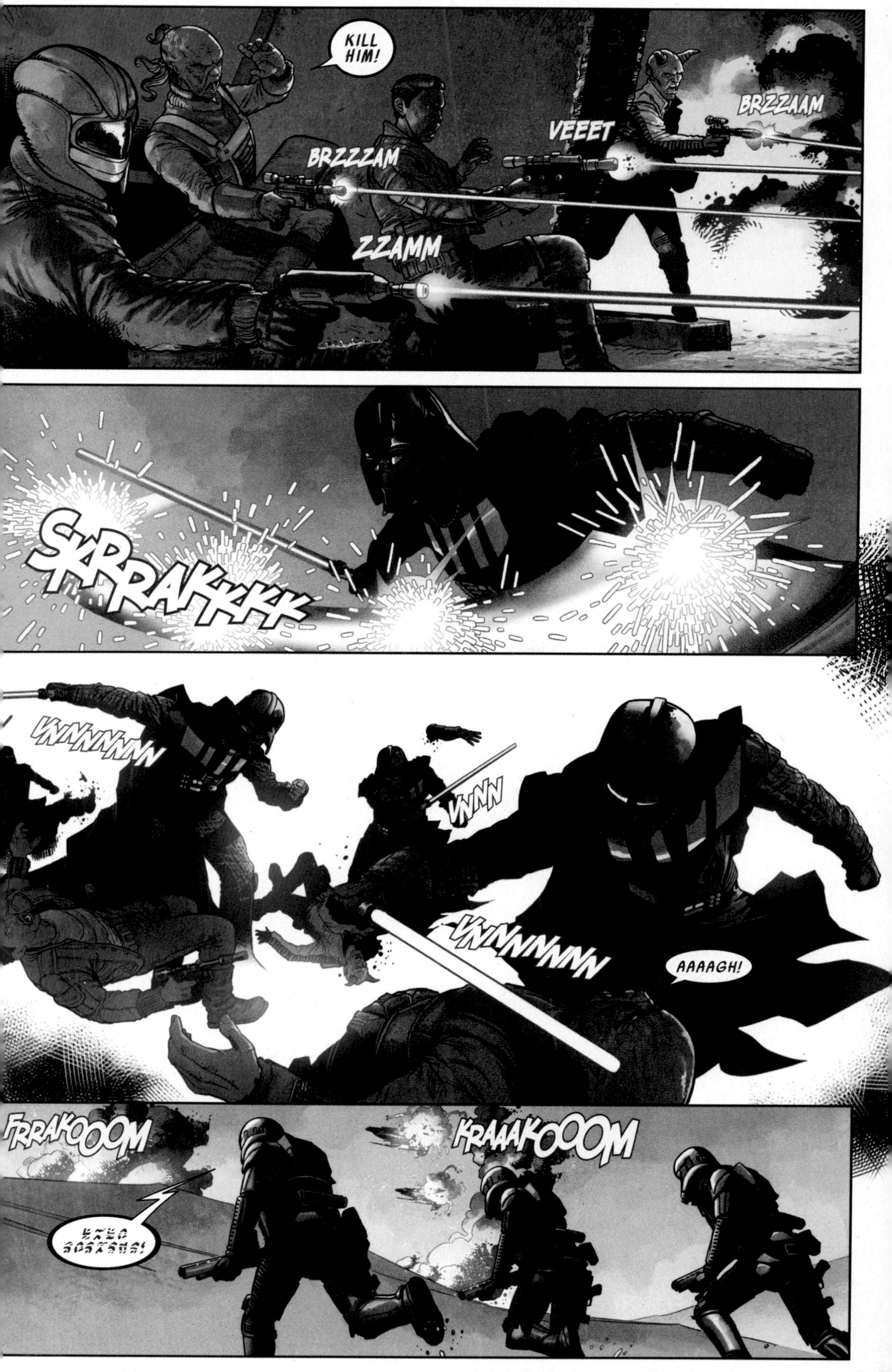
KILL HIM!
BRZZZAM
VEEET
BRZZAAM
ZZAMM
SKRRAKKKK
VNNNNNNN
VNNN
VNNNNNNN
AAAAGH!
FRRRAKOOOM
KRAAAKOOOM

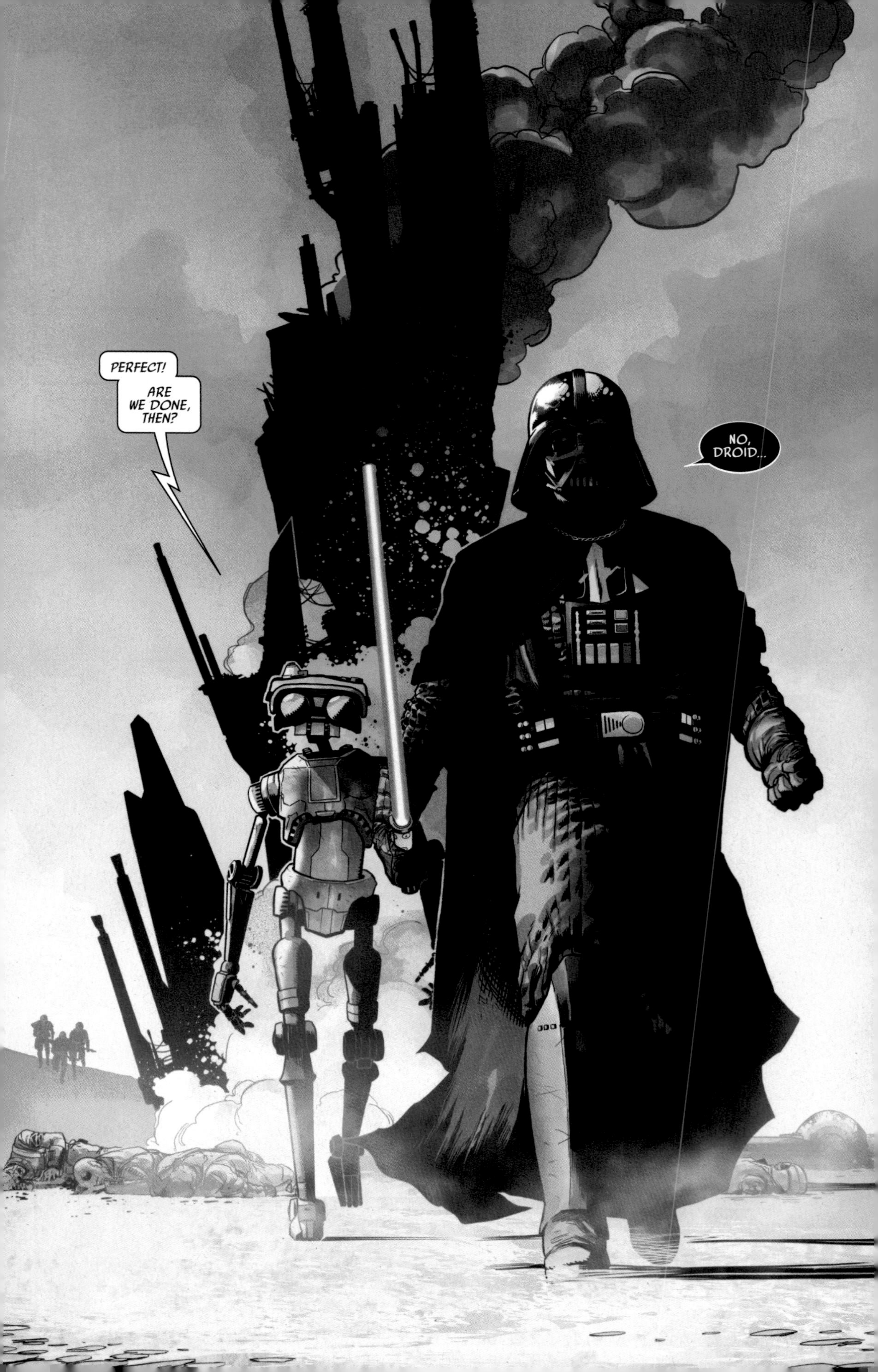
PERFECT!
ARE WE DONE, THEN?
NO, DROID...

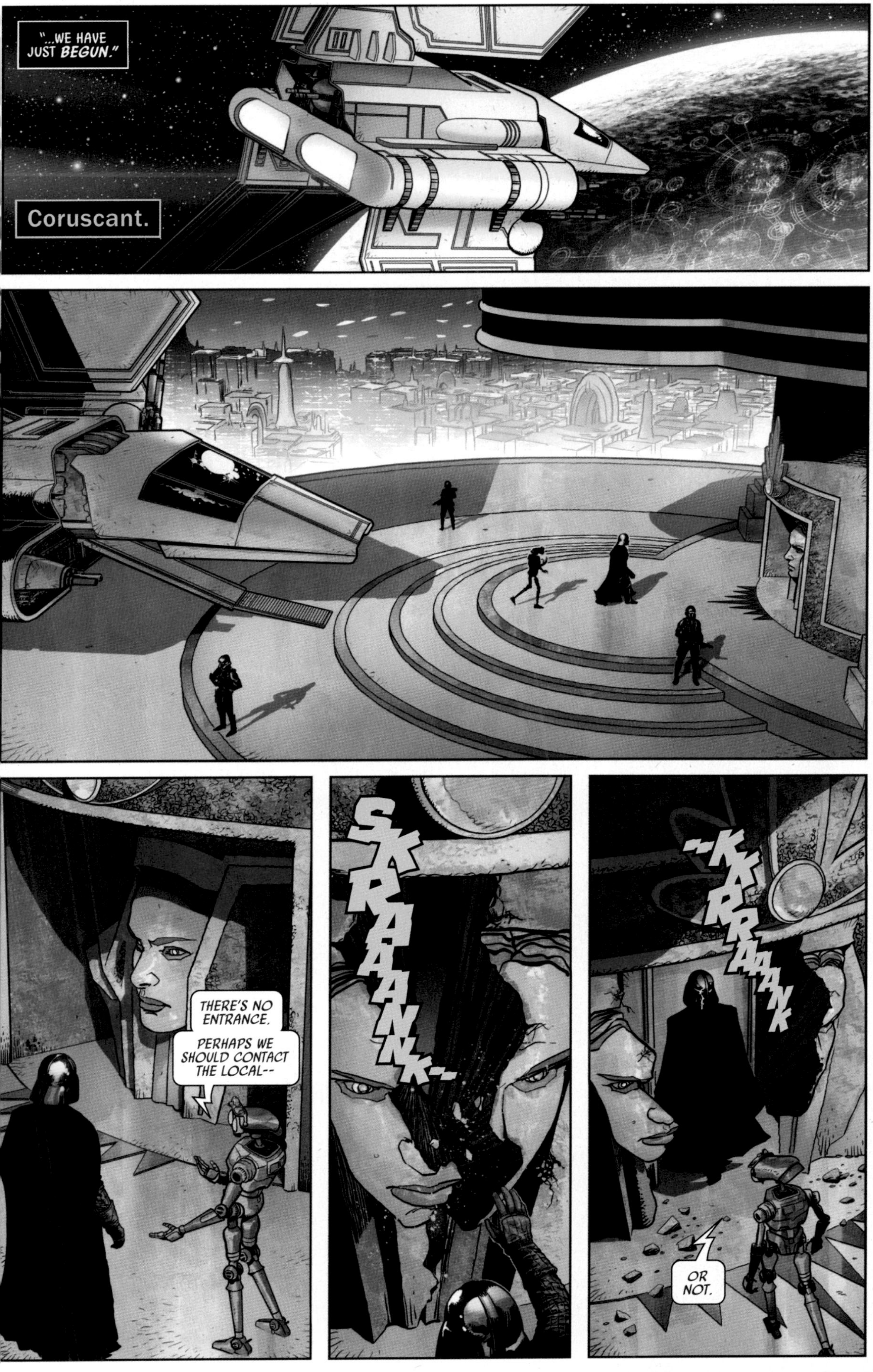
"...WE HAVE JUST BEGUN."
Coruscant.
THERE'S NO ENTRANCE.
PERHAPS WE SHOULD CONTACT THE LOCAL--
SKRAAAANK--
--KKRAAAANK
OR NOT.

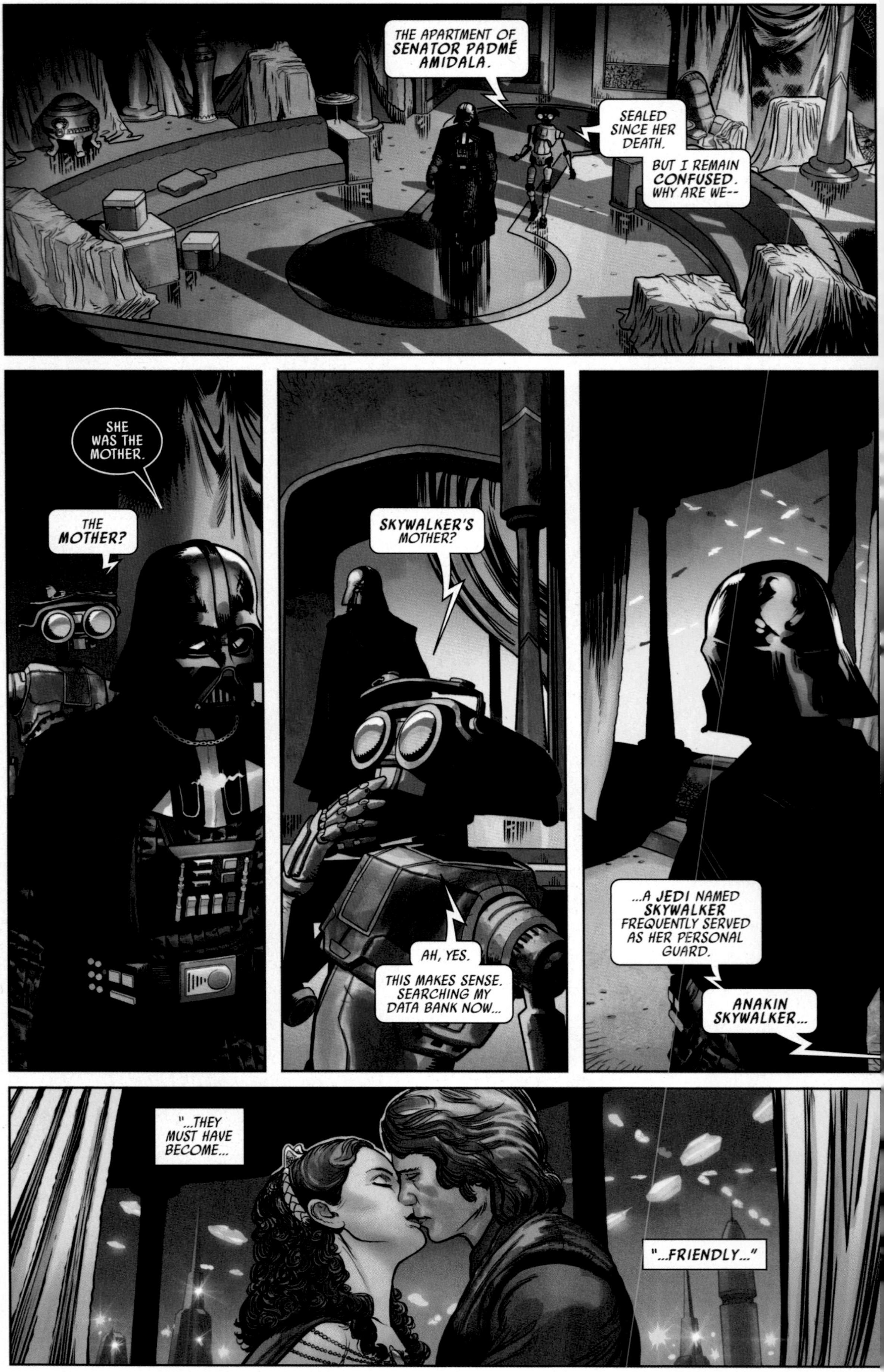

THE APARTMENT OF SENATOR PADMÉ AMIDALA.
SEALED SINCE HER DEATH.
BUT I REMAIN CONFUSED. WHY ARE WE--
SHE WAS THE MOTHER.
THE MOTHER?
SKYWALKER'S MOTHER?
AH, YES.
THIS MAKES SENSE. SEARCHING MY DATA BANK NOW...
...A JEDI NAMED SKYWALKER FREQUENTLY SERVED AS HER PERSONAL GUARD.
ANAKIN SKYWALKER...
"...THEY MUST HAVE BECOME...
"...FRIENDLY..."

ONLY HER MOST *TRUSTED ALLIES* COULD HAVE KNOWN SHE WAS *PREGNANT*...

...AND *STOLEN THE BOY* BEFORE SHE *DIED*.

DID THEY BRING HER *HERE*?

DID THEY LEAVE A *TRACE*?

ALAS, I CANNOT CONFIRM ONE WAY OR ANOTHER...

VEEEE VEEEET

...BECAUSE THE *SECURITY RECORDINGS* FOR THE TIME PERIOD DIRECTLY AFTER HER *REPORTED DEATH* ARE *MISSING*.

BUT THAT TELLS US SOMEONE WANTED TO *HIDE* SOMETHING.

PERHAPS SHE *DID* RETURN.

OR PERHAPS SOMEONE *ELSE* CAME HERE AFTER HER DEATH...

...LOOKING FOR...

WRRRR

AHA!

WHAT?

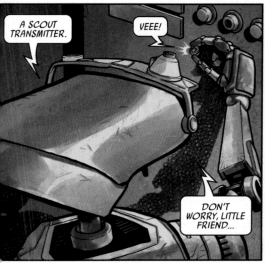

A SCOUT TRANSMITTER.

VEEE!

DON'T WORRY, LITTLE FRIEND...

SHIINK

EEEEEE!

WE JUST WANT TO KNOW *WHOM* YOU'RE REPORTING TO.

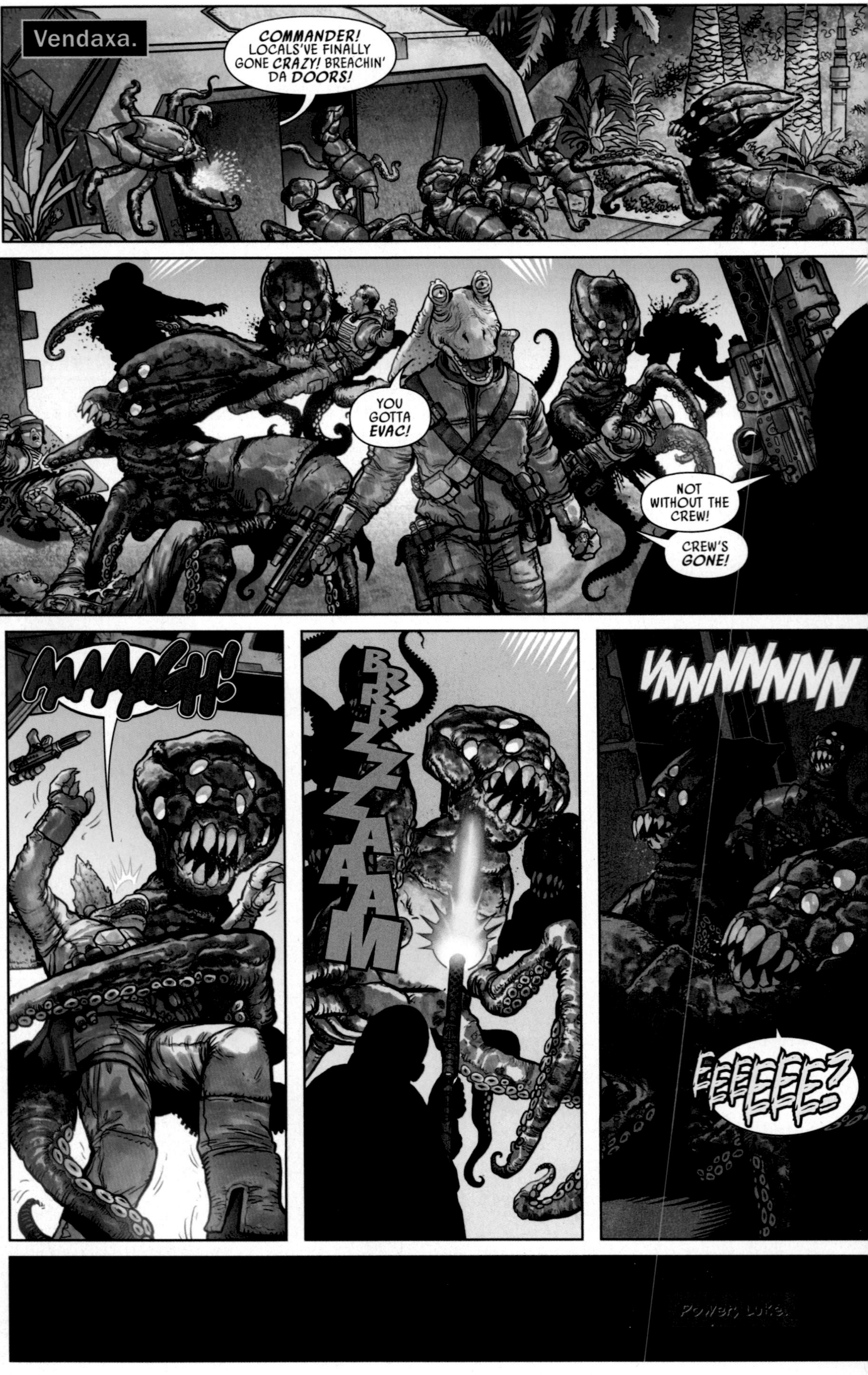
Vendaxa.
COMMANDER! LOCALS'VE FINALLY GONE CRAZY! BREACHIN' DA DOORS!
YOU GOTTA EVAC!
NOT WITHOUT THE CREW!
CREW'S GONE!
AAAAGH!
BRRRZZZAAAM
VNNNNNNN
EEEEEEE?
Power, Luke.

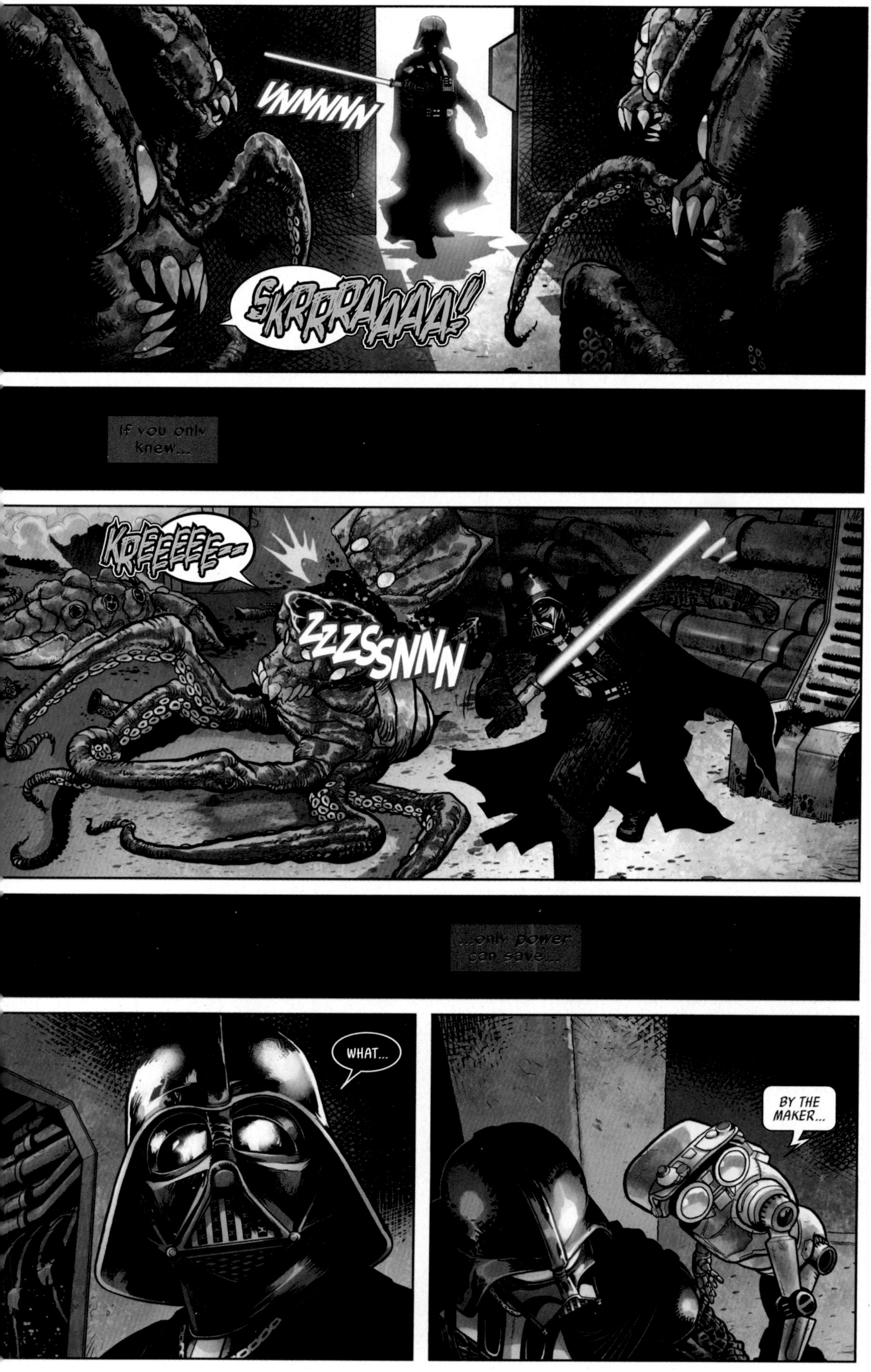
VNNNNN
SKRRRAAAAA!
If you only knew...
KREEEEEE--
ZZZSSNNNN
...only power can save...
WHAT...
BY THE MAKER...

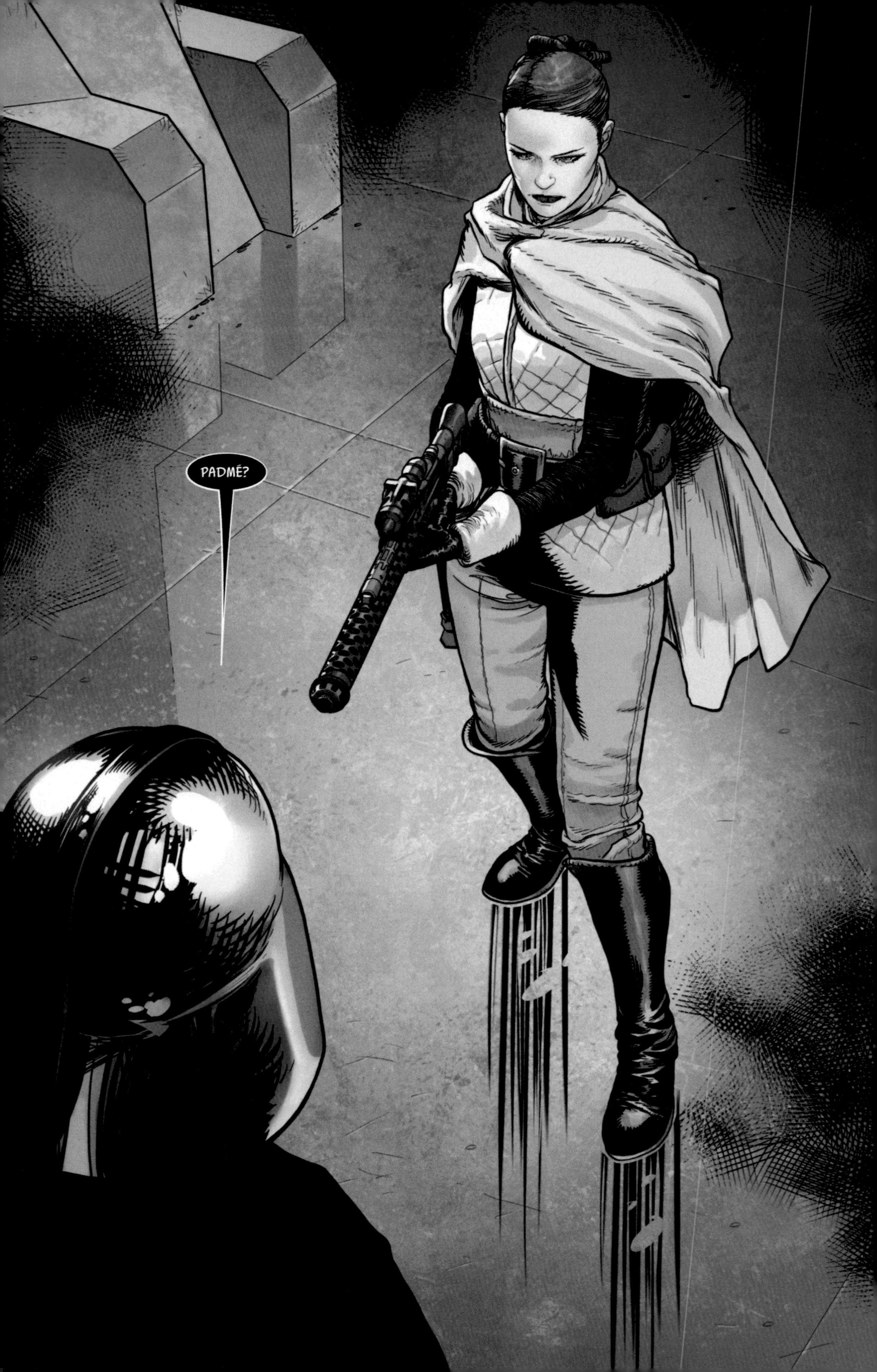
PADMÉ?

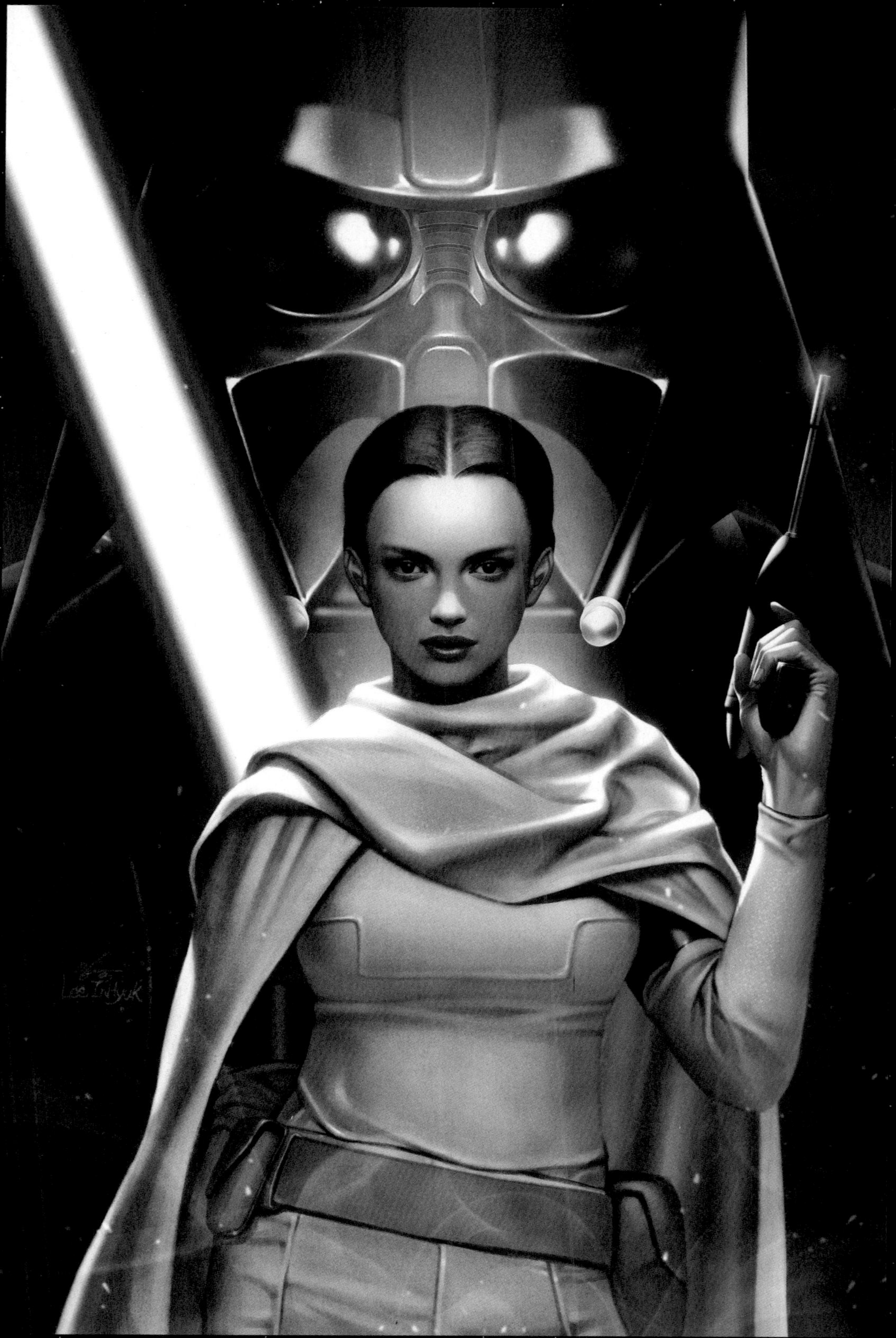

2

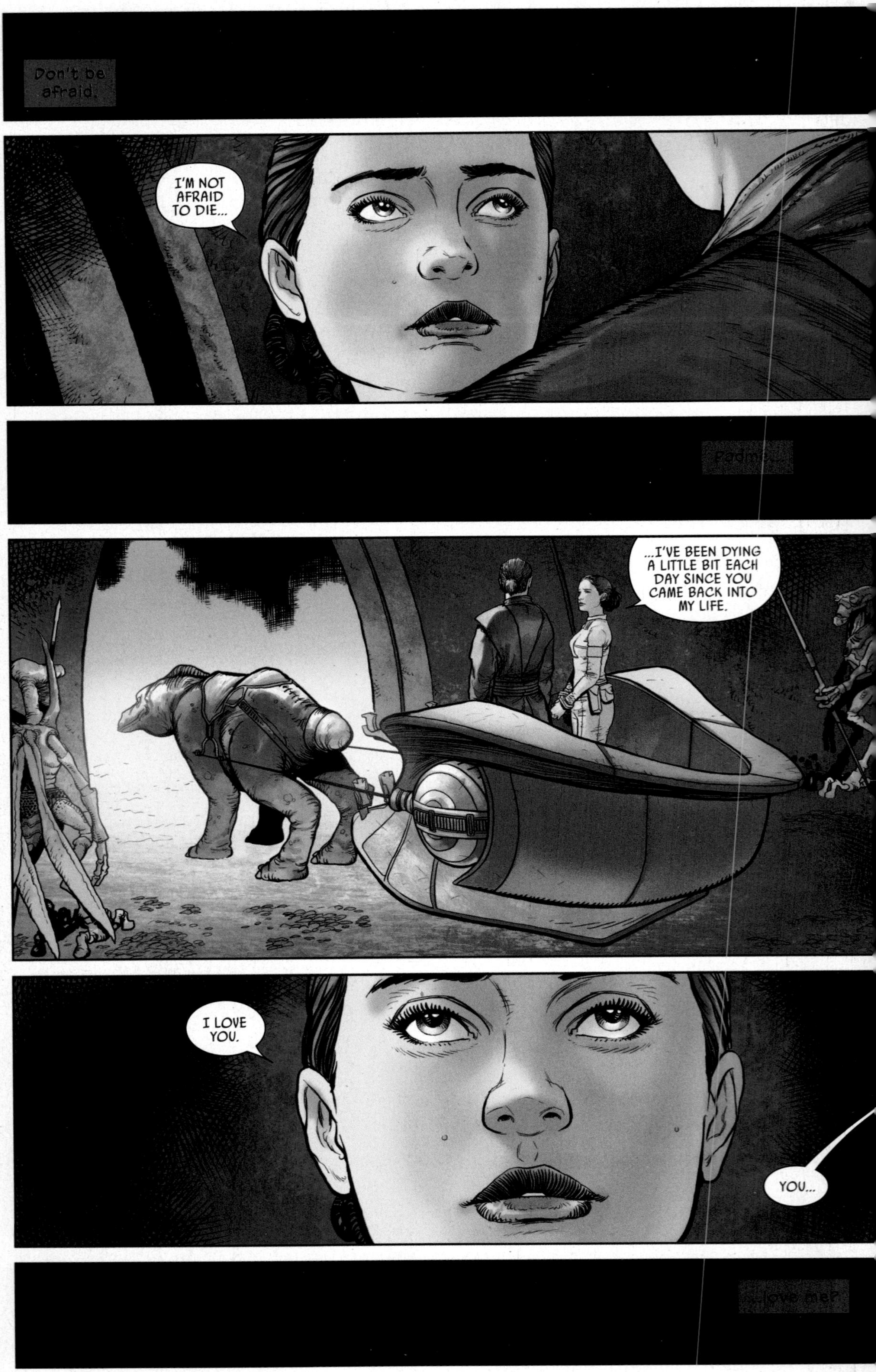
Don't be afraid.
I'M NOT AFRAID TO DIE...
Padmé...
...I'VE BEEN DYING A LITTLE BIT EACH DAY SINCE YOU CAME BACK INTO MY LIFE.
I LOVE YOU.
YOU...
...love me?

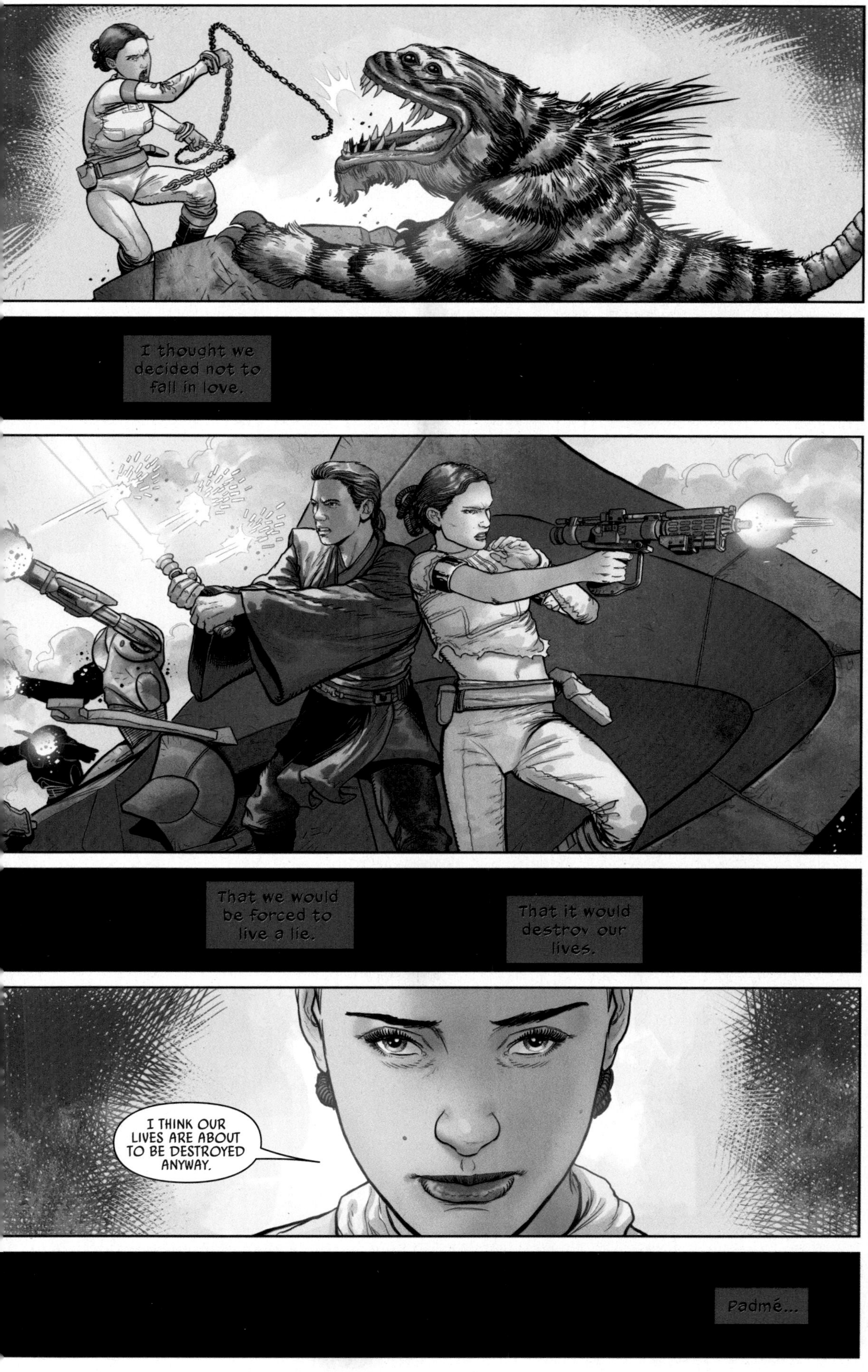
I thought we decided not to fall in love.
That we would be forced to live a lie.
That it would destroy our lives.
I THINK OUR LIVES ARE ABOUT TO BE DESTROYED ANYWAY.
Padmé...

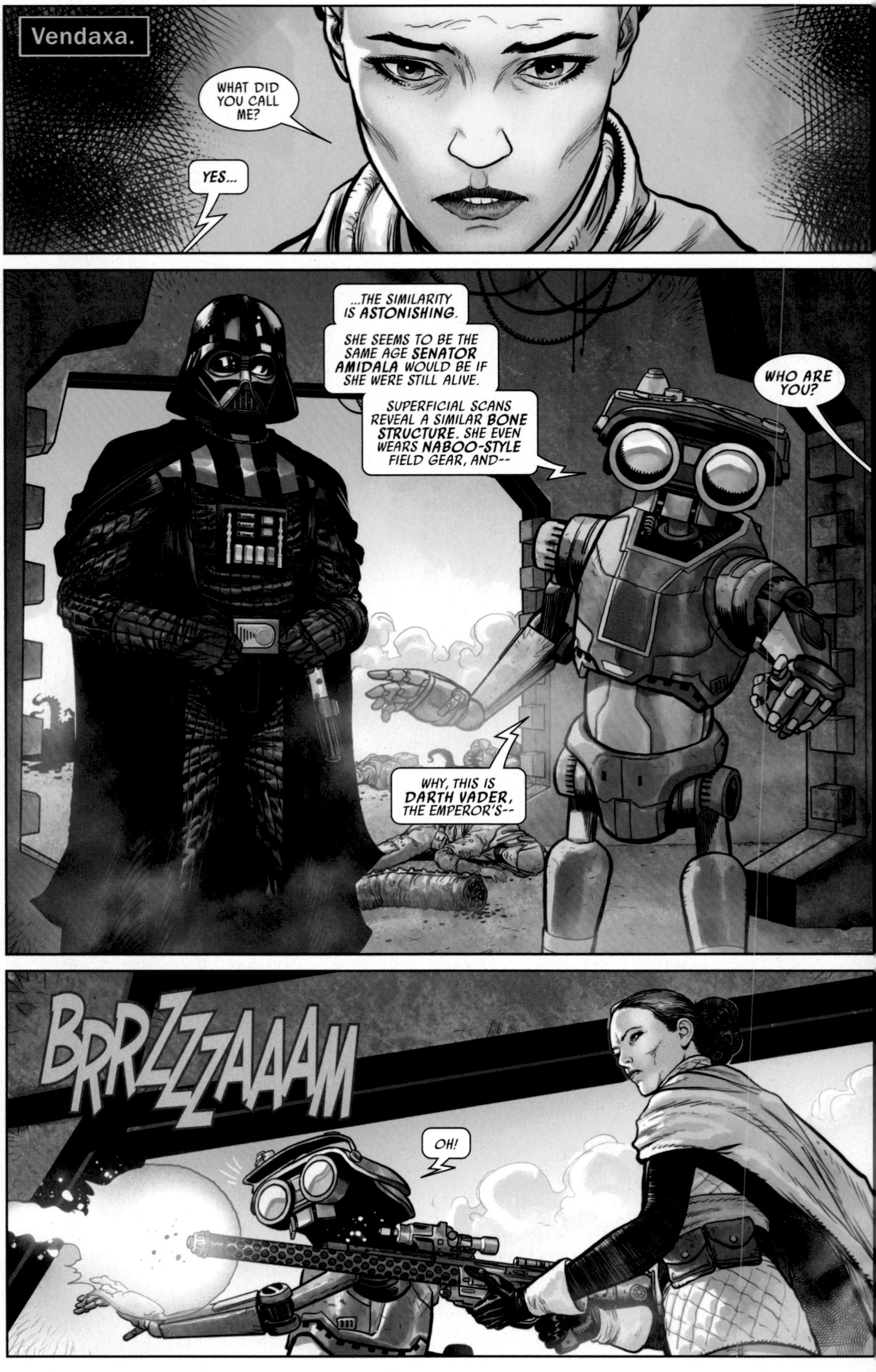
Vendaxa.
WHAT DID YOU CALL ME?
YES...
...THE SIMILARITY IS ASTONISHING.
SHE SEEMS TO BE THE SAME AGE SENATOR AMIDALA WOULD BE IF SHE WERE STILL ALIVE.
SUPERFICIAL SCANS REVEAL A SIMILAR BONE STRUCTURE. SHE EVEN WEARS NABOO-STYLE FIELD GEAR, AND--
WHO ARE YOU?
WHY, THIS IS DARTH VADER, THE EMPEROR'S--
BRRZZZAAAM
OH!

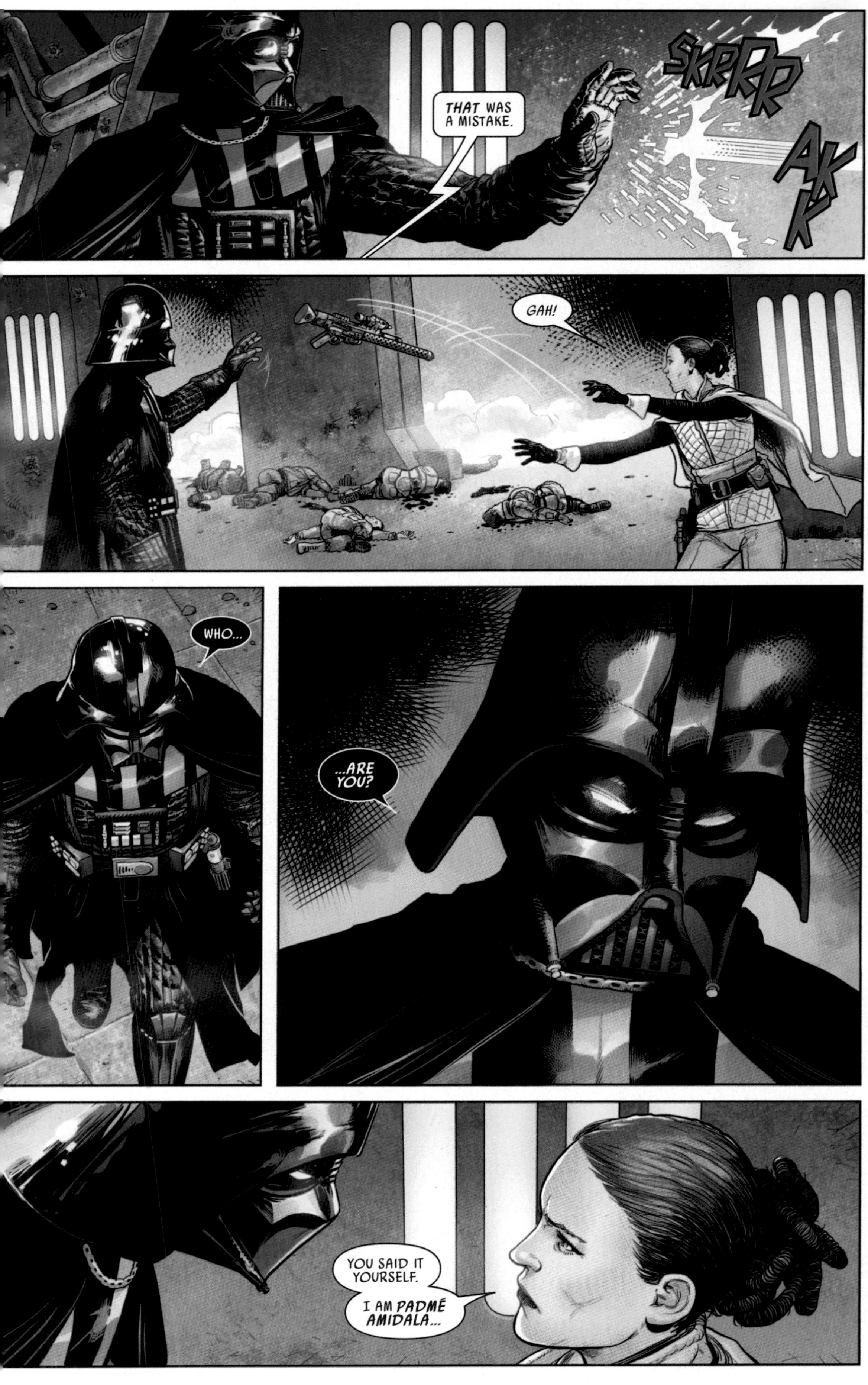
THAT WAS A MISTAKE.
SKRRR
AKK
GAH!
WHO...
...ARE YOU?
YOU SAID IT YOURSELF.
I AM PADMÉ AMIDALA...

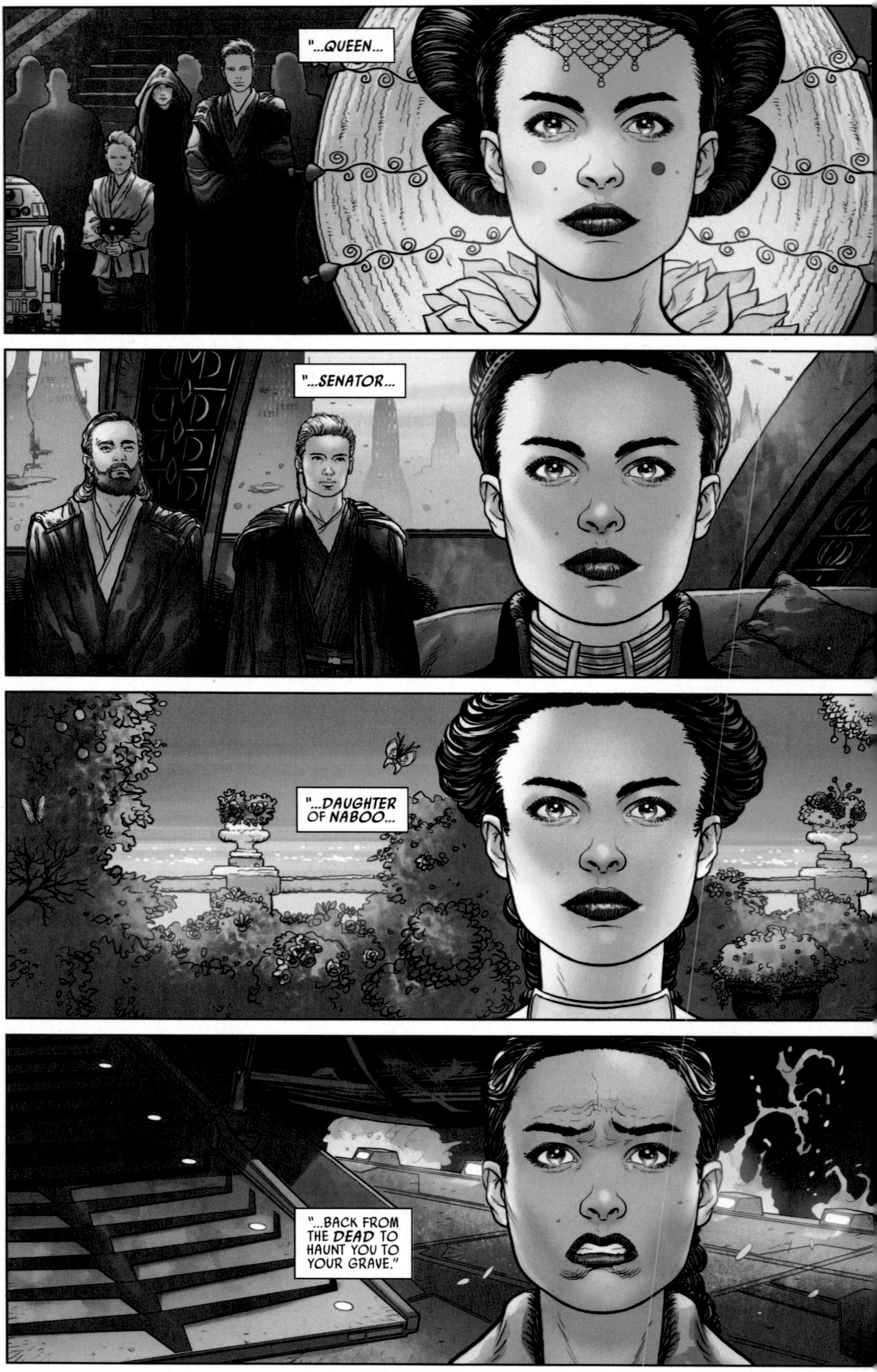
"...QUEEN...
"...SENATOR...
"...DAUGHTER OF NABOO...
"...BACK FROM THE DEAD TO HAUNT YOU TO YOUR GRAVE."

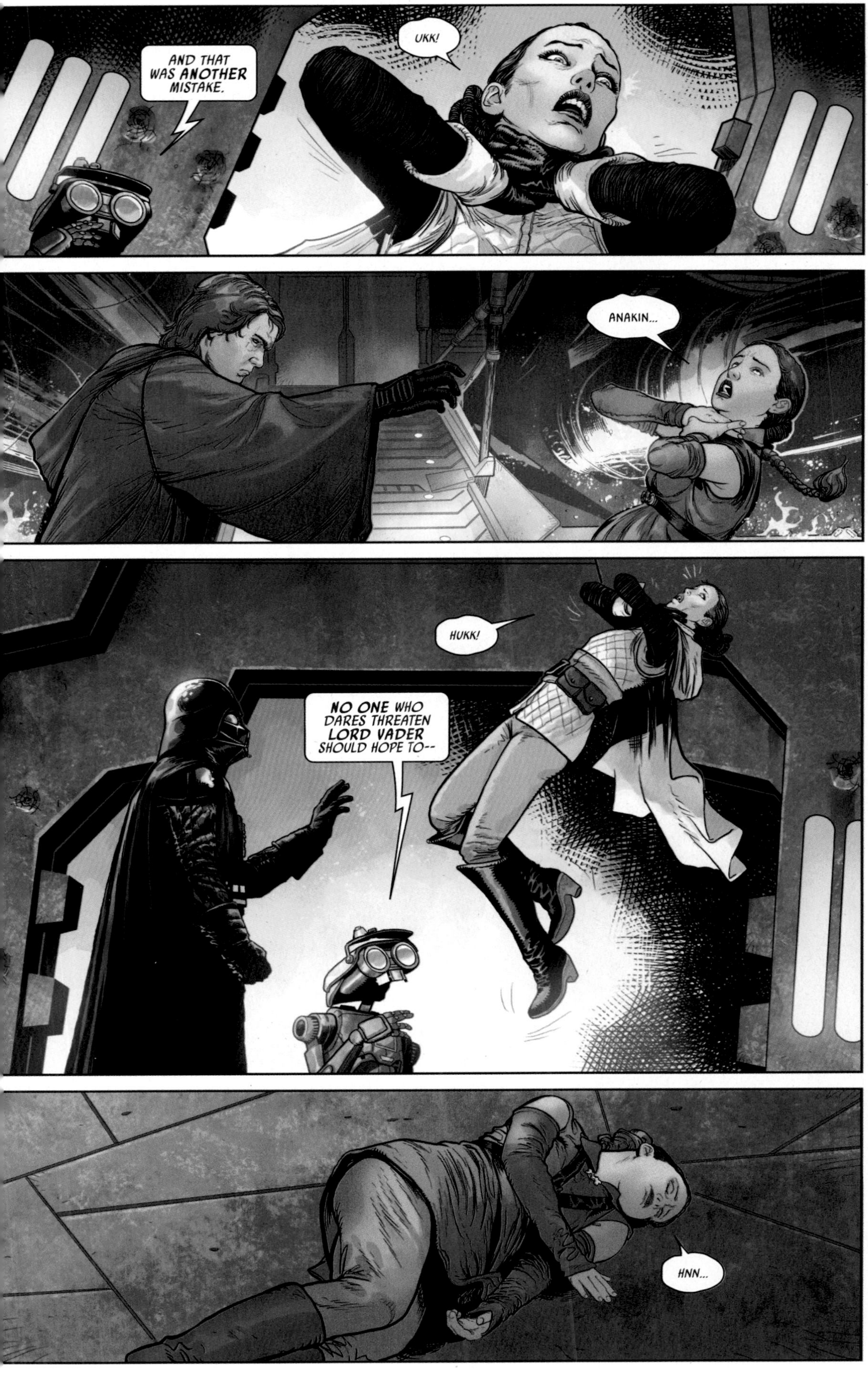
AND THAT WAS ANOTHER MISTAKE.
UKK!
ANAKIN...
HUKK!
NO ONE WHO DARES THREATEN LORD VADER SHOULD HOPE TO--
HNN...

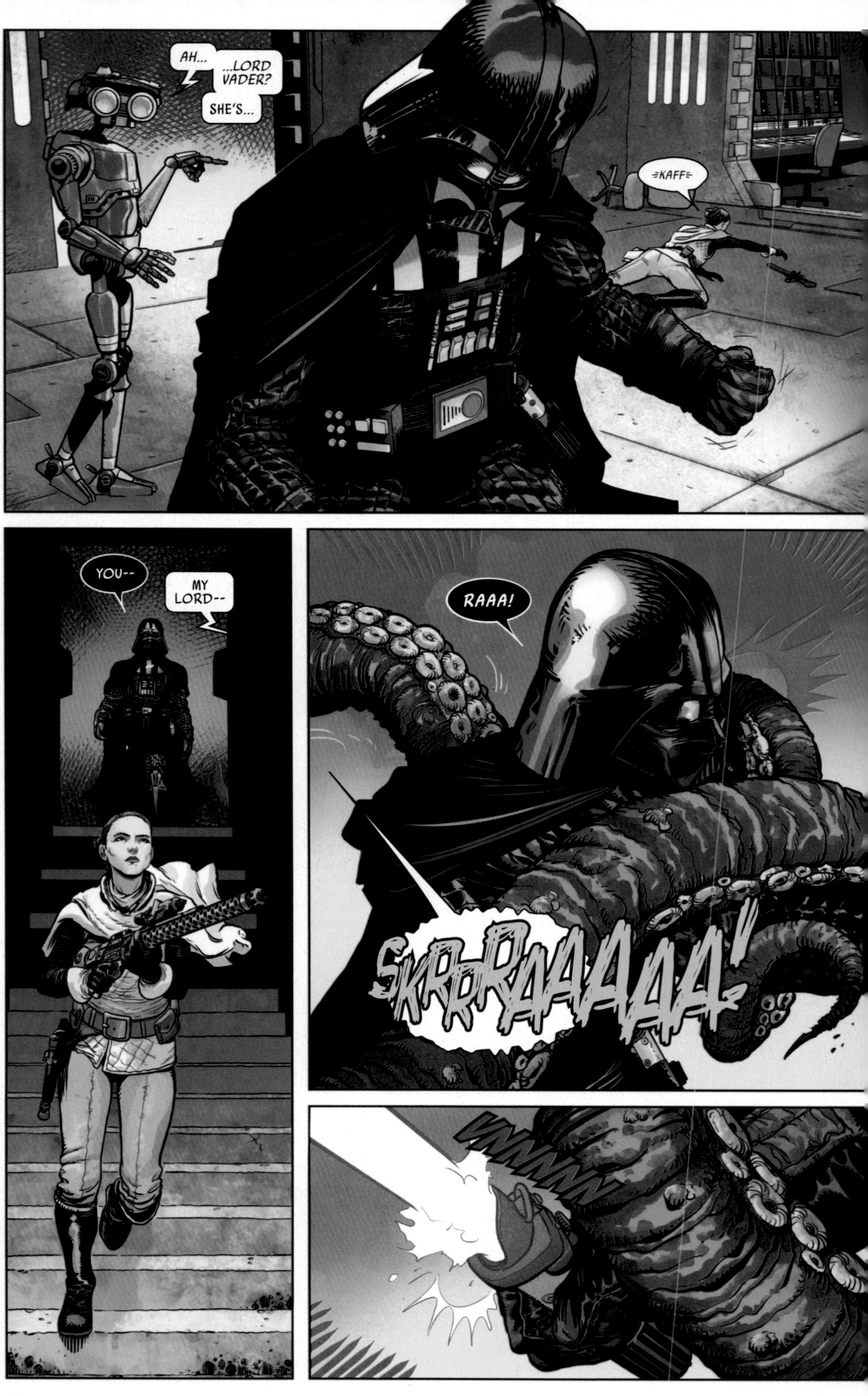
AH...
...LORD VADER?
SHE'S...
=KAFF=
YOU--
MY LORD--
RAAA!
SKRRRAAAAAA!
VNNNNNN

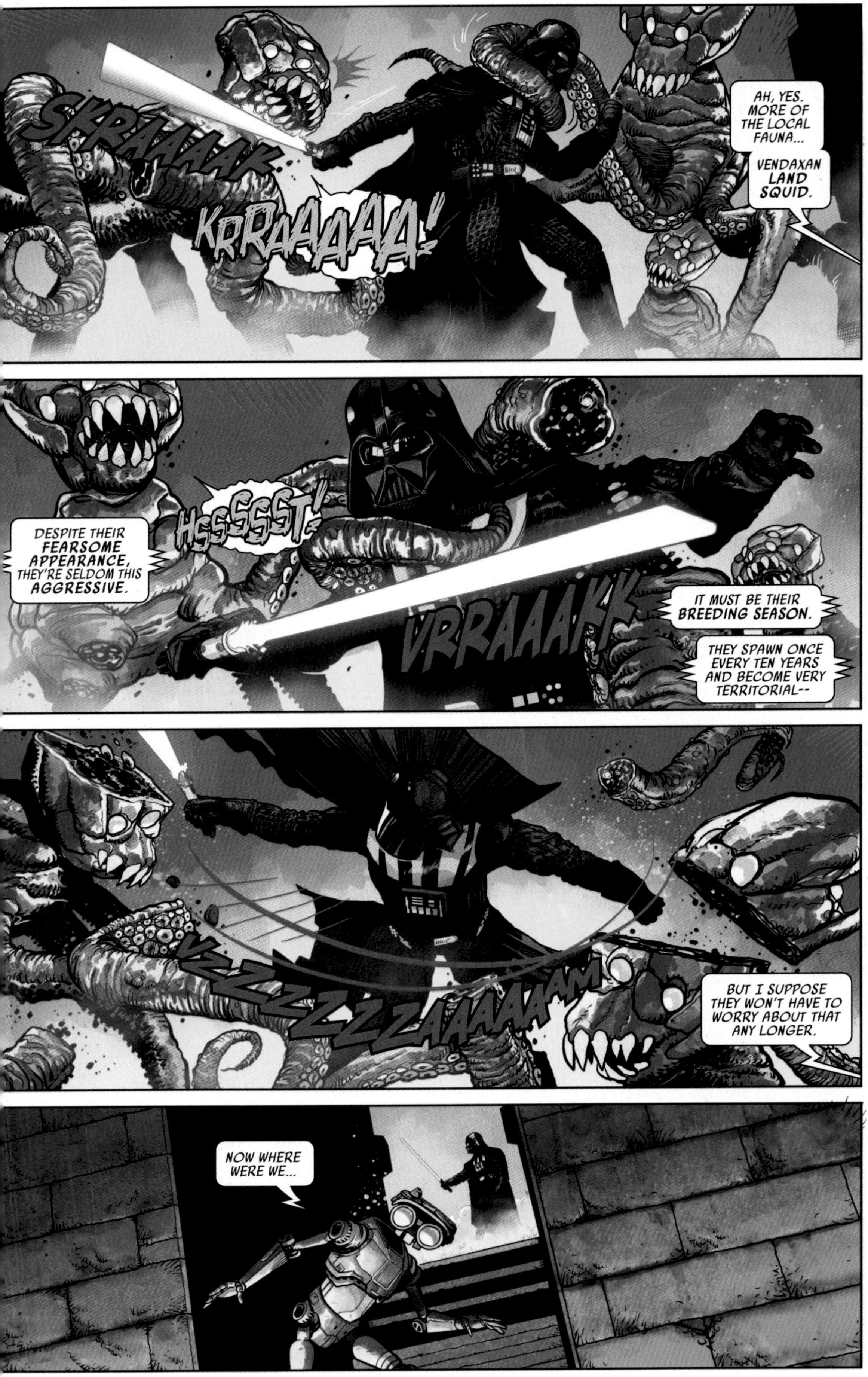
SKRAAAAK
KRRAAAAAA!
AH, YES. MORE OF THE LOCAL FAUNA...
VENDAXAN LAND SQUID.
HSSSSST!
DESPITE THEIR FEARSOME APPEARANCE, THEY'RE SELDOM THIS AGGRESSIVE.
VRRAAAKK
IT MUST BE THEIR BREEDING SEASON.
THEY SPAWN ONCE EVERY TEN YEARS AND BECOME VERY TERRITORIAL--
VZZZZZZAAAAAAM
BUT I SUPPOSE THEY WON'T HAVE TO WORRY ABOUT THAT ANY LONGER.
NOW WHERE WERE WE...

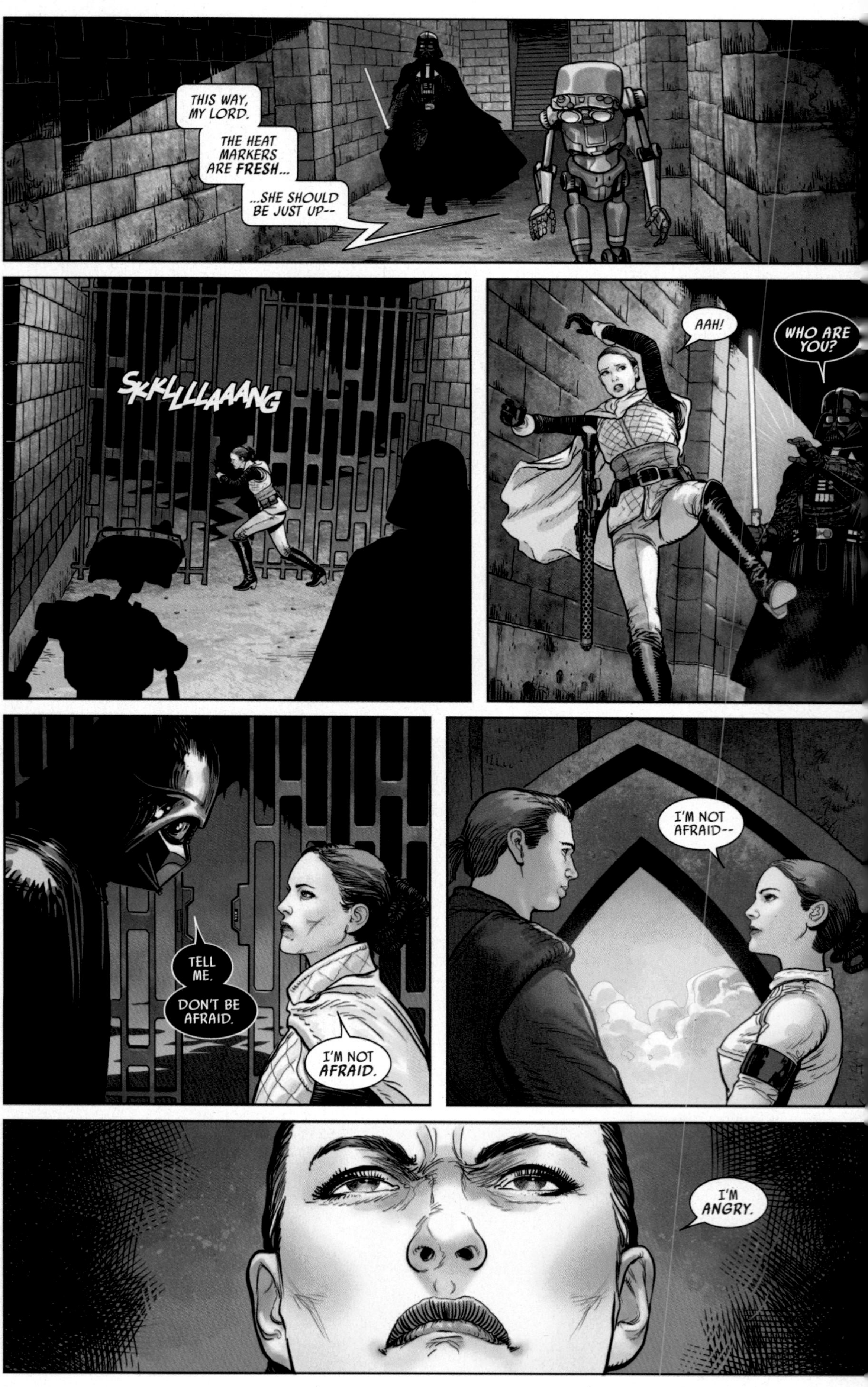

THIS WAY, MY LORD.
THE HEAT MARKERS ARE FRESH...
...SHE SHOULD BE JUST UP--
SKKLLLLAAANG
AAH!
WHO ARE YOU?
TELL ME.
DON'T BE AFRAID.
I'M NOT AFRAID.
I'M NOT AFRAID--
I'M ANGRY.

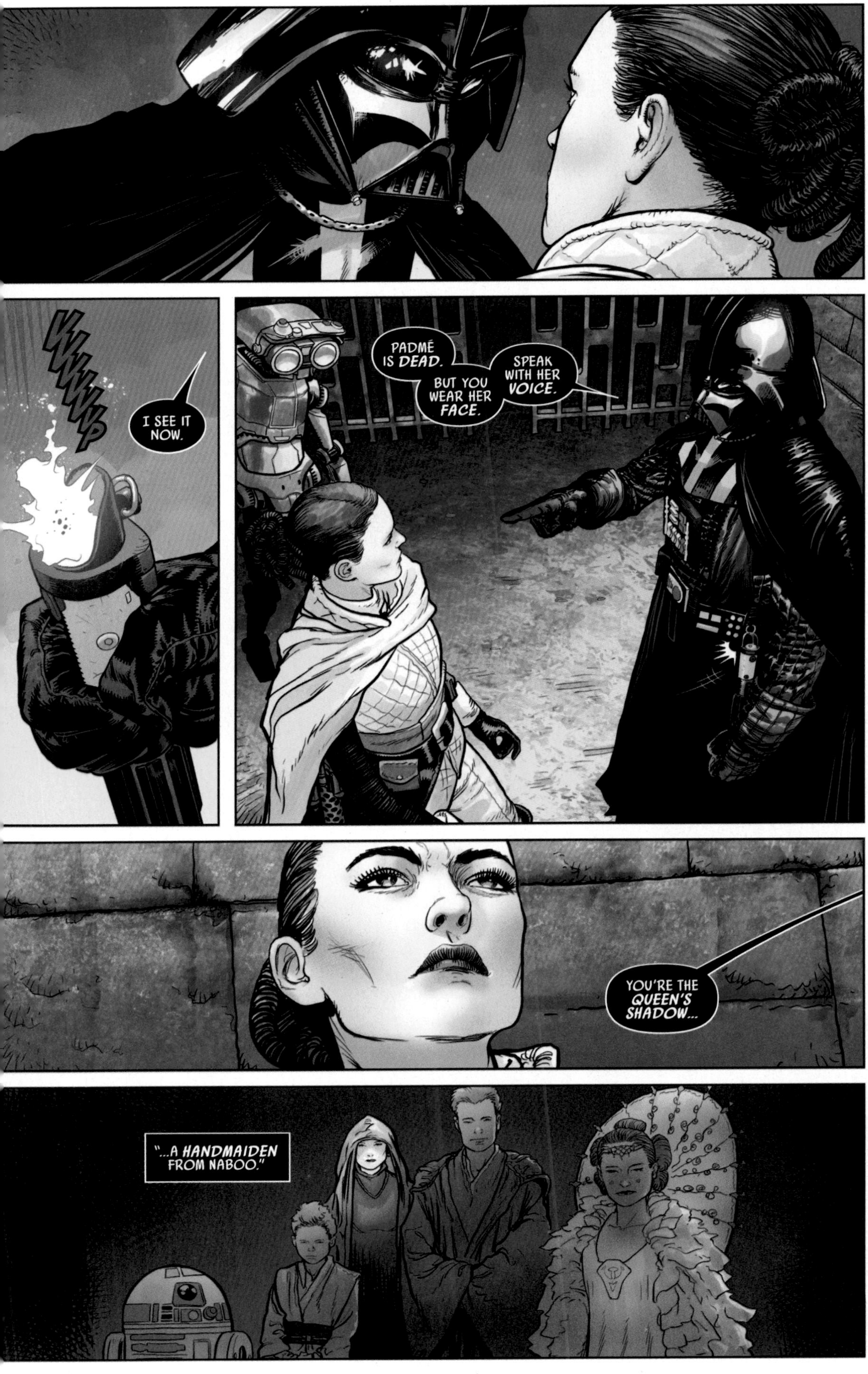
VVVVVP
I SEE IT NOW.
PADMÉ IS DEAD.
BUT YOU WEAR HER FACE.
SPEAK WITH HER VOICE.
YOU'RE THE QUEEN'S SHADOW...
"...A HANDMAIDEN FROM NABOO."

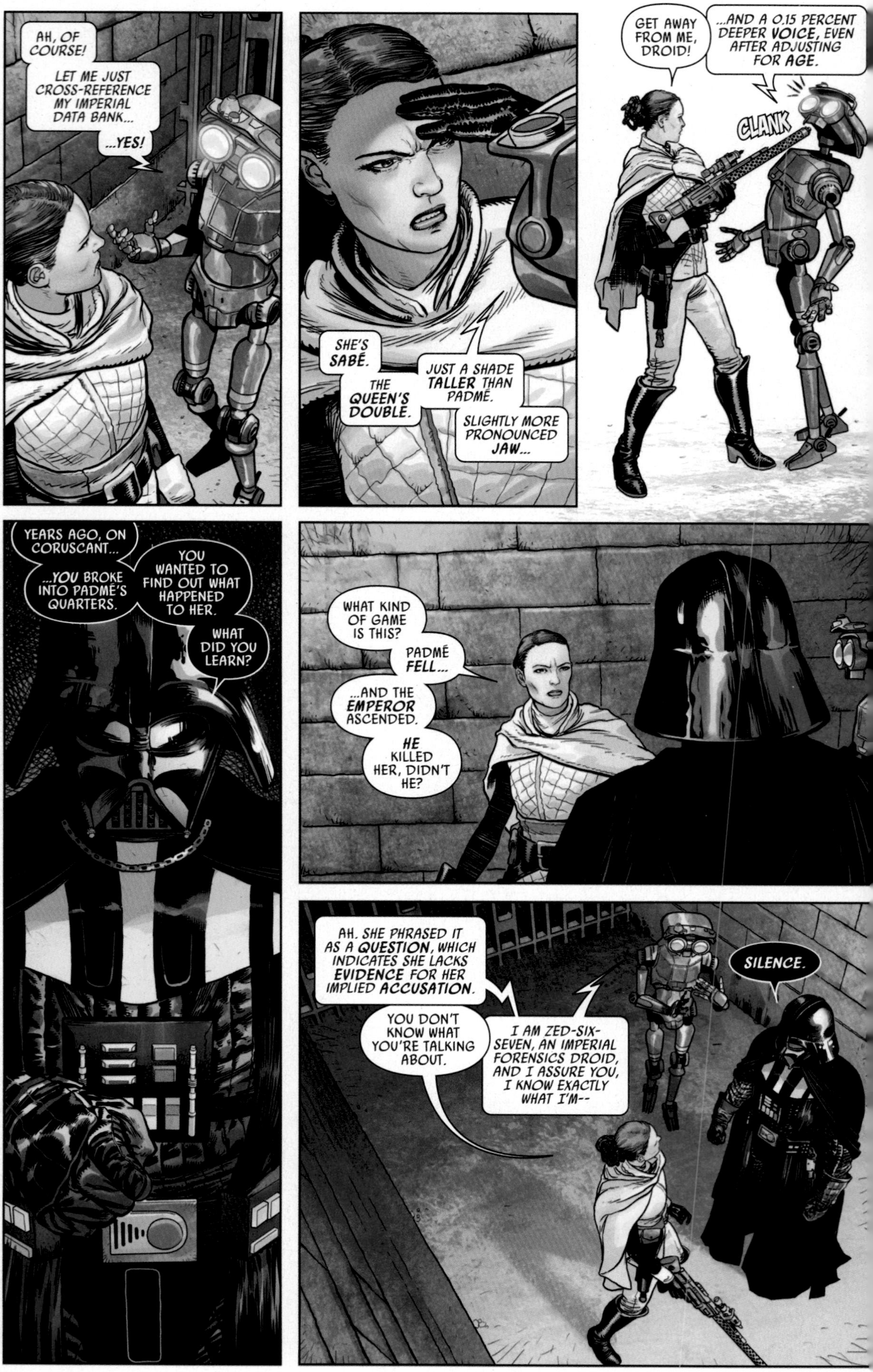
AH, OF COURSE!
LET ME JUST CROSS-REFERENCE MY IMPERIAL DATA BANK...
...YES!
SHE'S SABÉ.
THE QUEEN'S DOUBLE.
JUST A SHADE TALLER THAN PADMÉ.
SLIGHTLY MORE PRONOUNCED JAW...
GET AWAY FROM ME, DROID!
...AND A 0.15 PERCENT DEEPER VOICE, EVEN AFTER ADJUSTING FOR AGE.
CLANK
YEARS AGO, ON CORUSCANT...
...YOU BROKE INTO PADMÉ'S QUARTERS.
YOU WANTED TO FIND OUT WHAT HAPPENED TO HER.
WHAT DID YOU LEARN?
WHAT KIND OF GAME IS THIS?
PADMÉ FELL...
...AND THE EMPEROR ASCENDED.
HE KILLED HER, DIDN'T HE?
AH. SHE PHRASED IT AS A QUESTION, WHICH INDICATES SHE LACKS EVIDENCE FOR HER IMPLIED ACCUSATION.
YOU DON'T KNOW WHAT YOU'RE TALKING ABOUT.
I AM ZED-SIX-SEVEN, AN IMPERIAL FORENSICS DROID, AND I ASSURE YOU, I KNOW EXACTLY WHAT I'M--
SILENCE.

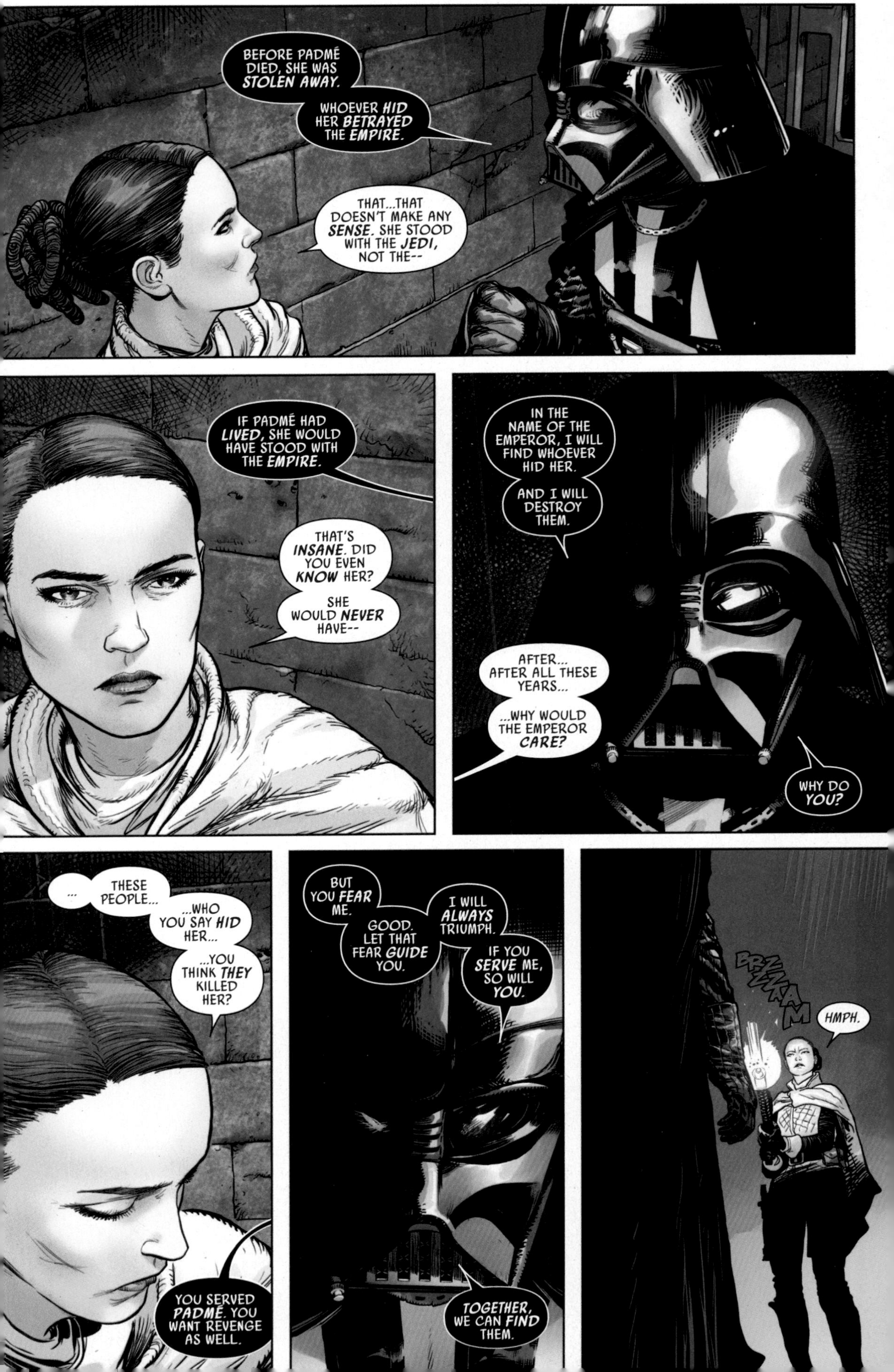
BEFORE PADMÉ DIED, SHE WAS STOLEN AWAY.
WHOEVER HID HER BETRAYED THE EMPIRE.
THAT...THAT DOESN'T MAKE ANY SENSE. SHE STOOD WITH THE JEDI, NOT THE--
IF PADMÉ HAD LIVED, SHE WOULD HAVE STOOD WITH THE EMPIRE.
THAT'S INSANE. DID YOU EVEN KNOW HER?
SHE WOULD NEVER HAVE--
IN THE NAME OF THE EMPEROR, I WILL FIND WHOEVER HID HER.
AND I WILL DESTROY THEM.
AFTER... AFTER ALL THESE YEARS...
...WHY WOULD THE EMPEROR CARE?
WHY DO YOU?
...
THESE PEOPLE...
...WHO YOU SAY HID HER...
...YOU THINK THEY KILLED HER?
YOU SERVED PADMÉ. YOU WANT REVENGE AS WELL.
BUT YOU FEAR ME.
GOOD. LET THAT FEAR GUIDE YOU.
I WILL ALWAYS TRIUMPH.
IF YOU SERVE ME, SO WILL YOU.
TOGETHER, WE CAN FIND THEM.
BRZZZAM
HMPH.

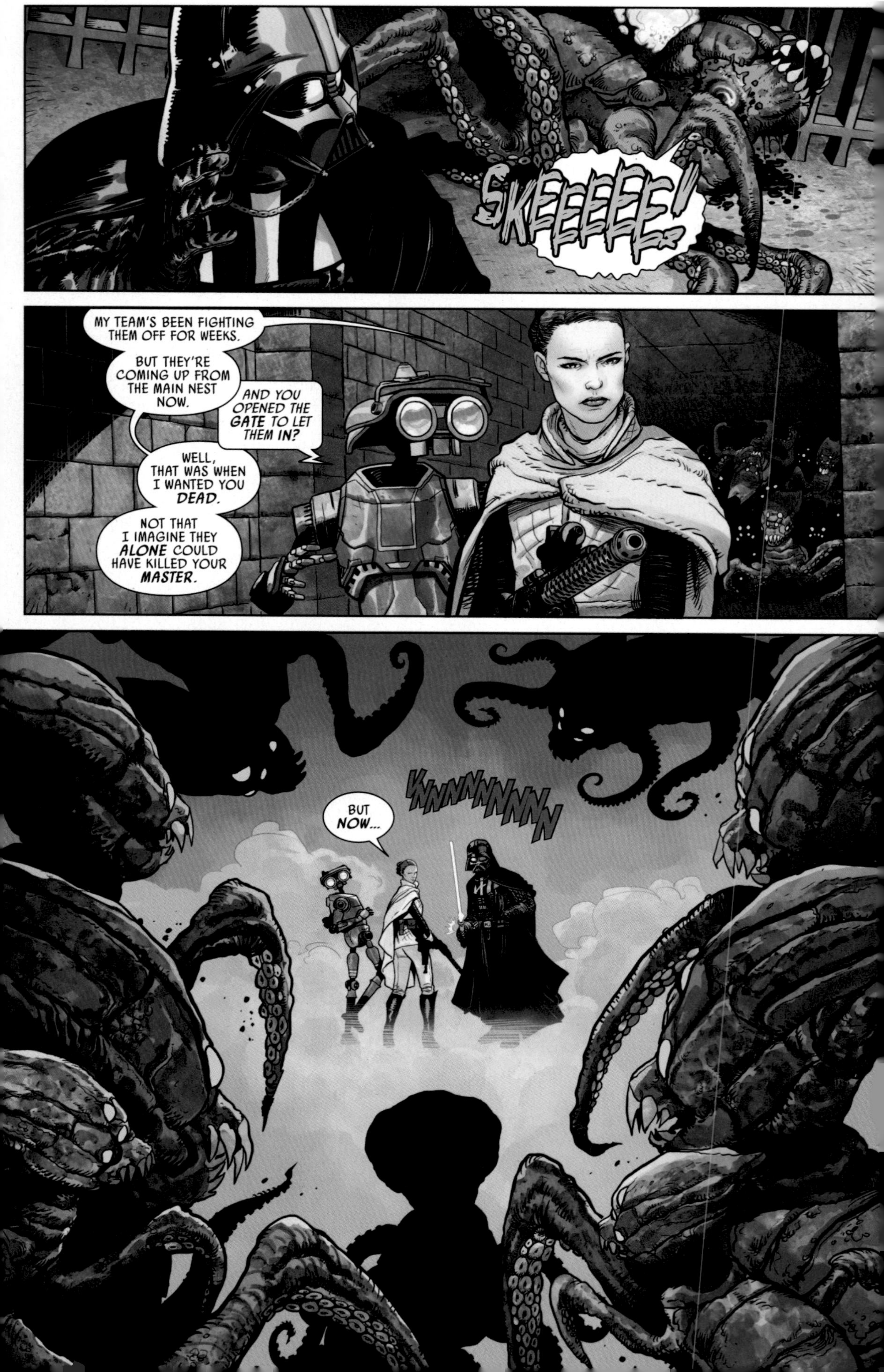
SKEEEEEE!
MY TEAM'S BEEN FIGHTING THEM OFF FOR WEEKS.
BUT THEY'RE COMING UP FROM THE MAIN NEST NOW.
AND YOU OPENED THE GATE TO LET THEM IN?
WELL, THAT WAS WHEN I WANTED YOU DEAD.
NOT THAT I IMAGINE THEY ALONE COULD HAVE KILLED YOUR MASTER.
BUT NOW...
VNNNNNNNNN

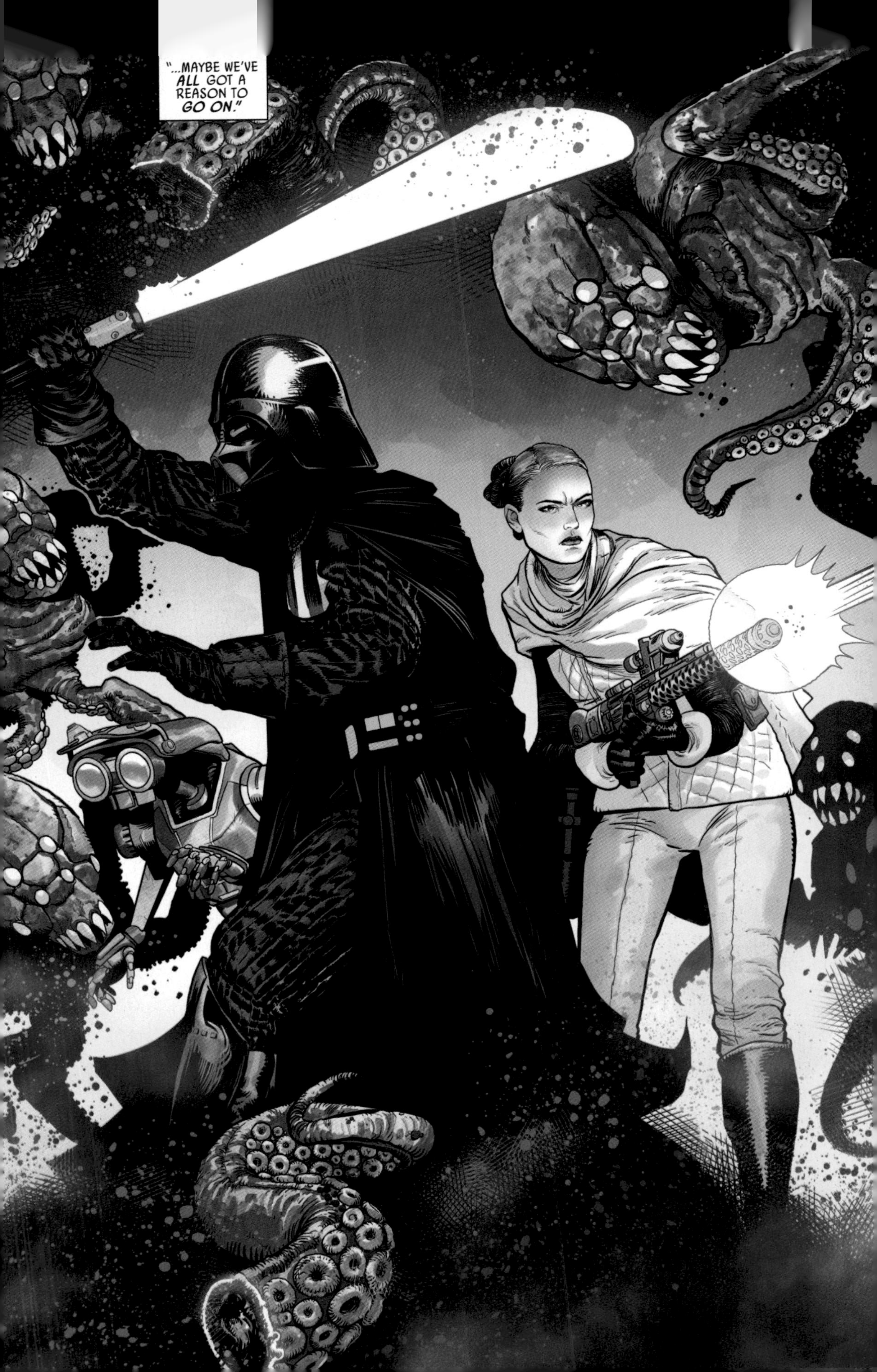
"...MAYBE WE'VE ALL GOT A REASON TO GO ON."

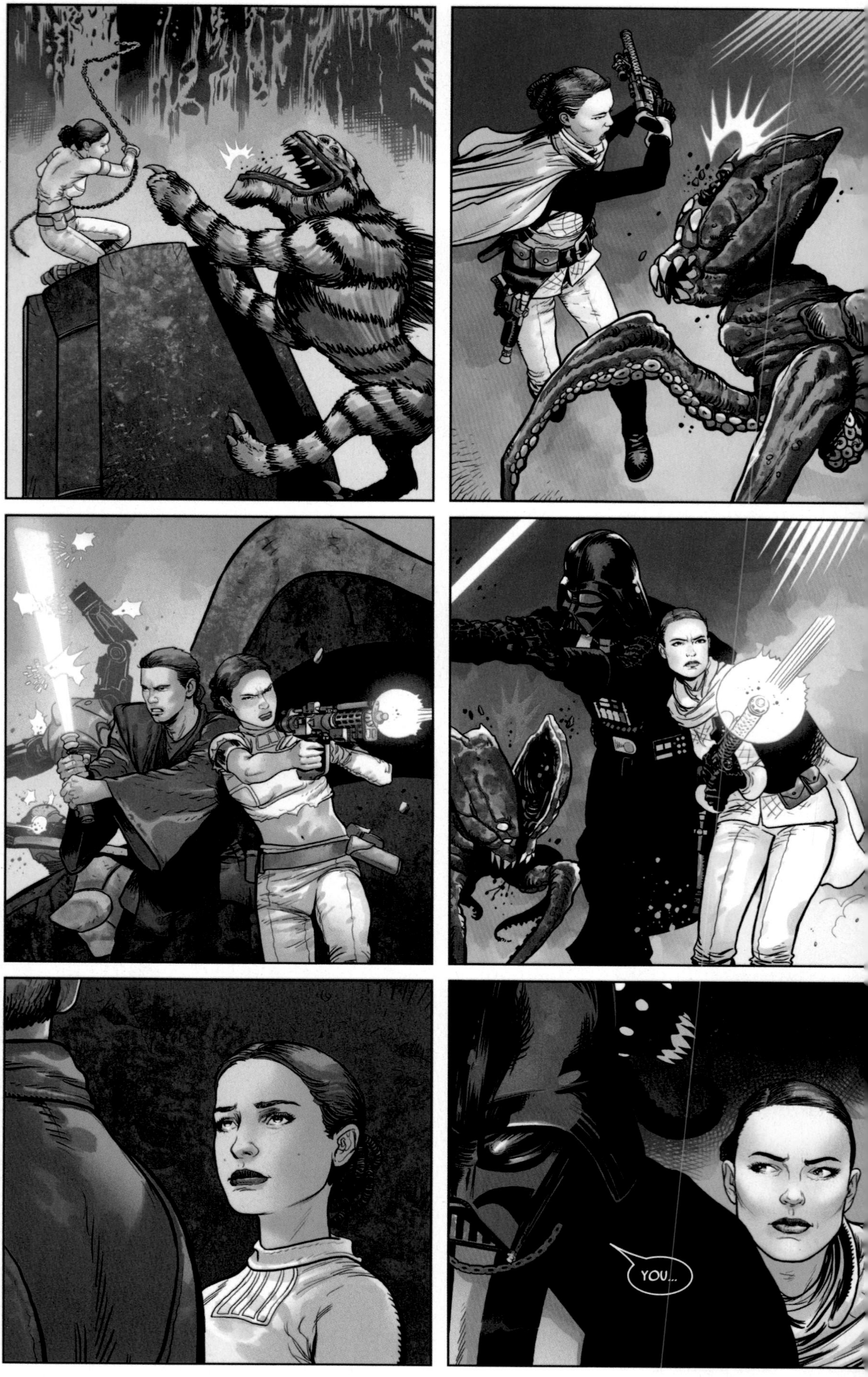
YOU...

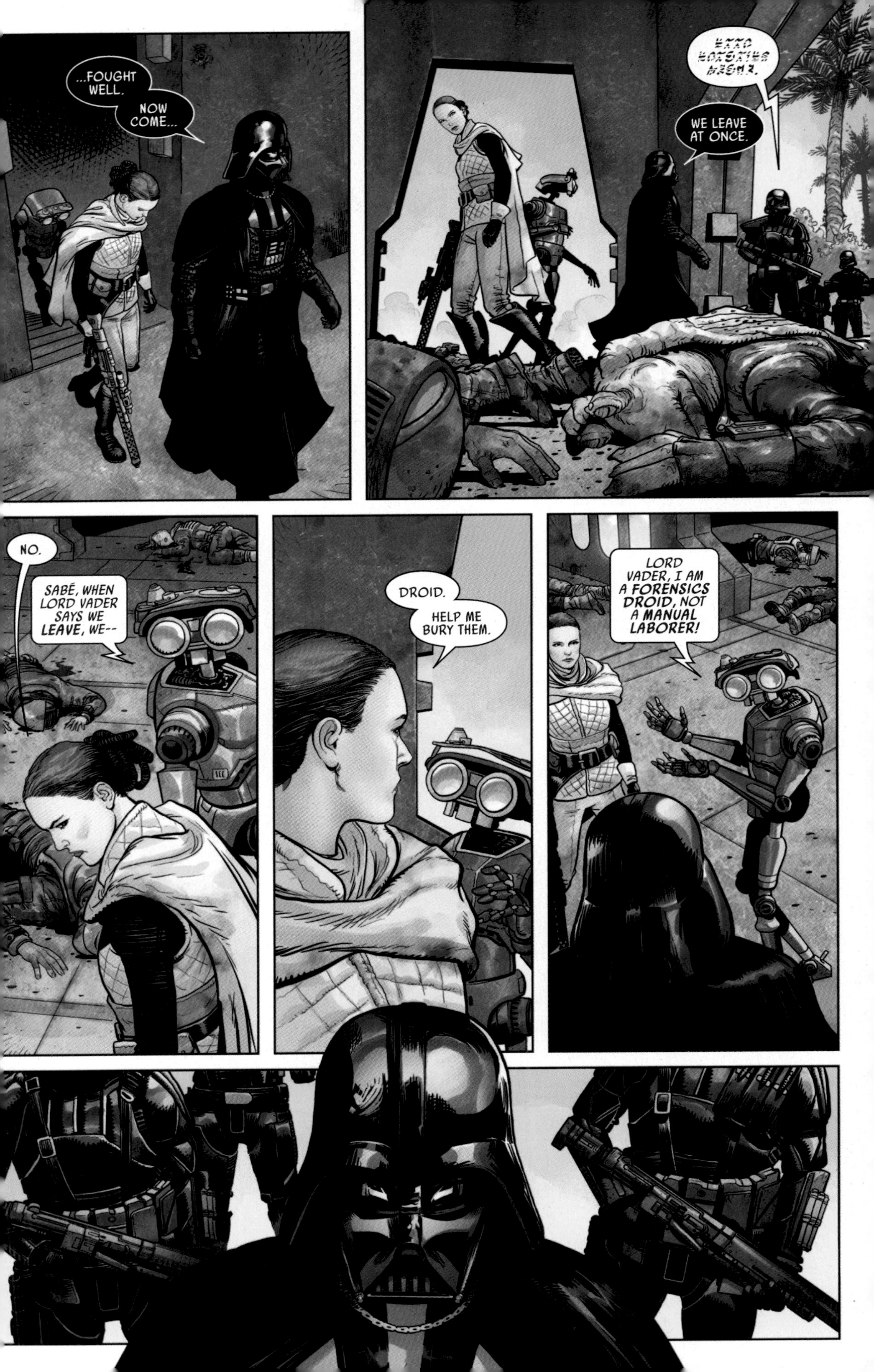
...FOUGHT WELL.
NOW COME...
WE LEAVE AT ONCE.
NO.
SABÉ, WHEN LORD VADER SAYS WE LEAVE, WE--
DROID.
HELP ME BURY THEM.
LORD VADER, I AM A FORENSICS DROID, NOT A MANUAL LABORER!

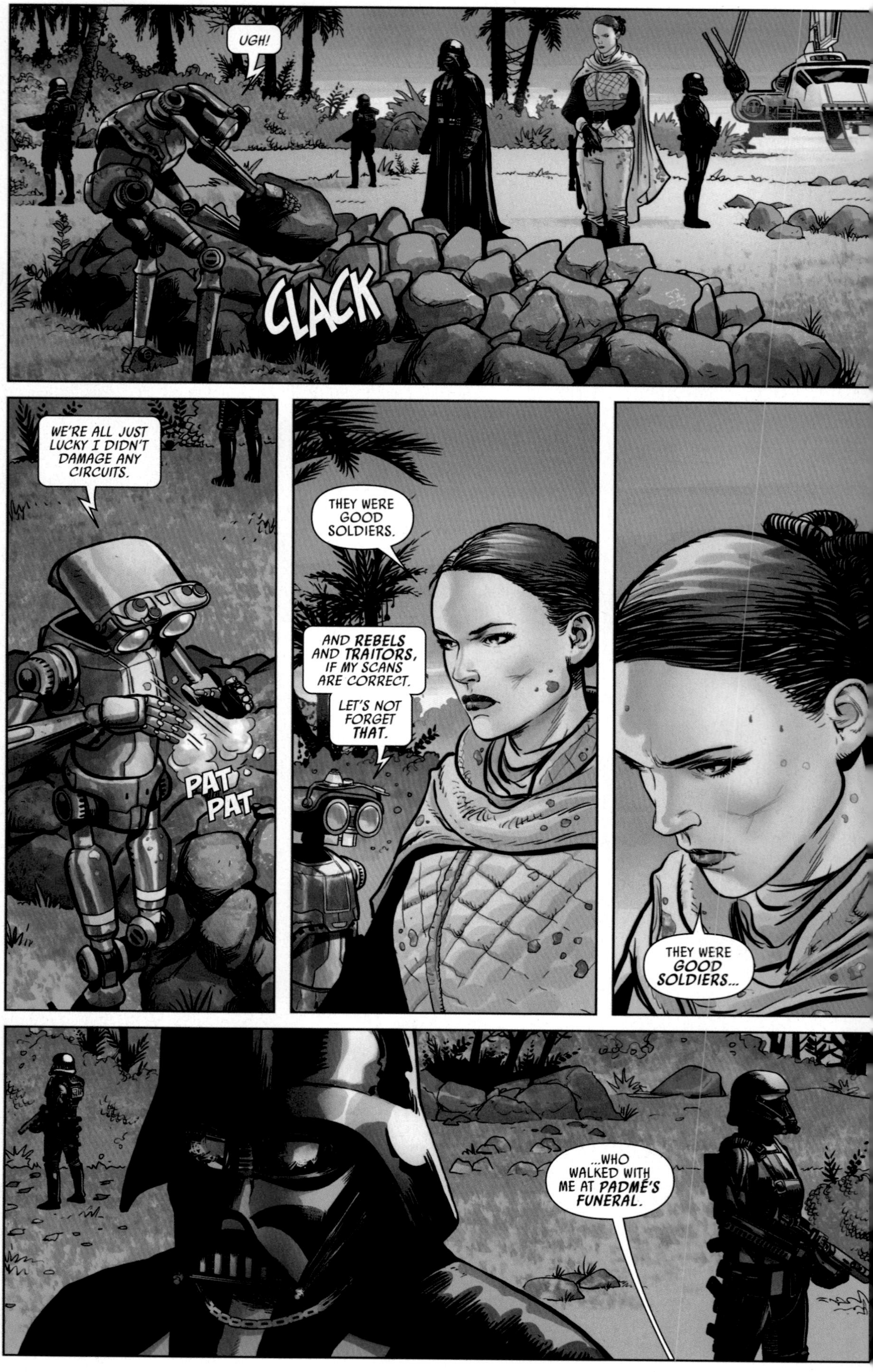

UGH!
CLACK
WE'RE ALL JUST LUCKY I DIDN'T DAMAGE ANY CIRCUITS.
PAT PAT
THEY WERE GOOD SOLDIERS.
AND REBELS AND TRAITORS, IF MY SCANS ARE CORRECT.
LET'S NOT FORGET THAT.
THEY WERE GOOD SOLDIERS...
...WHO WALKED WITH ME AT PADMÉ'S FUNERAL.

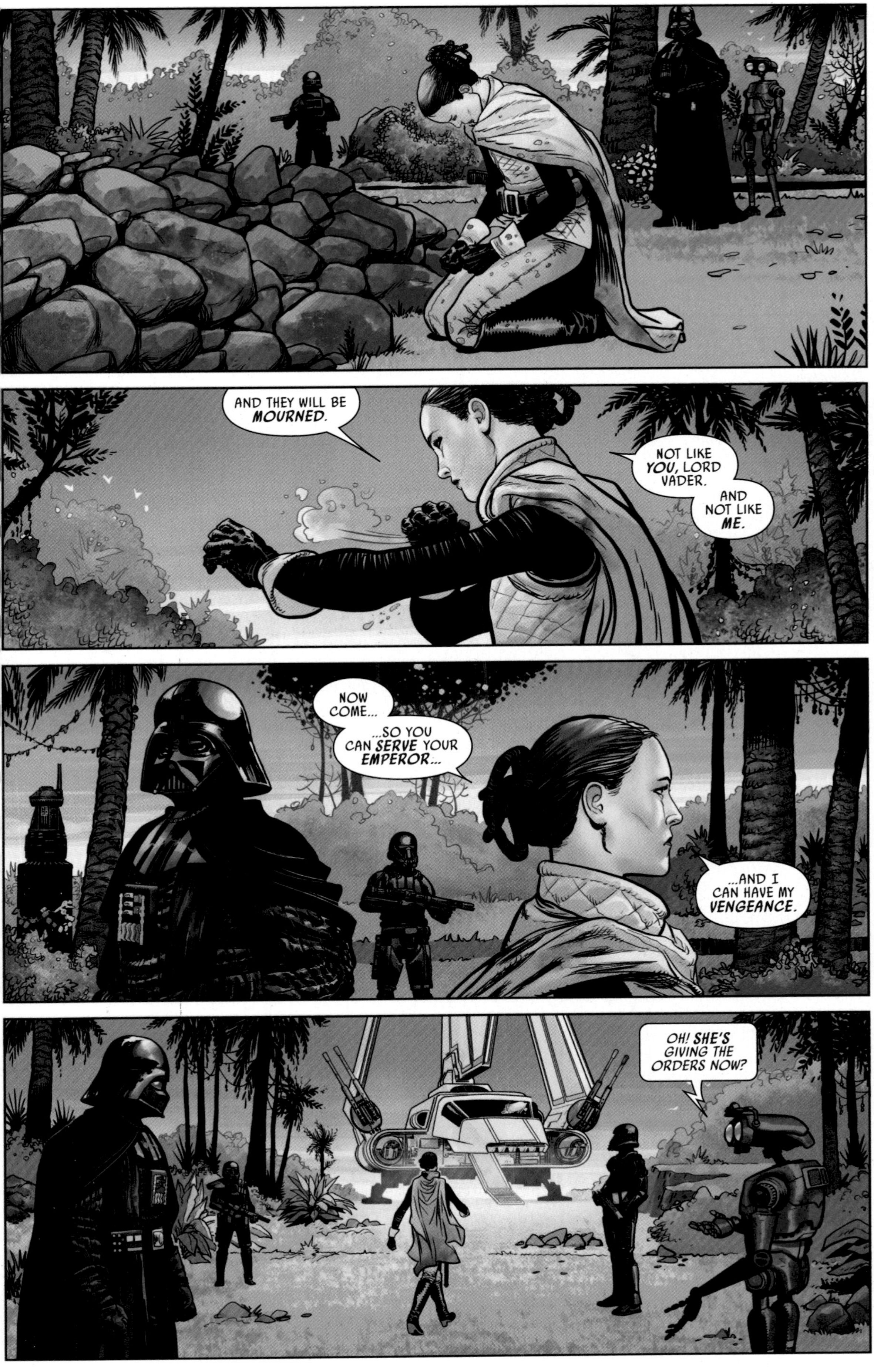
AND THEY WILL BE MOURNED.
NOT LIKE YOU, LORD VADER.
AND NOT LIKE ME.
NOW COME...
...SO YOU CAN SERVE YOUR EMPEROR...
...AND I CAN HAVE MY VENGEANCE.
OH! SHE'S GIVING THE ORDERS NOW?

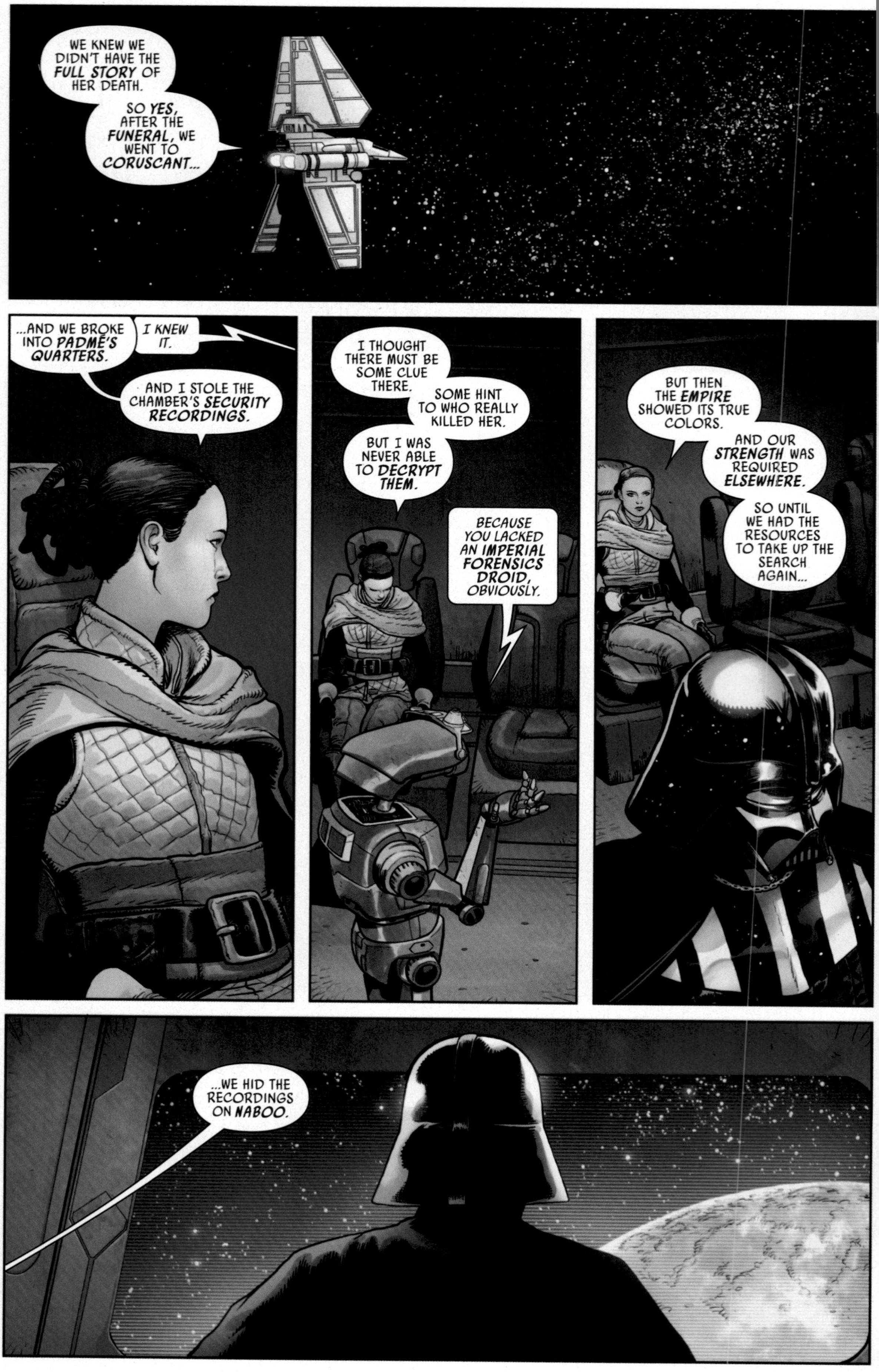

WE KNEW WE DIDN'T HAVE THE FULL STORY OF HER DEATH.
SO YES, AFTER THE FUNERAL, WE WENT TO CORUSCANT...
...AND WE BROKE INTO PADMÉ'S QUARTERS.
I KNEW IT.
AND I STOLE THE CHAMBER'S SECURITY RECORDINGS.
I THOUGHT THERE MUST BE SOME CLUE THERE.
SOME HINT TO WHO REALLY KILLED HER.
BUT I WAS NEVER ABLE TO DECRYPT THEM.
BECAUSE YOU LACKED AN IMPERIAL FORENSICS DROID, OBVIOUSLY.
BUT THEN THE EMPIRE SHOWED ITS TRUE COLORS.
AND OUR STRENGTH WAS REQUIRED ELSEWHERE.
SO UNTIL WE HAD THE RESOURCES TO TAKE UP THE SEARCH AGAIN...
...WE HID THE RECORDINGS ON NABOO.

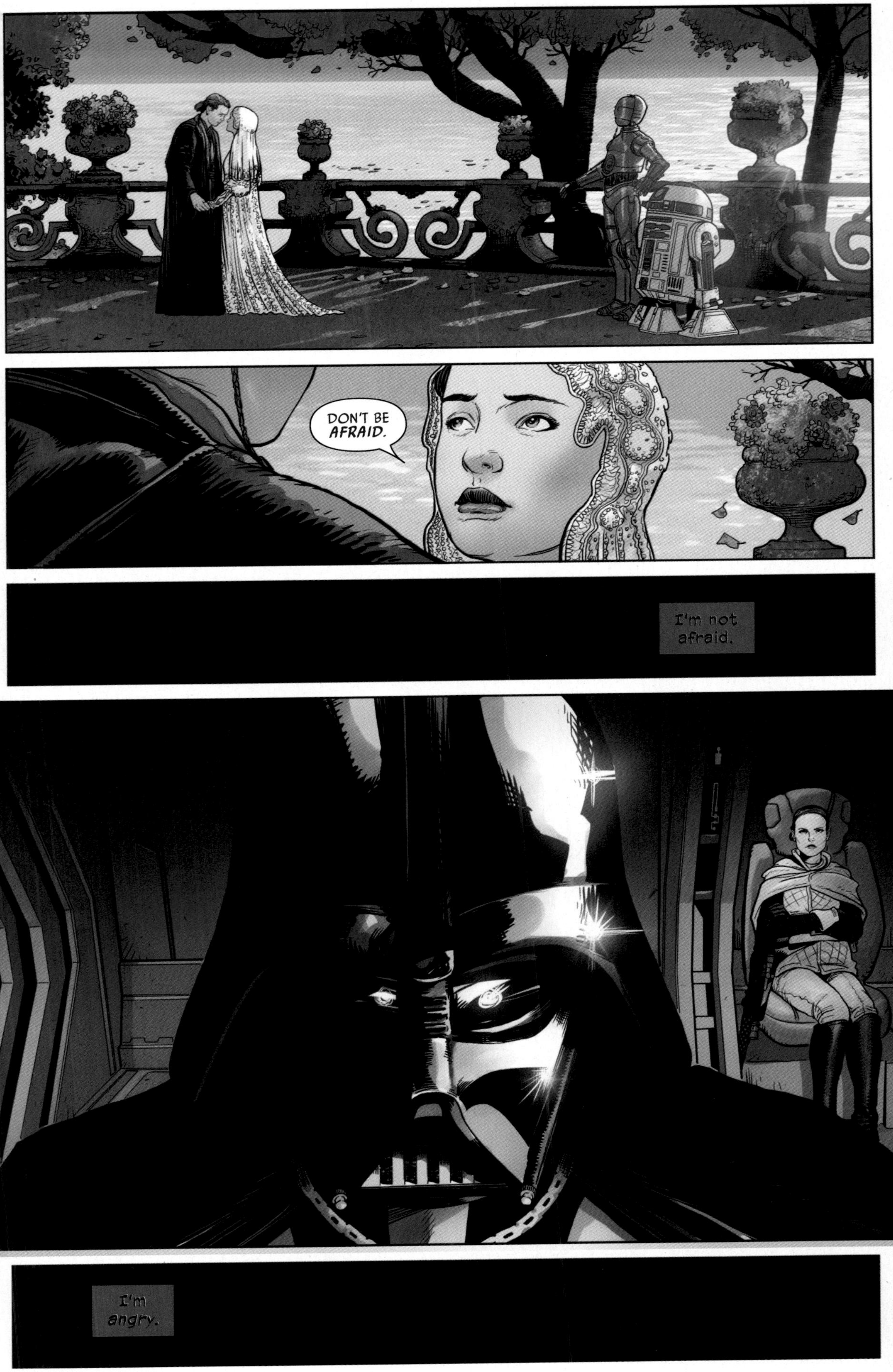
DON'T BE AFRAID.
I'm not afraid.
I'm angry.

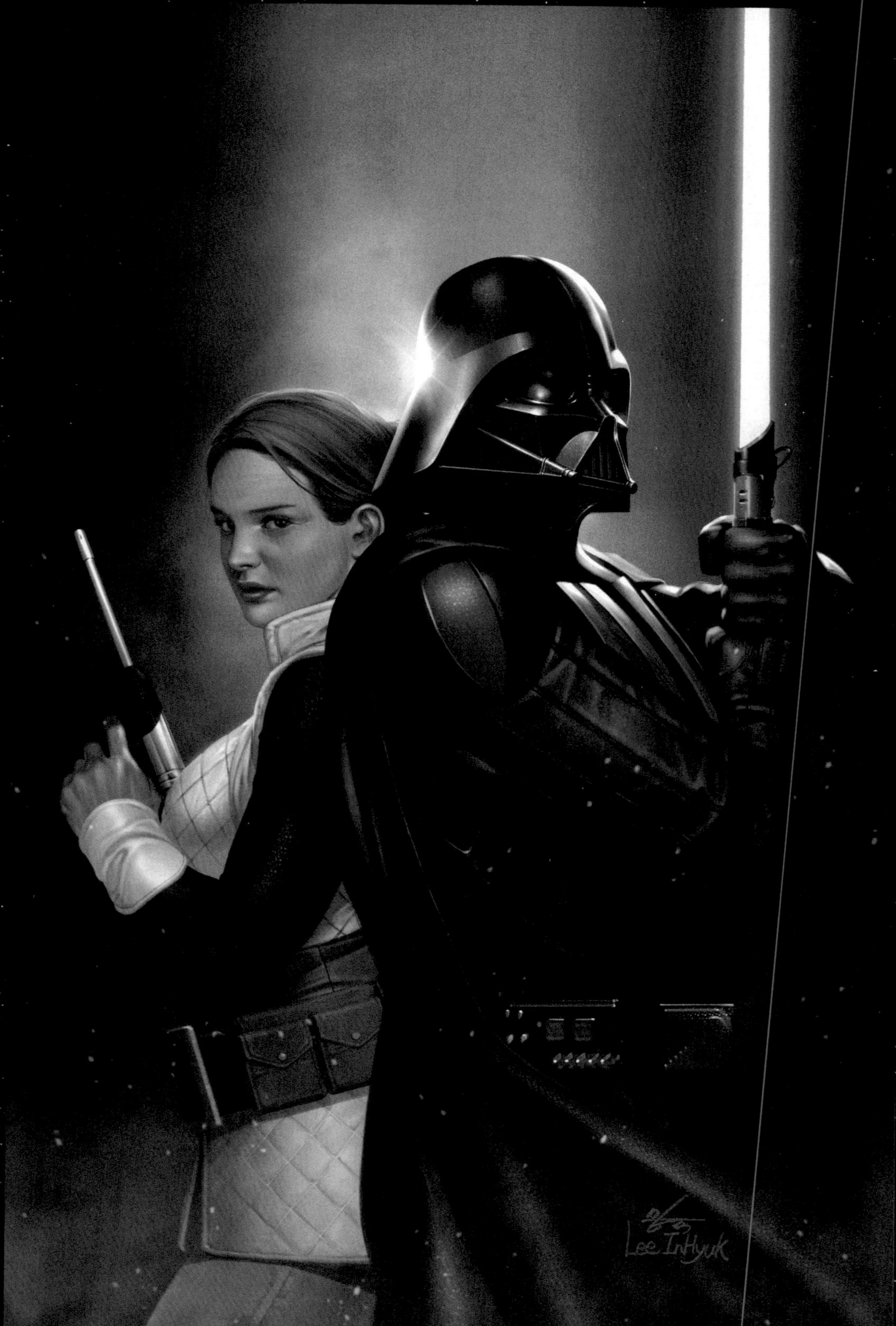
Lee InHyuk

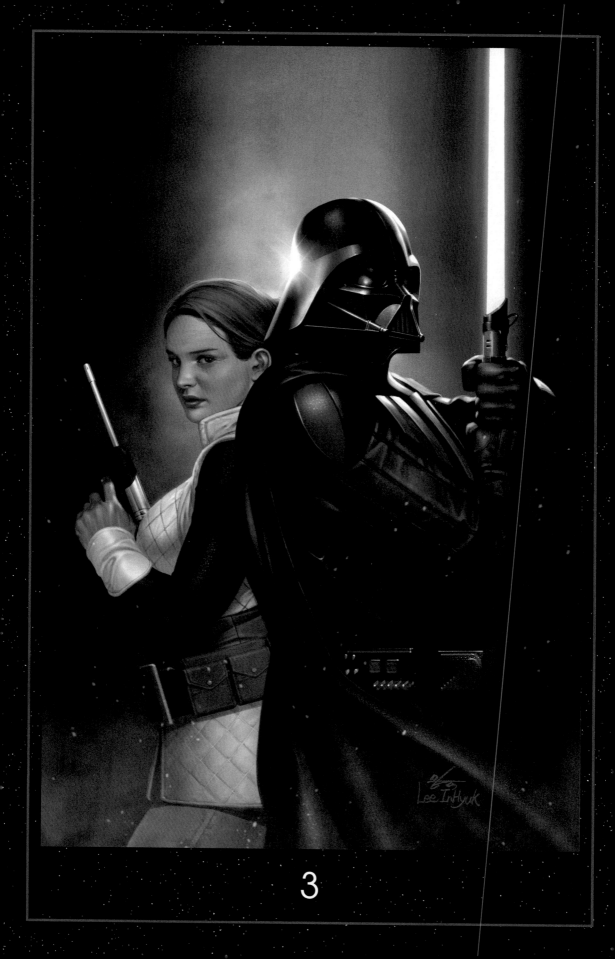

3

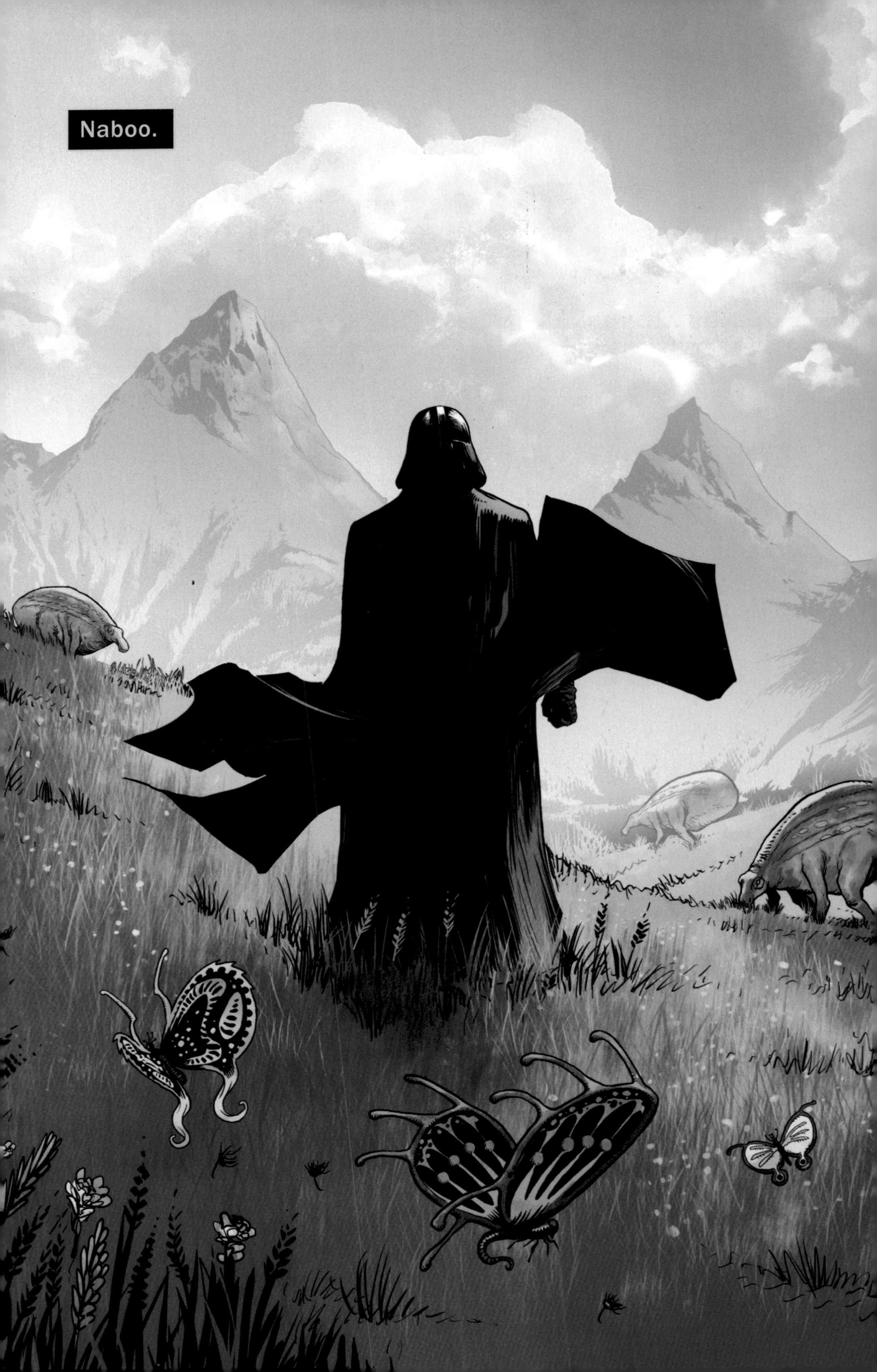
Naboo.

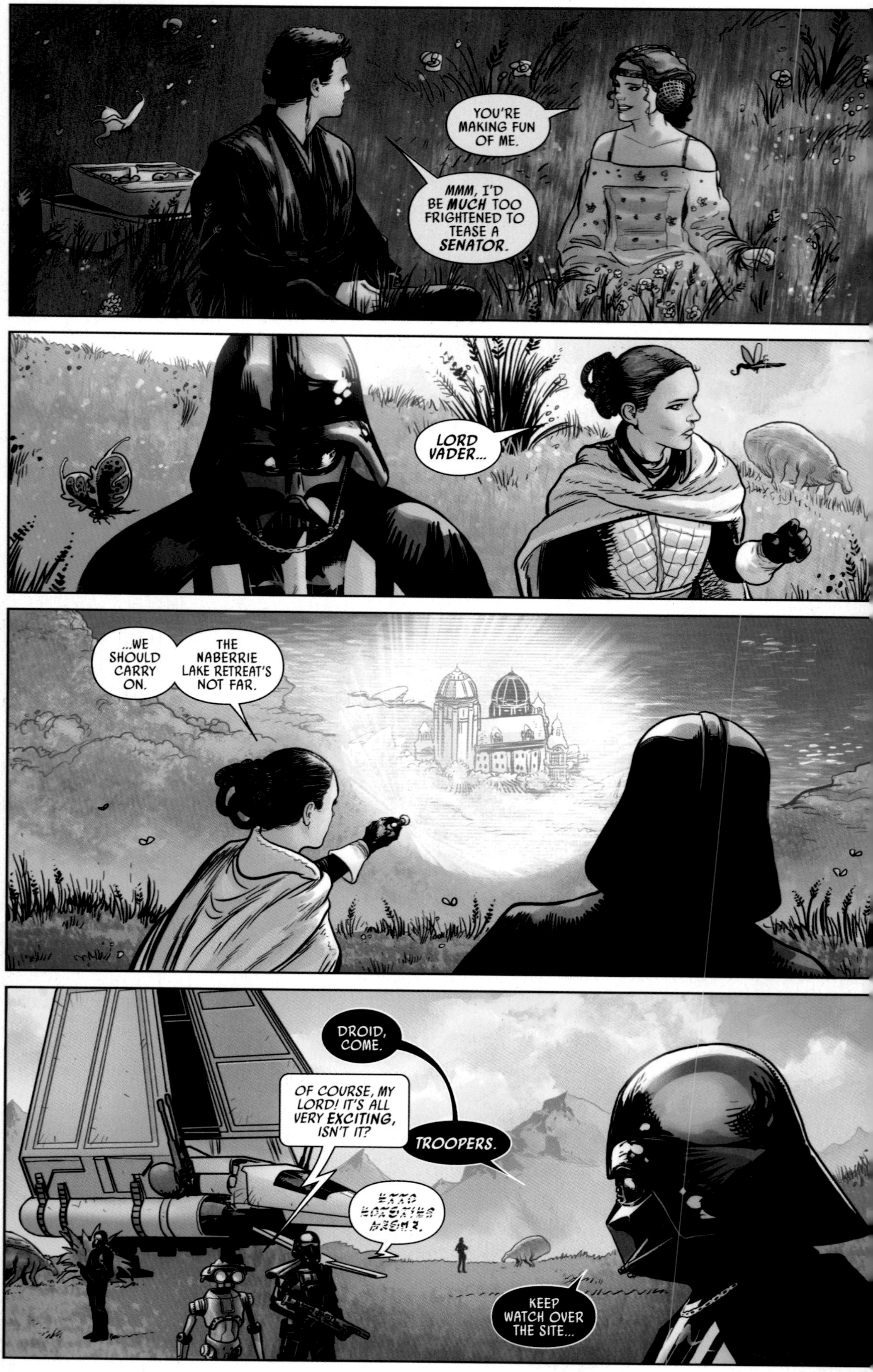
YOU'RE MAKING FUN OF ME.
MMM, I'D BE MUCH TOO FRIGHTENED TO TEASE A SENATOR.
LORD VADER...
...WE SHOULD CARRY ON.
THE NABERRIE LAKE RETREAT'S NOT FAR.
DROID, COME.
OF COURSE, MY LORD! IT'S ALL VERY EXCITING, ISN'T IT?
TROOPERS.
KEEP WATCH OVER THE SITE...

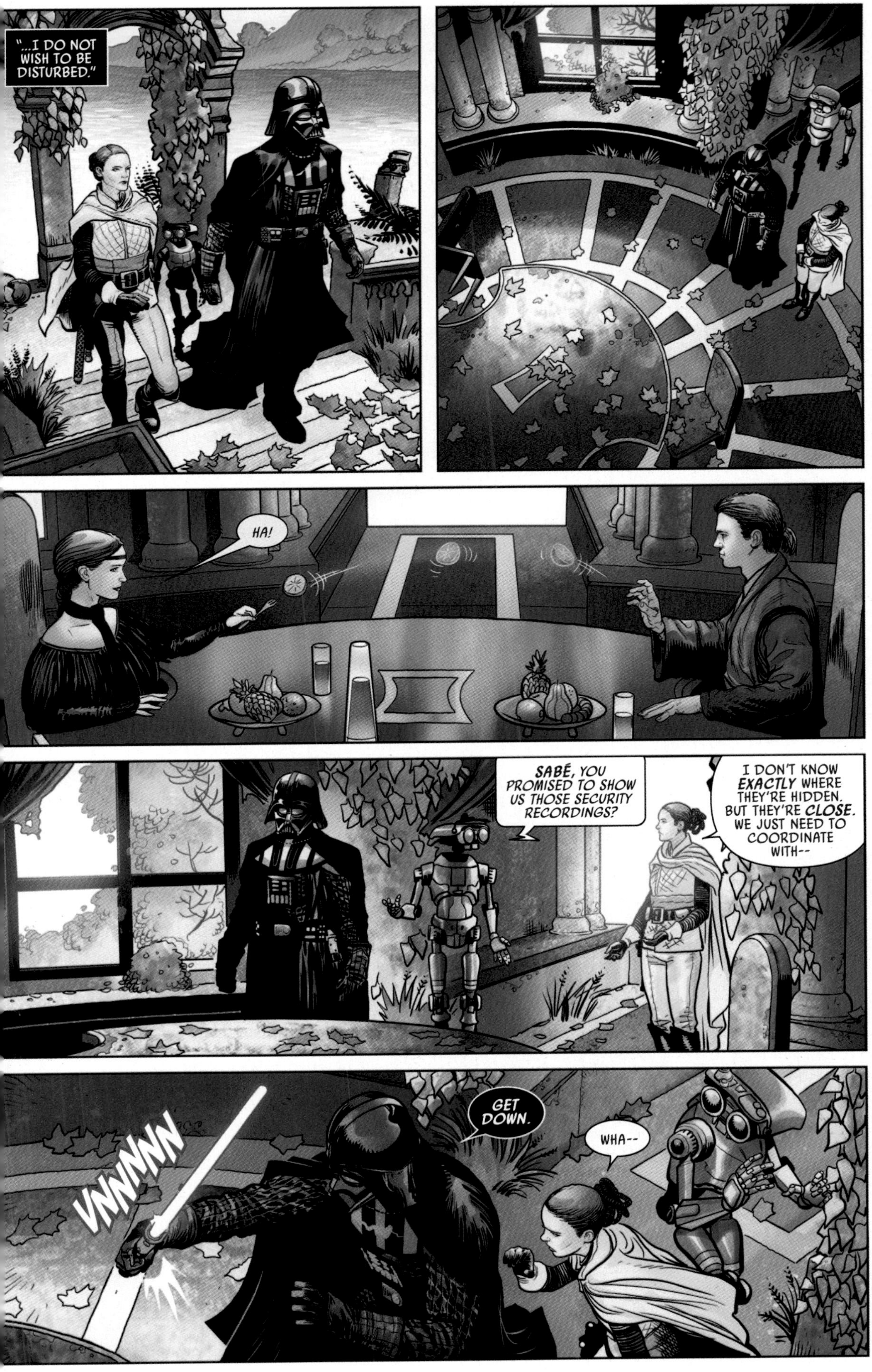
"...I DO NOT WISH TO BE DISTURBED."
HA!
SABÉ, YOU PROMISED TO SHOW US THOSE SECURITY RECORDINGS?
I DON'T KNOW EXACTLY WHERE THEY'RE HIDDEN. BUT THEY'RE CLOSE. WE JUST NEED TO COORDINATE WITH--
VNNNNN
GET DOWN.
WHA--

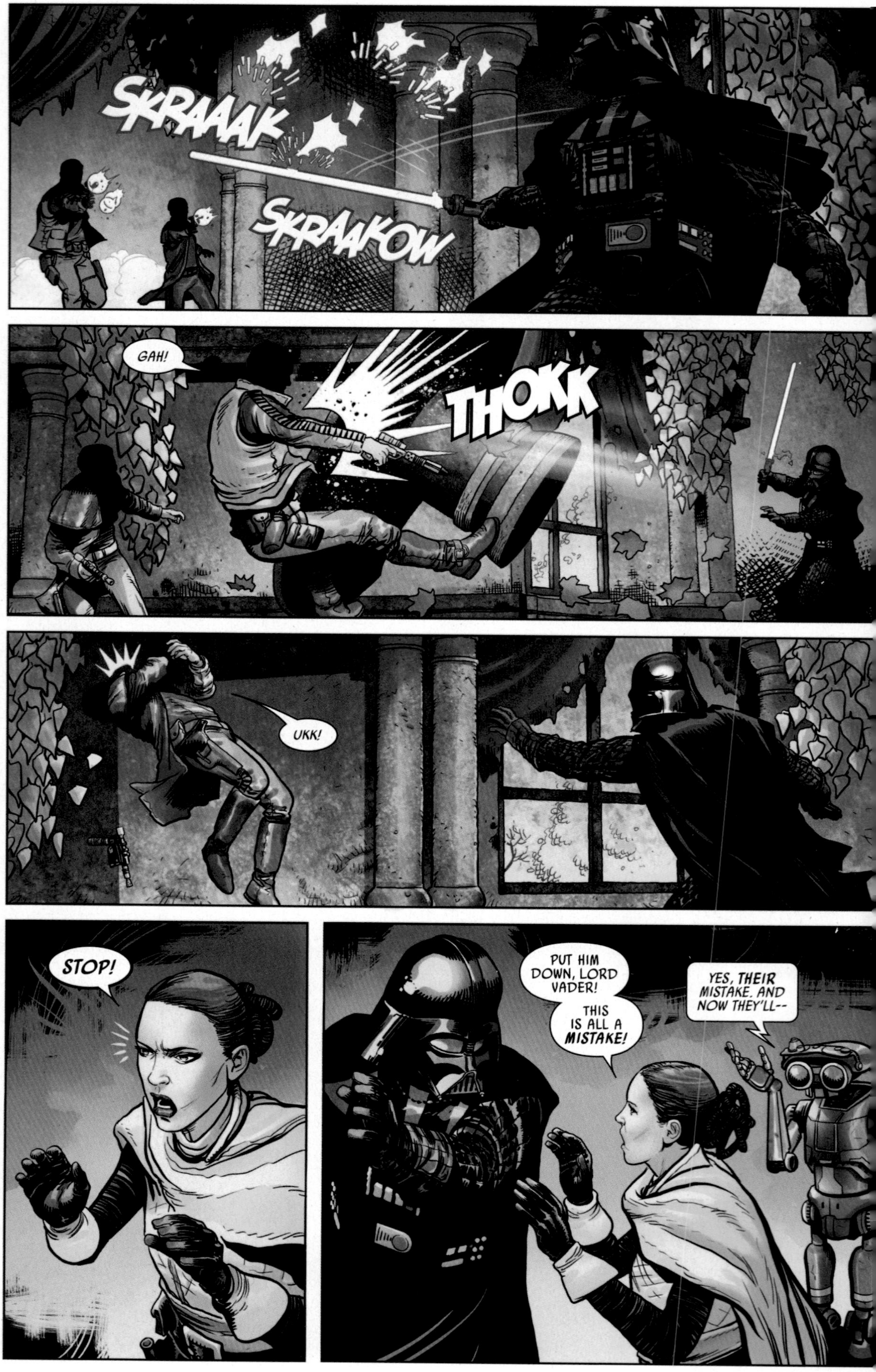
SKRAAAK
SKRAAKOW
GAH!
THOKK
UKK!
STOP!
PUT HIM DOWN, LORD VADER!
THIS IS ALL A MISTAKE!
YES, THEIR MISTAKE. AND NOW THEY'LL--

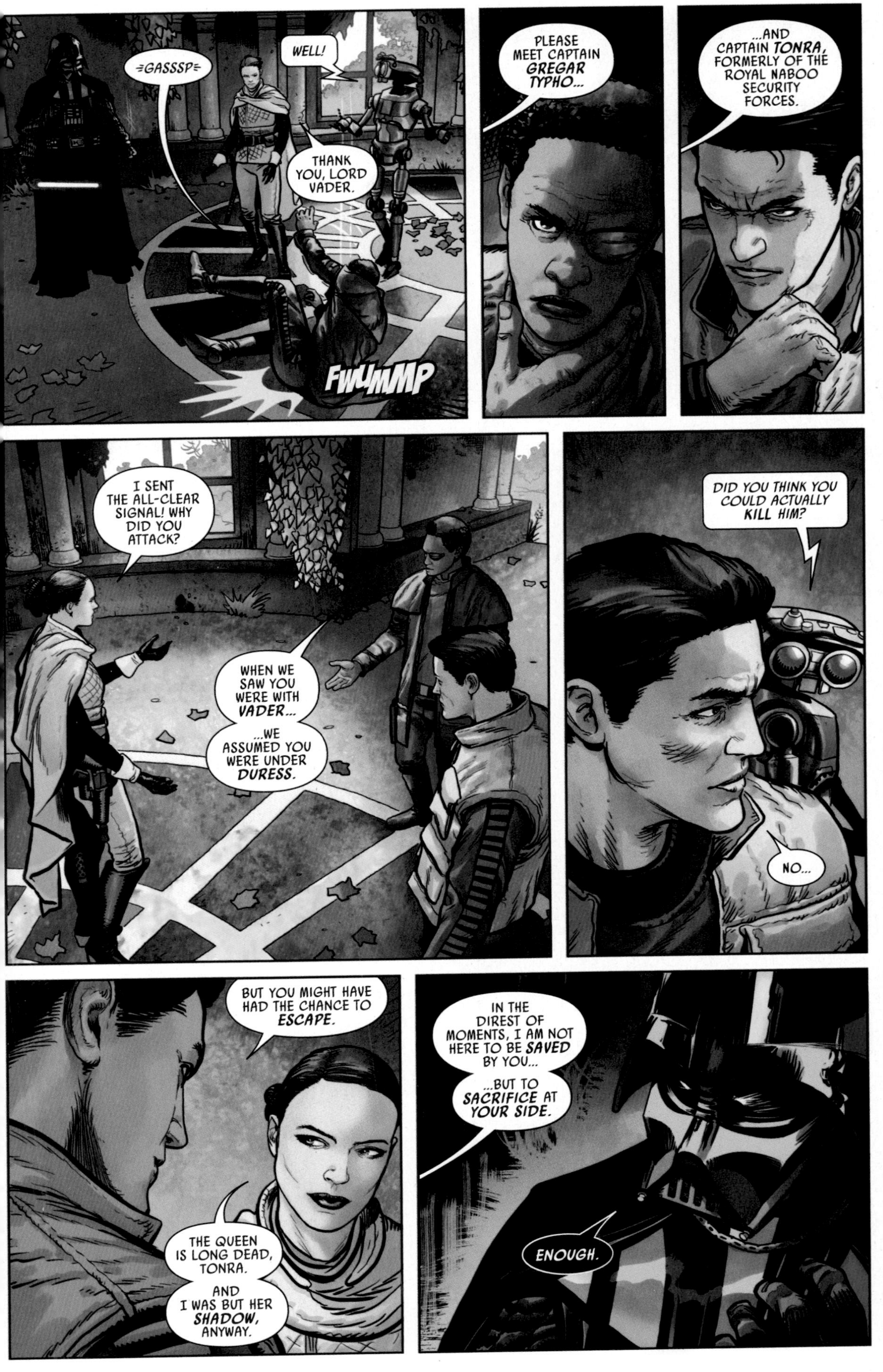

=GASSSP=
WELL!
THANK YOU, LORD VADER.
FWUMMP
PLEASE MEET CAPTAIN GREGAR TYPHO...
...AND CAPTAIN TONRA, FORMERLY OF THE ROYAL NABOO SECURITY FORCES.
I SENT THE ALL-CLEAR SIGNAL! WHY DID YOU ATTACK?
WHEN WE SAW YOU WERE WITH VADER...
...WE ASSUMED YOU WERE UNDER DURESS.
DID YOU THINK YOU COULD ACTUALLY KILL HIM?
NO...
BUT YOU MIGHT HAVE HAD THE CHANCE TO ESCAPE.
THE QUEEN IS LONG DEAD, TONRA.
AND I WAS BUT HER SHADOW, ANYWAY.
IN THE DIREST OF MOMENTS, I AM NOT HERE TO BE SAVED BY YOU...
...BUT TO SACRIFICE AT YOUR SIDE.
ENOUGH.

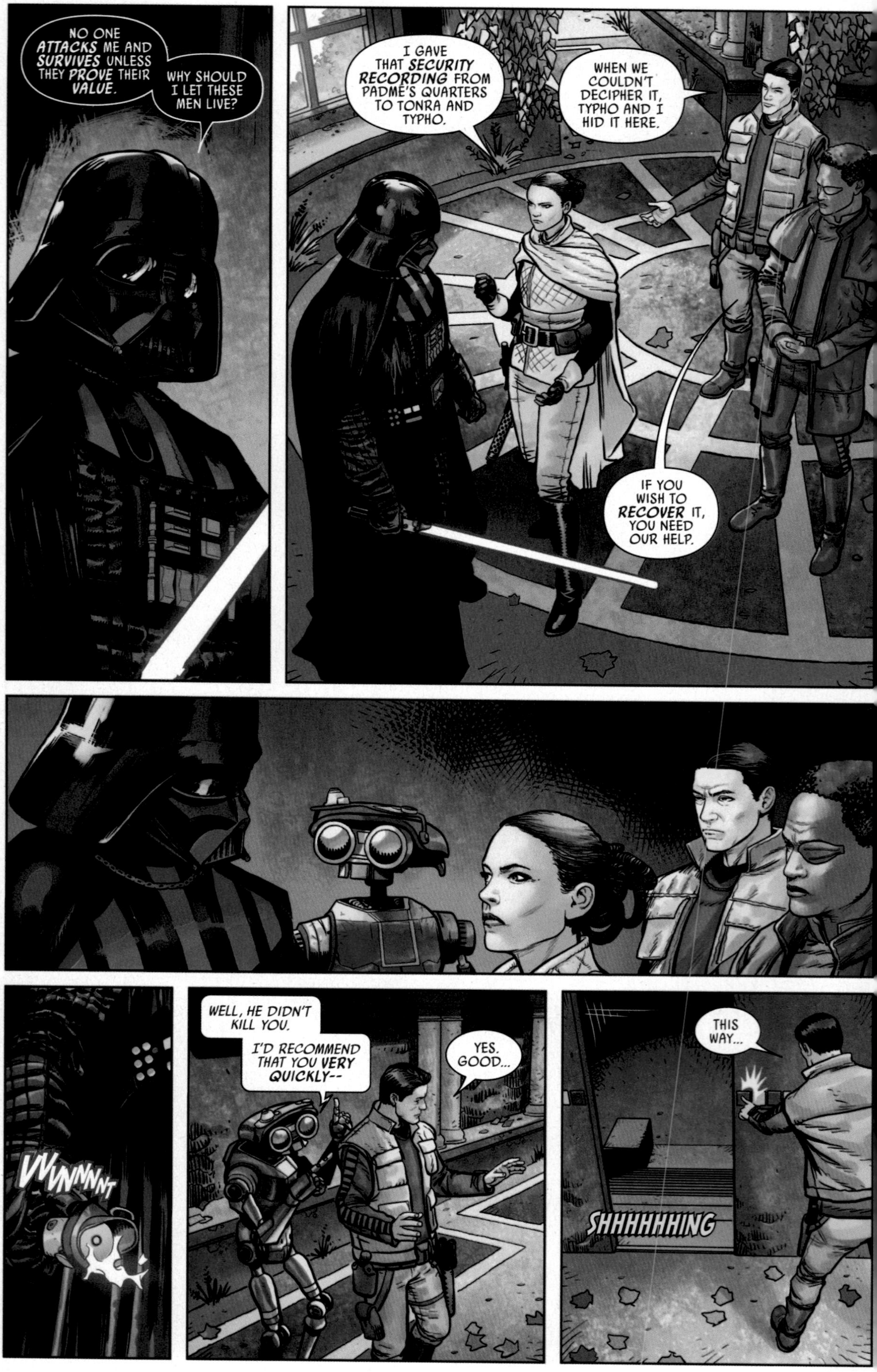
NO ONE ATTACKS ME AND SURVIVES UNLESS THEY PROVE THEIR VALUE.
WHY SHOULD I LET THESE MEN LIVE?
I GAVE THAT SECURITY RECORDING FROM PADMÉ'S QUARTERS TO TONRA AND TYPHO.
WHEN WE COULDN'T DECIPHER IT, TYPHO AND I HID IT HERE.
IF YOU WISH TO RECOVER IT, YOU NEED OUR HELP.
VVVNNNNT
WELL, HE DIDN'T KILL YOU.
I'D RECOMMEND THAT YOU VERY QUICKLY--
YES. GOOD...
THIS WAY...
SHHHHHHING

WE... ...WE ALWAYS SUSPECTED PADMÉ WAS *MURDERED.*

ARE YOU SEEKING HER KILLERS?

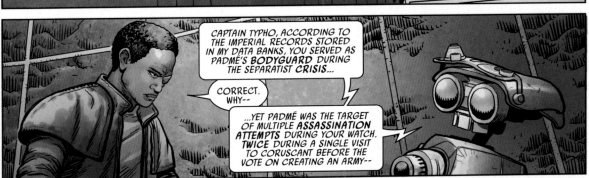

CAPTAIN TYPHO, ACCORDING TO THE IMPERIAL RECORDS STORED IN MY DATA BANKS, YOU SERVED AS PADMÉ'S *BODYGUARD* DURING THE SEPARATIST *CRISIS...*

CORRECT. WHY--

...YET PADMÉ WAS THE TARGET OF MULTIPLE *ASSASSINATION ATTEMPTS* DURING YOUR WATCH. *TWICE* DURING A SINGLE VISIT TO CORUSCANT BEFORE THE VOTE ON CREATING AN ARMY--

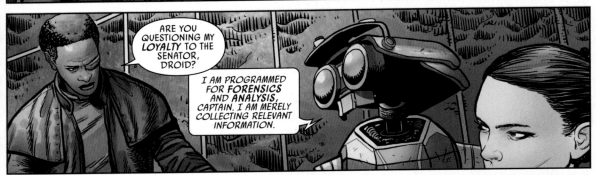

ARE YOU QUESTIONING MY *LOYALTY* TO THE SENATOR, DROID?

I AM PROGRAMMED FOR *FORENSICS* AND *ANALYSIS,* CAPTAIN. I AM MERELY COLLECTING RELEVANT INFORMATION.

MY TEAM THWARTED *COUNTLESS* THREATS.

THOSE ATTEMPTS YOU MENTIONED WERE STOPPED BY TWO HEROES...

...THE HANDMAIDEN *CORDÉ,* WHO GAVE HER LIFE THAT DAY...

...AND THE JEDI *ANAKIN SKYWALKER...*

...WHO GAVE HIS *OWN* A FEW YEARS LATER.

WHEN...

...DID YOU LAST SEE PADMÉ?

ON CORUSCANT. AFTER THE CLONE TROOPERS BURNED THE JEDI TEMPLE.

SHE INSISTED ON FLYING TO MUSTAFAR-- *ALONE.*

SAID IT WAS *PERSONAL.*

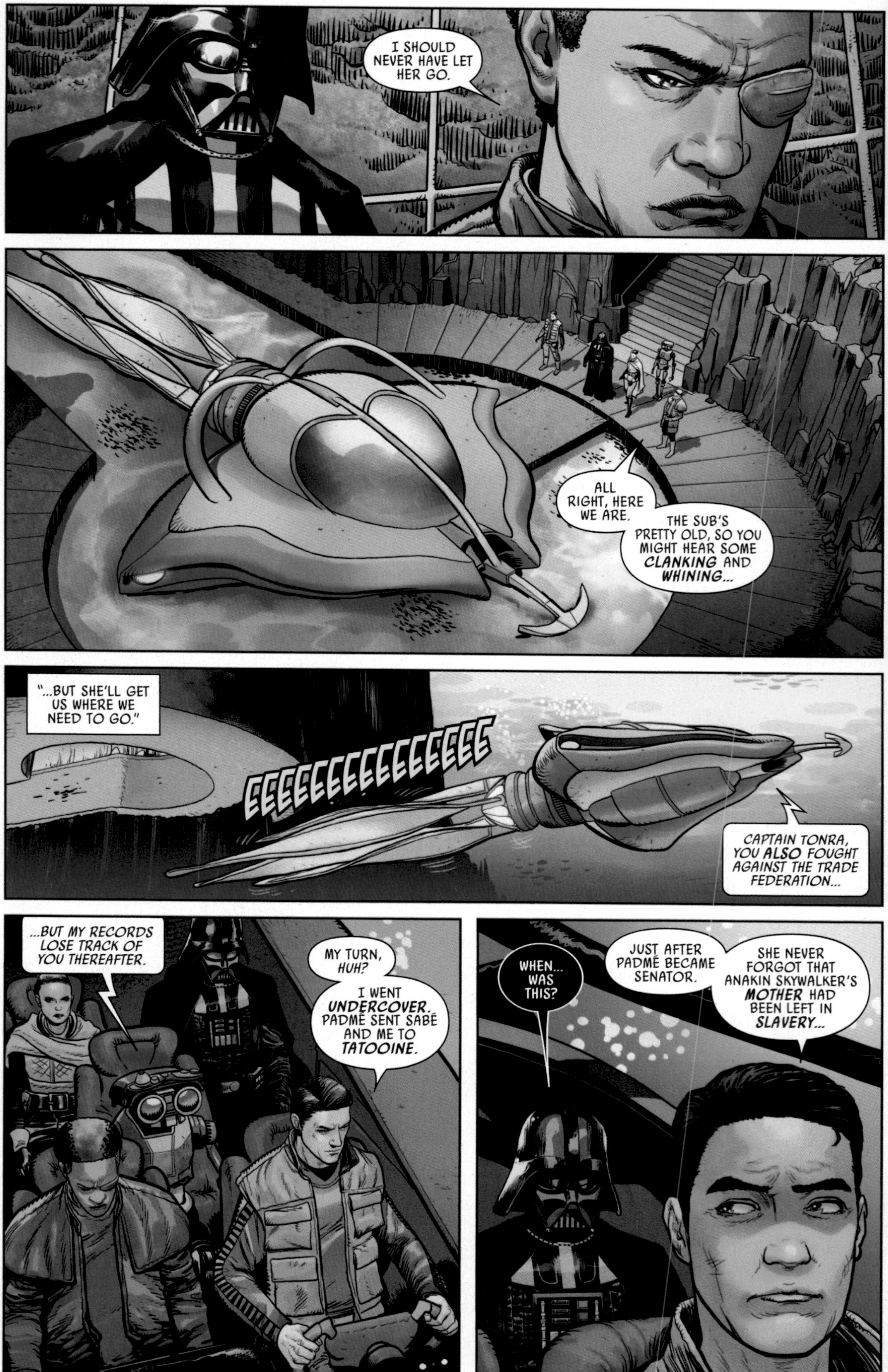
I SHOULD NEVER HAVE LET HER GO.
ALL RIGHT, HERE WE ARE.
THE SUB'S PRETTY OLD, SO YOU MIGHT HEAR SOME CLANKING AND WHINING...
"...BUT SHE'LL GET US WHERE WE NEED TO GO."
EEEEEEEEEEEEEEEEE
CAPTAIN TONRA, YOU ALSO FOUGHT AGAINST THE TRADE FEDERATION...
...BUT MY RECORDS LOSE TRACK OF YOU THEREAFTER.
MY TURN, HUH?
I WENT UNDERCOVER. PADMÉ SENT SABÉ AND ME TO TATOOINE.
WHEN... WAS THIS?
JUST AFTER PADMÉ BECAME SENATOR.
SHE NEVER FORGOT THAT ANAKIN SKYWALKER'S MOTHER HAD BEEN LEFT IN SLAVERY...

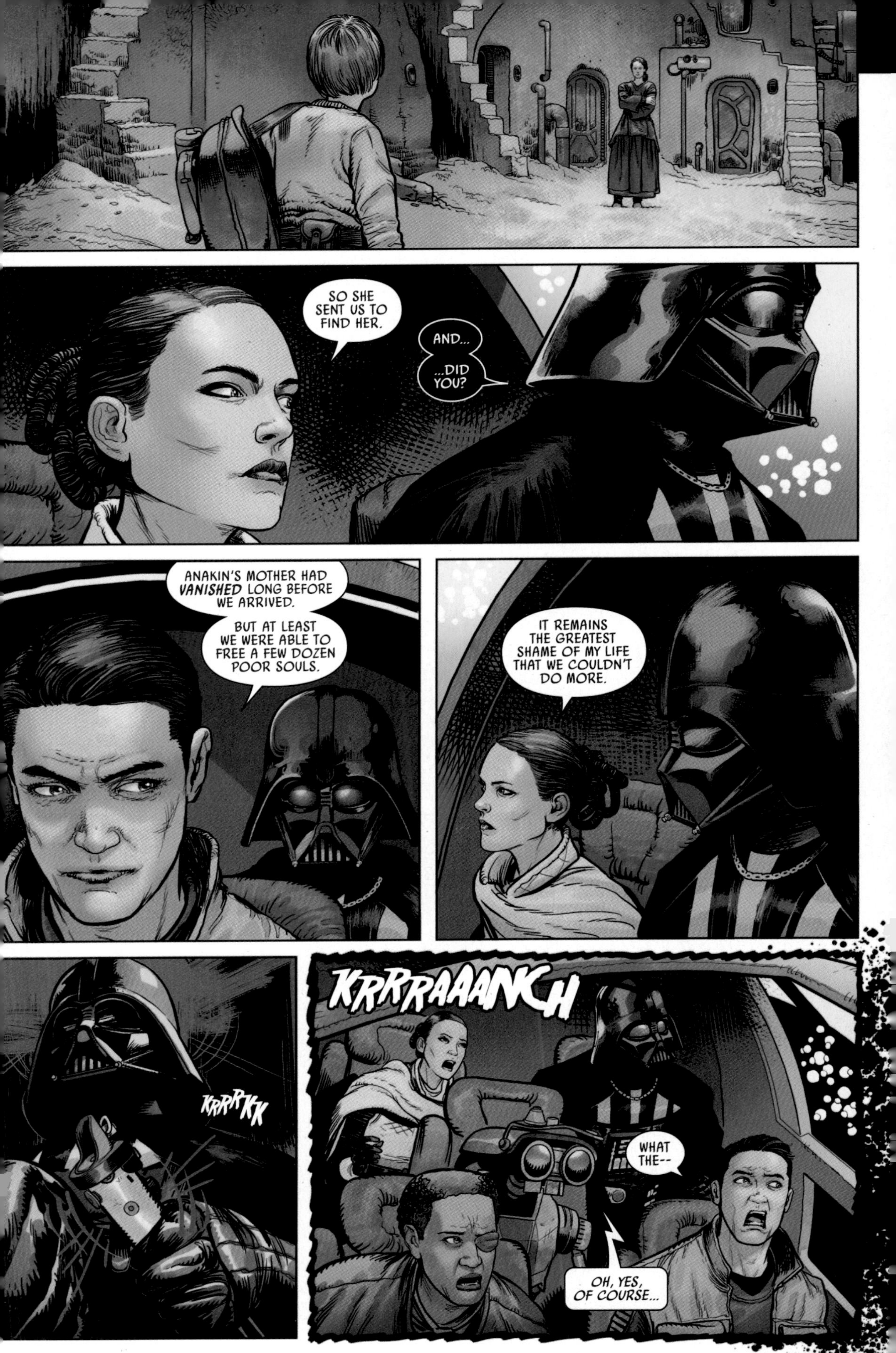

SO SHE SENT US TO FIND HER.
AND...
...DID YOU?
ANAKIN'S MOTHER HAD VANISHED LONG BEFORE WE ARRIVED.
BUT AT LEAST WE WERE ABLE TO FREE A FEW DOZEN POOR SOULS.
IT REMAINS THE GREATEST SHAME OF MY LIFE THAT WE COULDN'T DO MORE.
KRRRKK
KRRRAAANCH
WHAT THE--
OH, YES, OF COURSE...

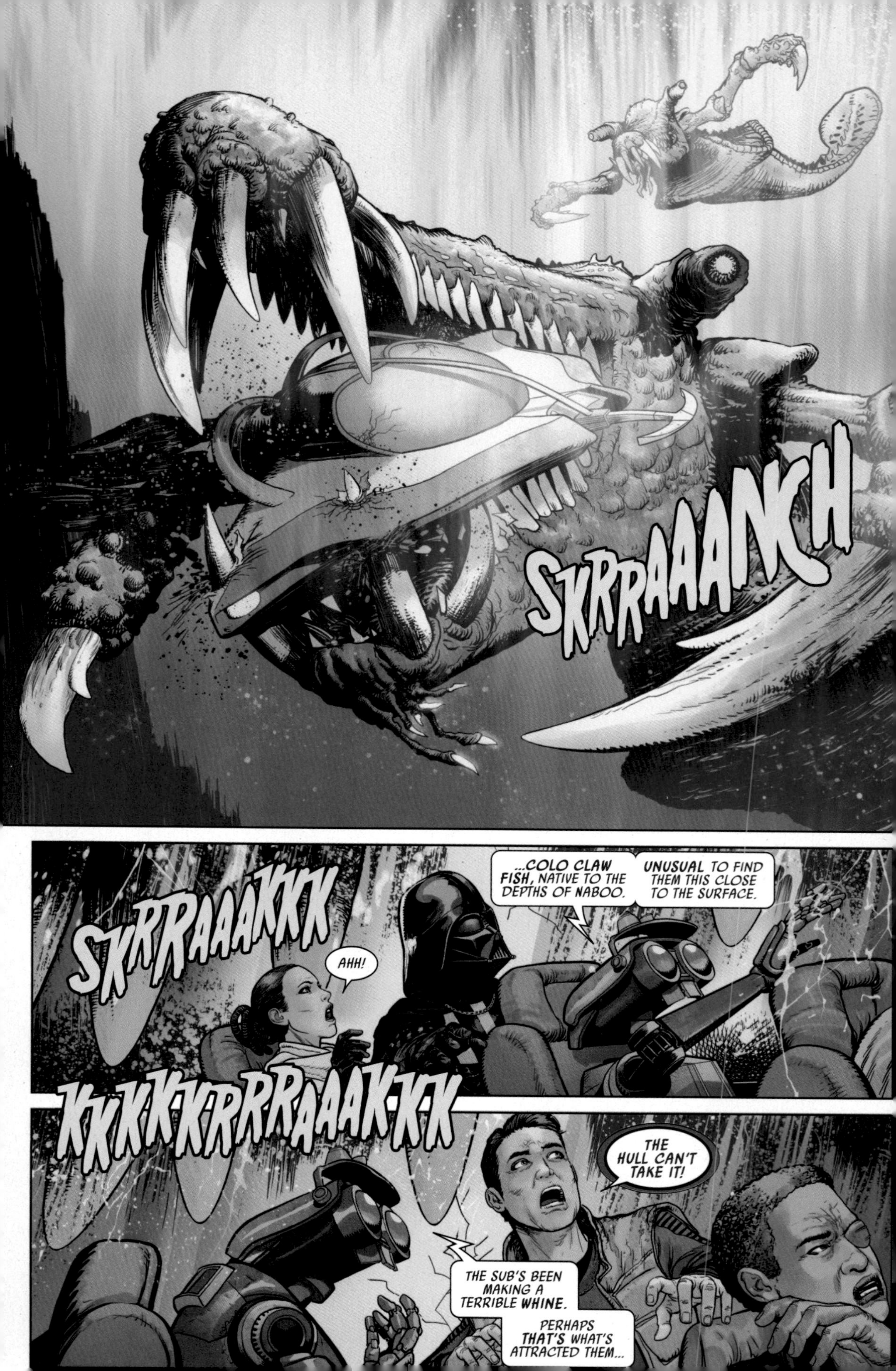
SKRRAAANCH
SKRRAAAKKK
AHH!
...COLO CLAW FISH, NATIVE TO THE DEPTHS OF NABOO.
UNUSUAL TO FIND THEM THIS CLOSE TO THE SURFACE.
KKKKKRRRRAAAKKK
THE HULL CAN'T TAKE IT!
THE SUB'S BEEN MAKING A TERRIBLE WHINE.
PERHAPS THAT'S WHAT'S ATTRACTED THEM...

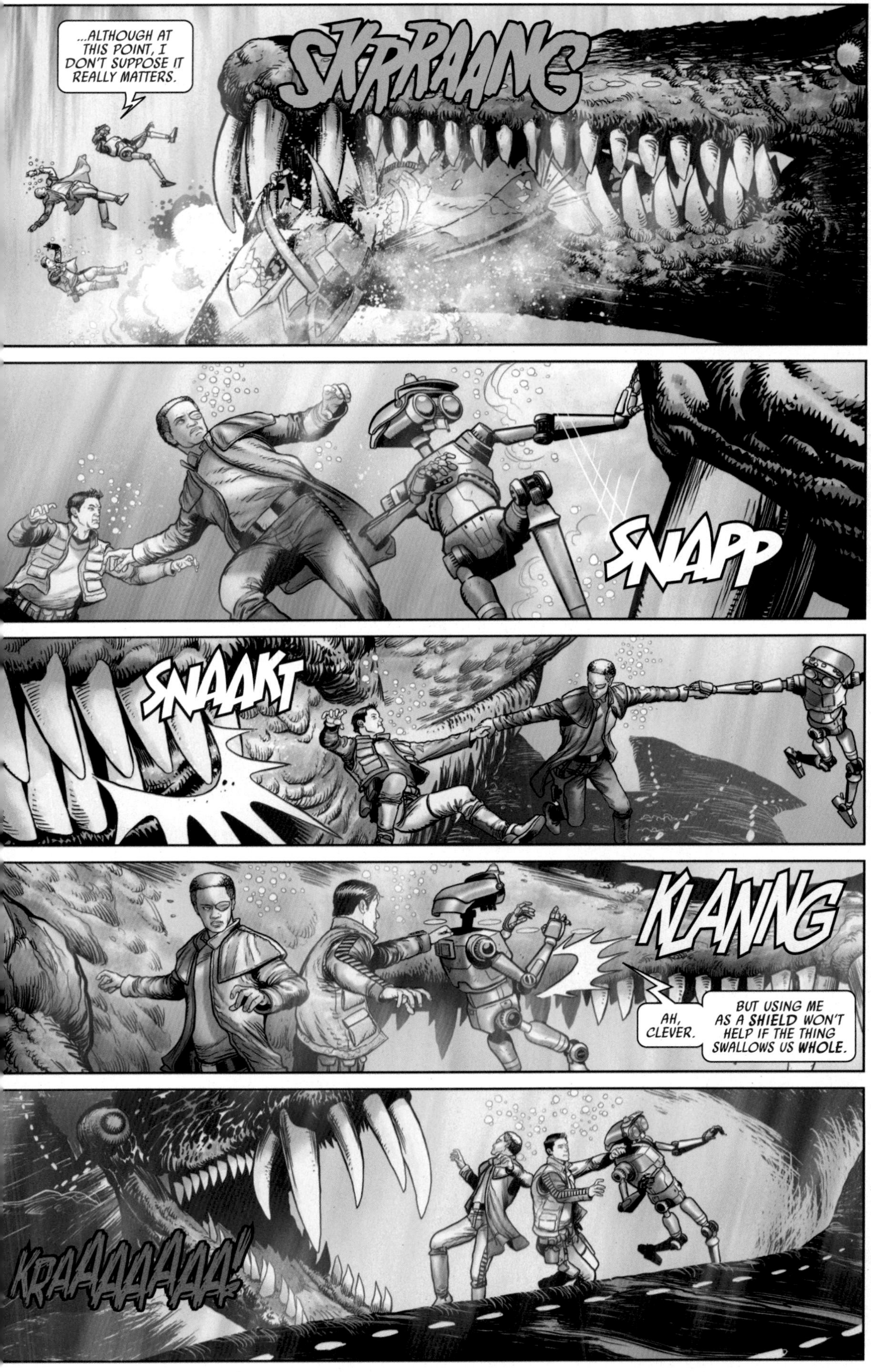
...ALTHOUGH AT THIS POINT, I DON'T SUPPOSE IT REALLY MATTERS.
SKRRAANG
SNAPP
SNAAKT
KLANNG
AH, CLEVER.
BUT USING ME AS A SHIELD WON'T HELP IF THE THING SWALLOWS US WHOLE.
KRAAAAAAAA!

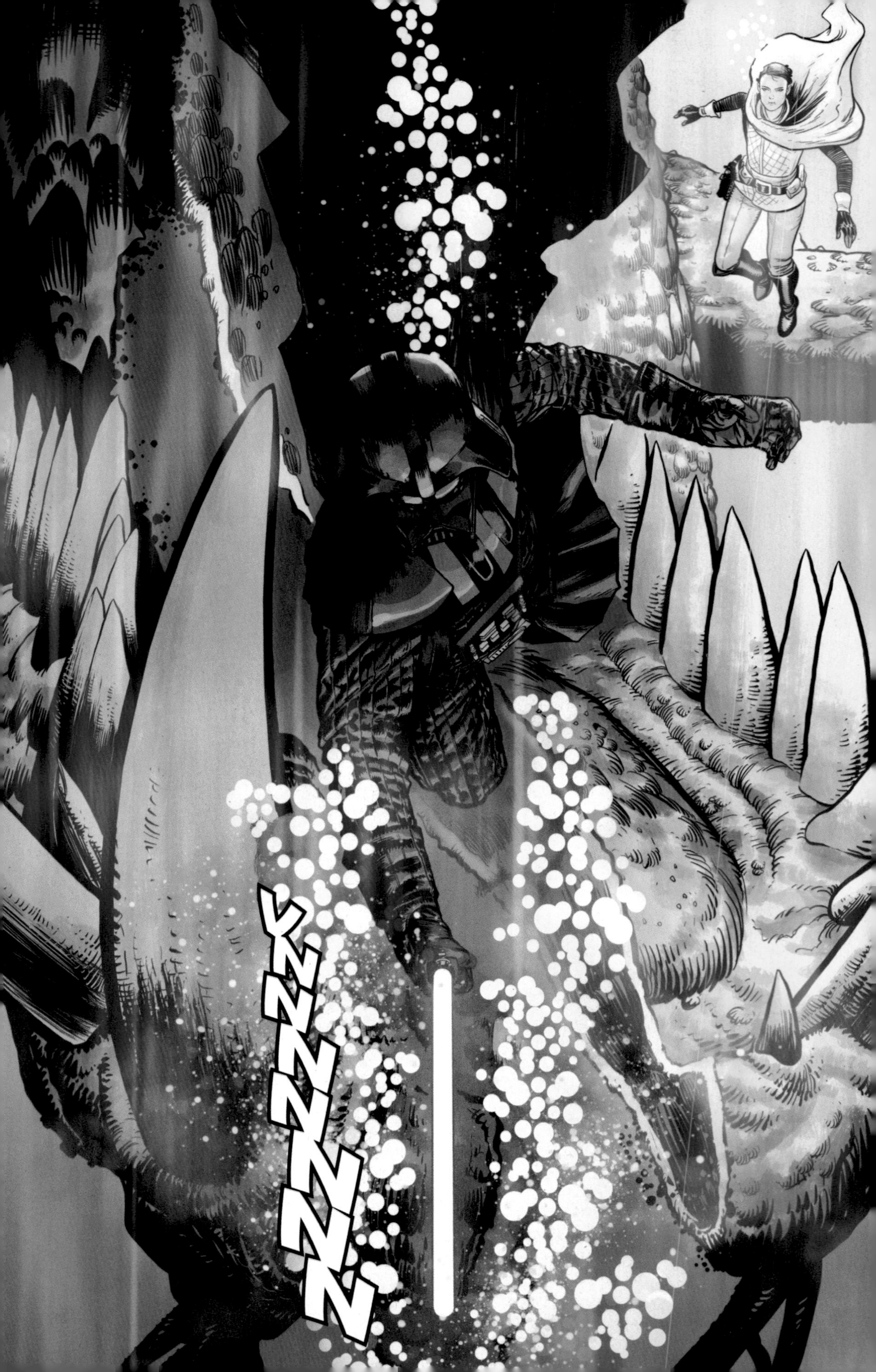
VNNNNNNNN

KAAAAAAA!

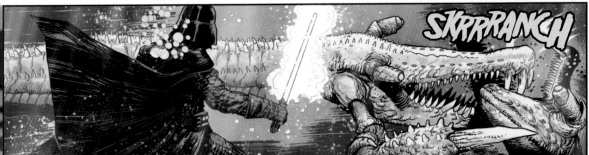

SKRRRANCH

VERY EXCITING! I HOPE YOU APPRECIATE LORD VADER NOW!

ALTHOUGH I DON'T KNOW HOW MUCH LONGER YOU ALL CAN SURVIVE WITHOUT AIR...

AH, PERFECT!

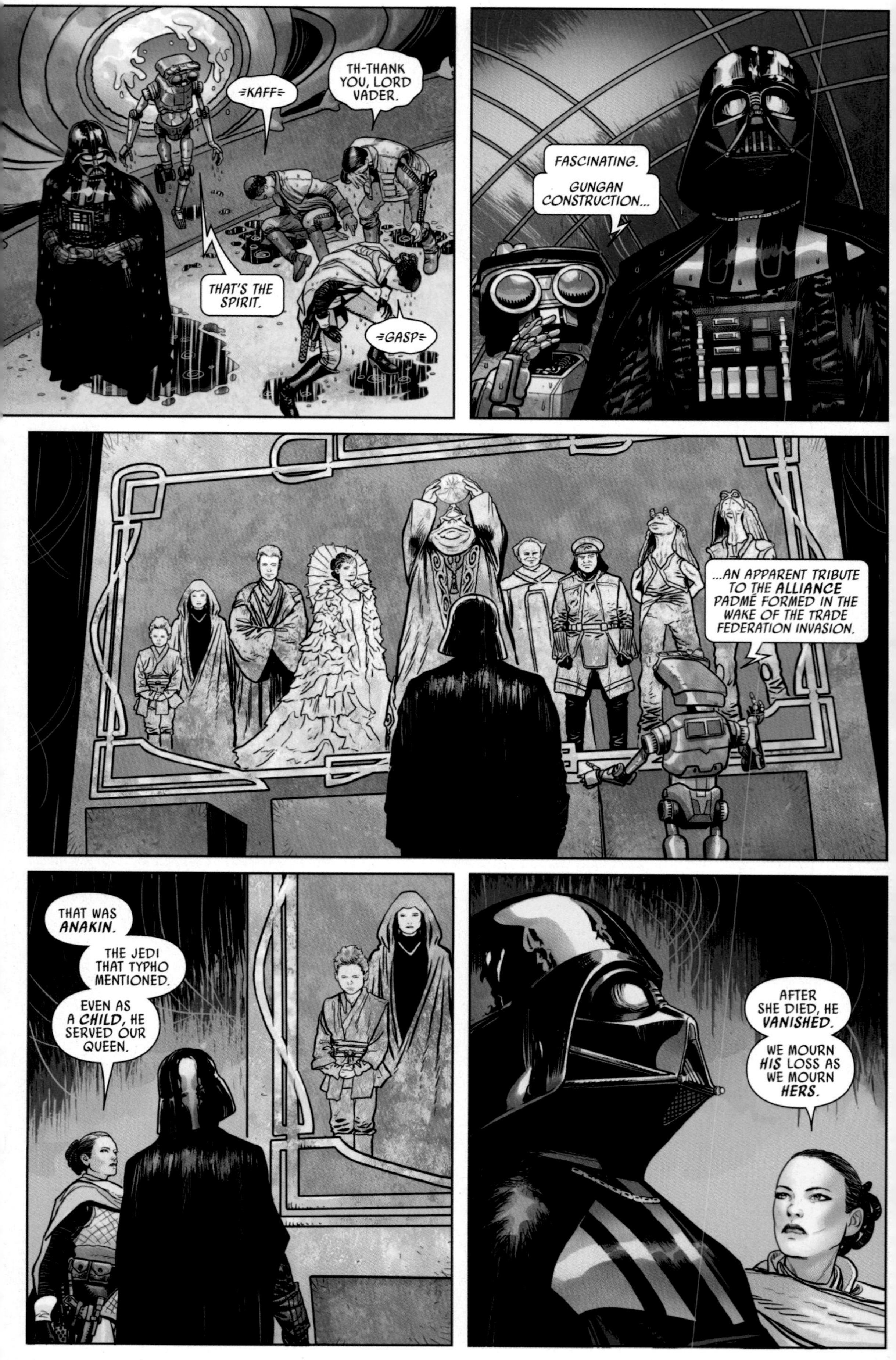

=KAFF=
TH-THANK YOU, LORD VADER.
THAT'S THE SPIRIT.
=GASP=
FASCINATING.
GUNGAN CONSTRUCTION...
...AN APPARENT TRIBUTE TO THE ALLIANCE PADMÉ FORMED IN THE WAKE OF THE TRADE FEDERATION INVASION.
THAT WAS ANAKIN.
THE JEDI THAT TYPHO MENTIONED.
EVEN AS A CHILD, HE SERVED OUR QUEEN.
AFTER SHE DIED, HE VANISHED.
WE MOURN HIS LOSS AS WE MOURN HERS.

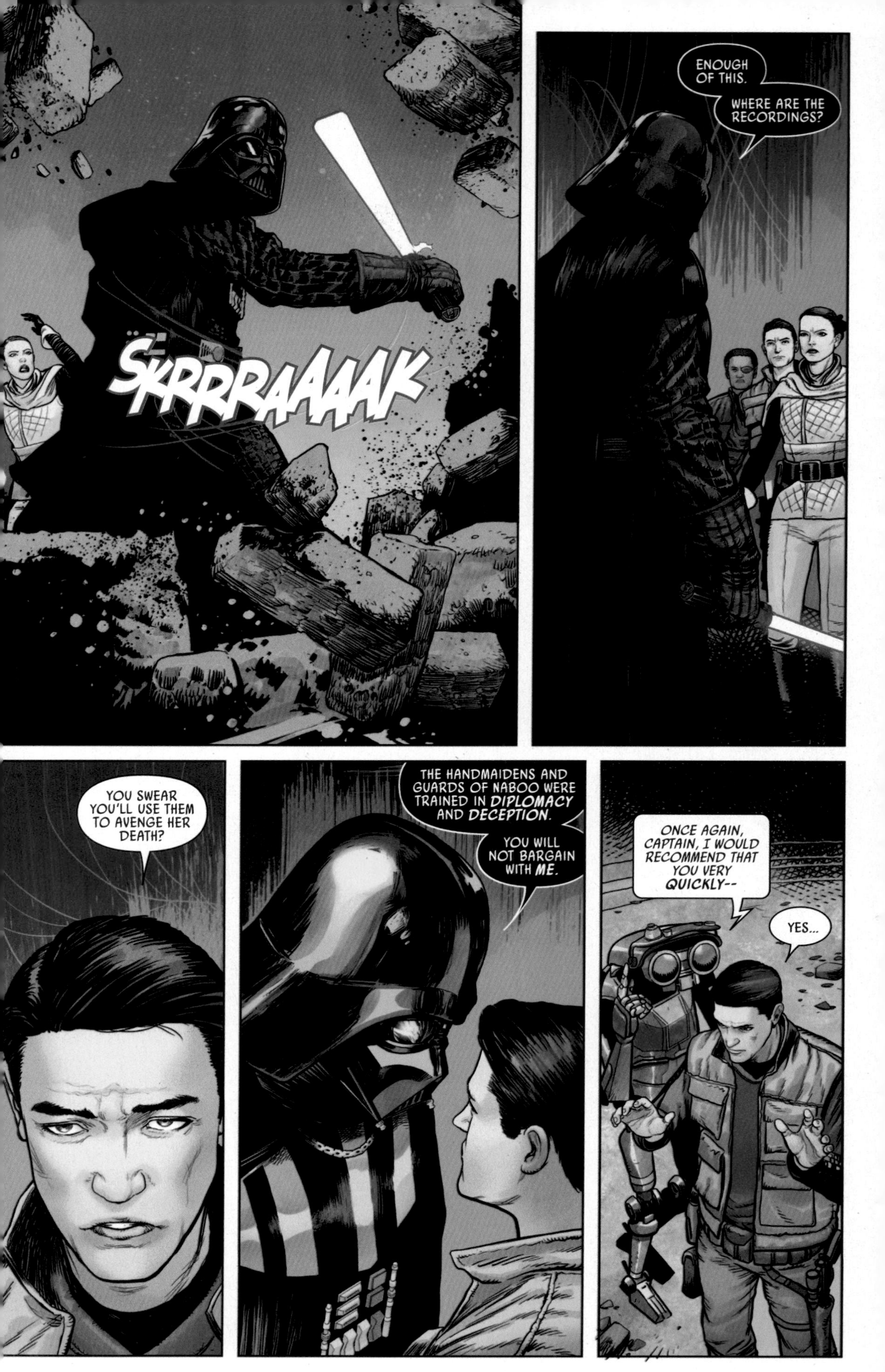
SKRRRAAAAK
ENOUGH OF THIS.
WHERE ARE THE RECORDINGS?
YOU SWEAR YOU'LL USE THEM TO AVENGE HER DEATH?
THE HANDMAIDENS AND GUARDS OF NABOO WERE TRAINED IN DIPLOMACY AND DECEPTION.
YOU WILL NOT BARGAIN WITH ME.
ONCE AGAIN, CAPTAIN, I WOULD RECOMMEND THAT YOU VERY QUICKLY--
YES...

CLICK

IT'S ALL YOURS.

AHA!

PERFECT.

SHIIINK

VEEE

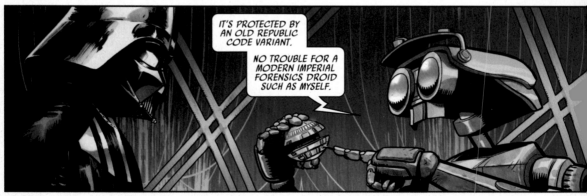

IT'S PROTECTED BY AN OLD REPUBLIC CODE VARIANT.

NO TROUBLE FOR A MODERN IMPERIAL FORENSICS DROID SUCH AS MYSELF.

BZZZTT

BZZZZZ

AND HERE WE ARE.

THE MISSING SURVEILLANCE DATA FROM PADMÉ'S APARTMENT.

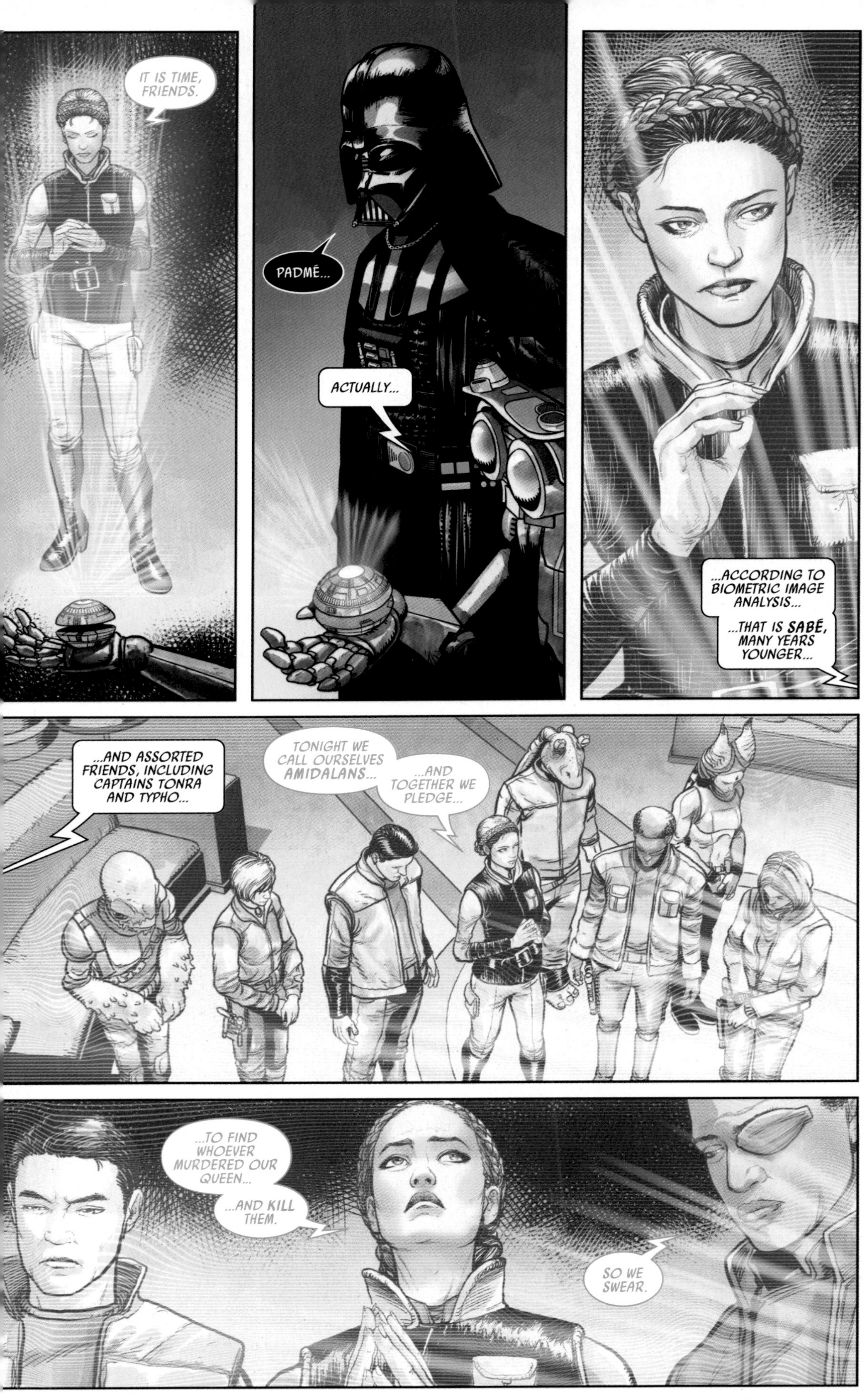
IT IS TIME, FRIENDS.
PADMÉ...
ACTUALLY...
...ACCORDING TO BIOMETRIC IMAGE ANALYSIS...
...THAT IS SABÉ, MANY YEARS YOUNGER...
...AND ASSORTED FRIENDS, INCLUDING CAPTAINS TONRA AND TYPHO...
TONIGHT WE CALL OURSELVES AMIDALANS...
...AND TOGETHER WE PLEDGE...
...TO FIND WHOEVER MURDERED OUR QUEEN...
...AND KILL THEM.
SO WE SWEAR.

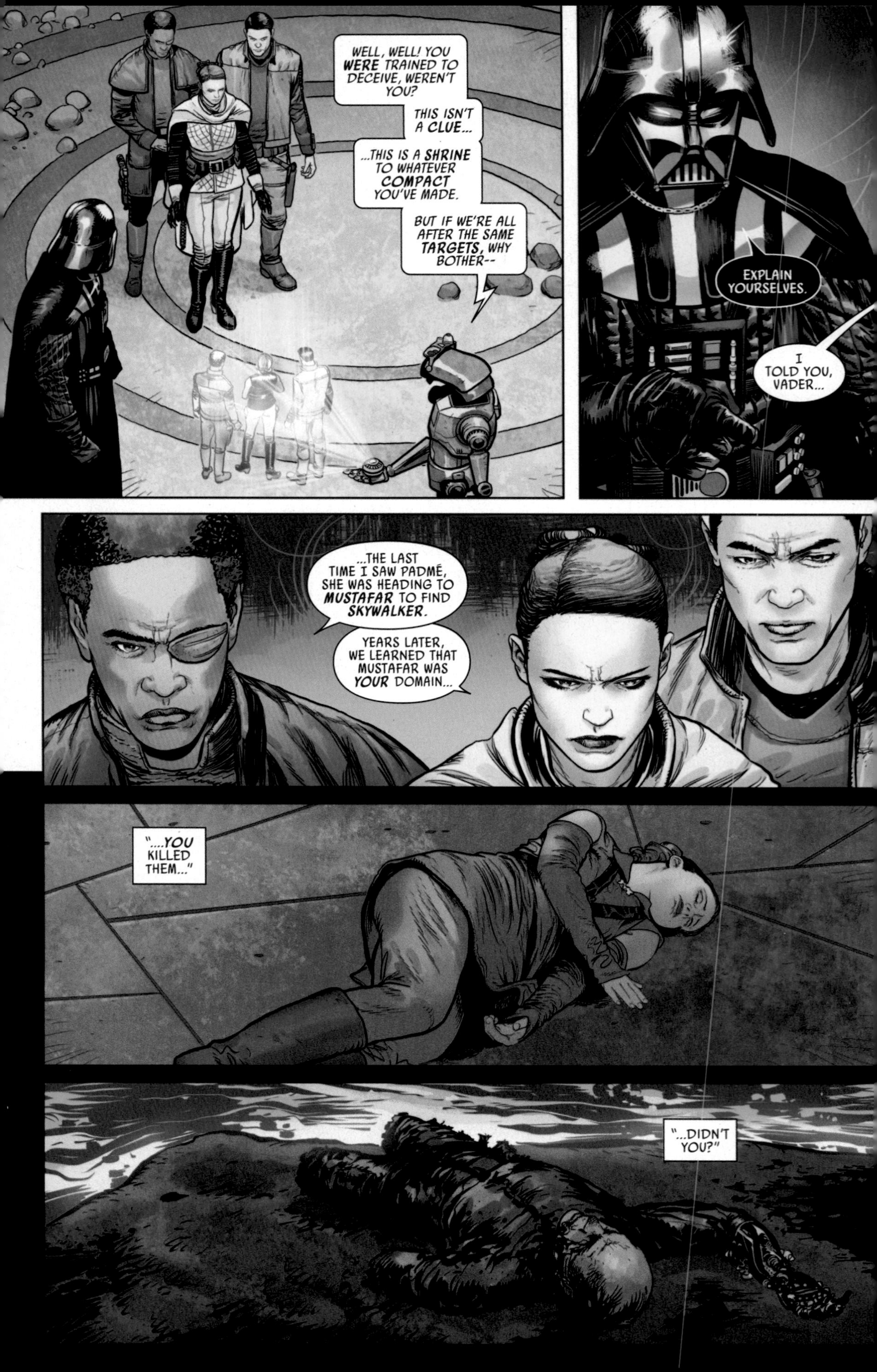

WELL, WELL! YOU WERE TRAINED TO DECEIVE, WEREN'T YOU?
THIS ISN'T A CLUE...
...THIS IS A SHRINE TO WHATEVER COMPACT YOU'VE MADE.
BUT IF WE'RE ALL AFTER THE SAME TARGETS, WHY BOTHER--
EXPLAIN YOURSELVES.
I TOLD YOU, VADER...
...THE LAST TIME I SAW PADMÉ, SHE WAS HEADING TO MUSTAFAR TO FIND SKYWALKER.
YEARS LATER, WE LEARNED THAT MUSTAFAR WAS YOUR DOMAIN...
"...YOU KILLED THEM..."
"...DIDN'T YOU?"

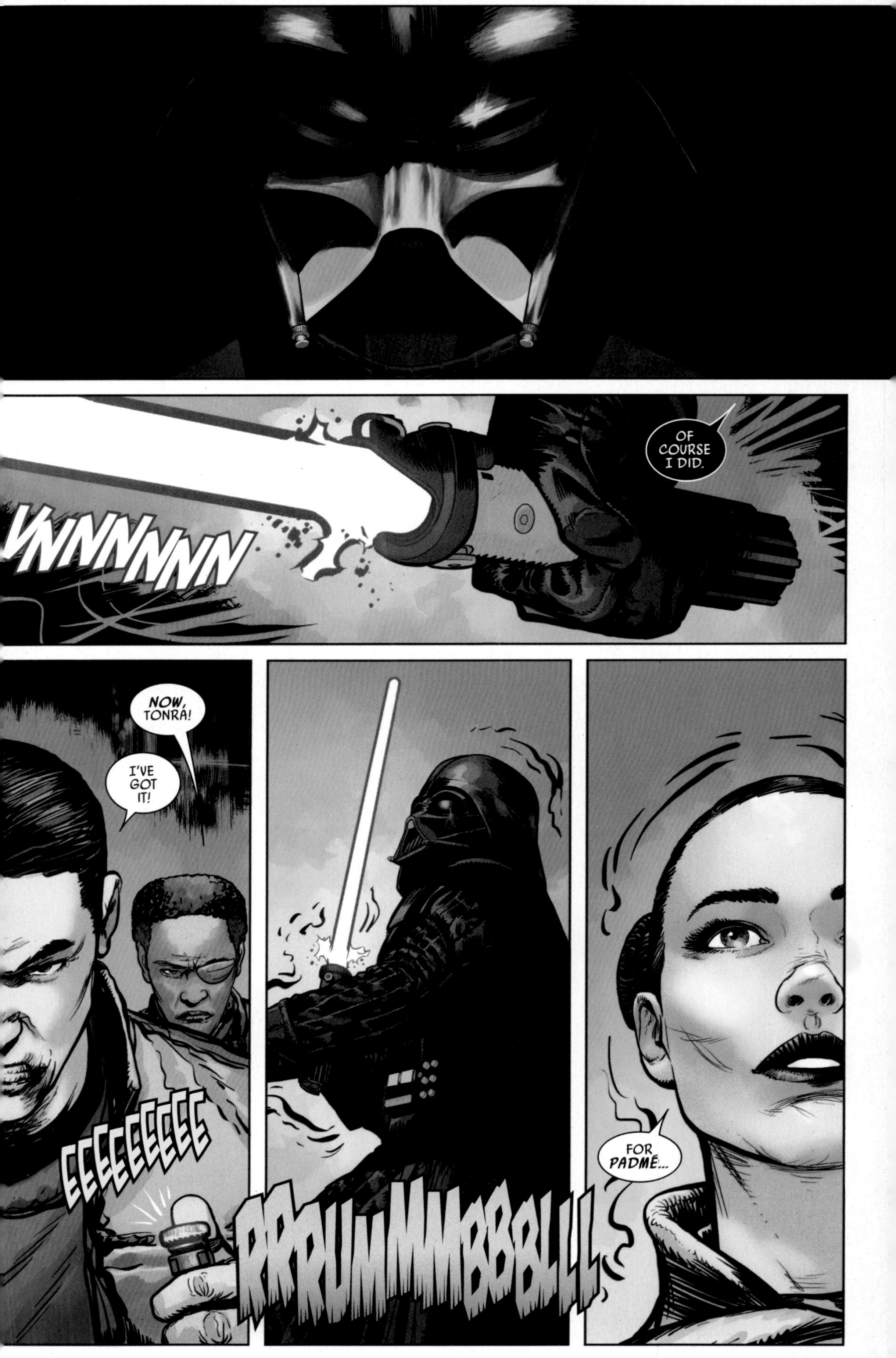
OF COURSE I DID.
VNNNNNN
NOW, TONRA!
I'VE GOT IT!
EEEEEEEEE
RRRUMMMBBLLL
FOR PADMÉ...

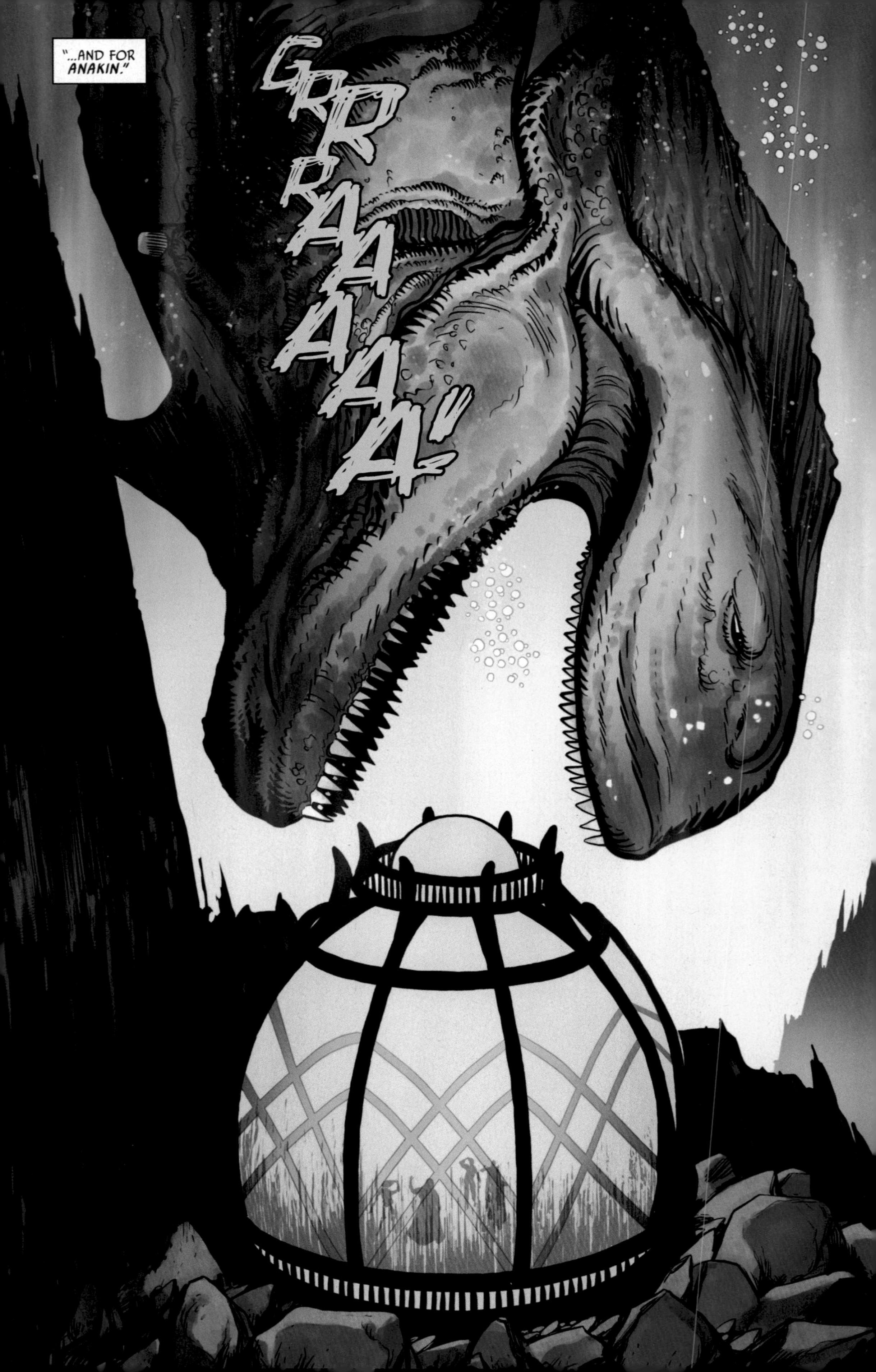
"...AND FOR ANAKIN."
GRRAAAAAA"

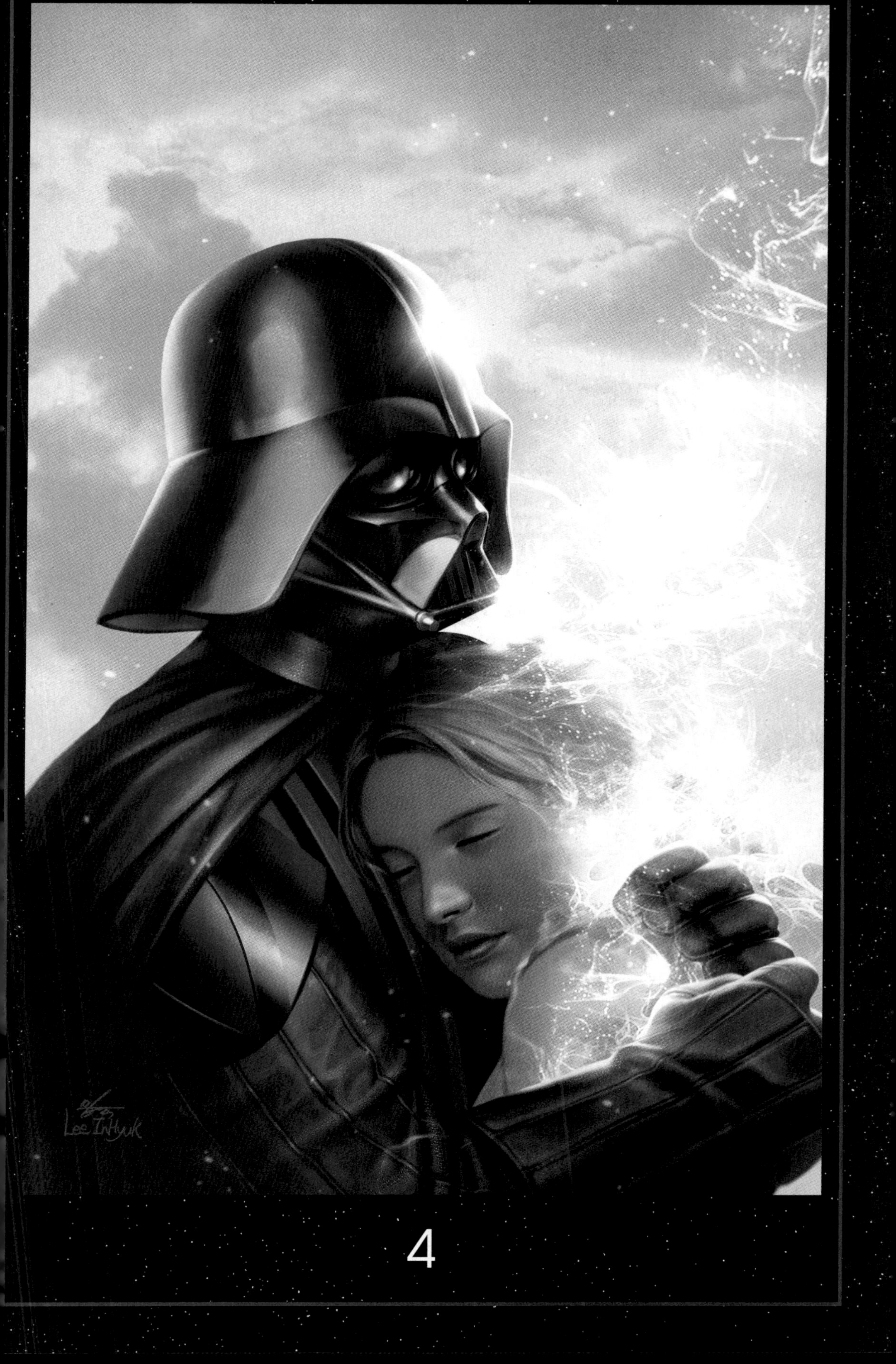
Lee InHyuk

4

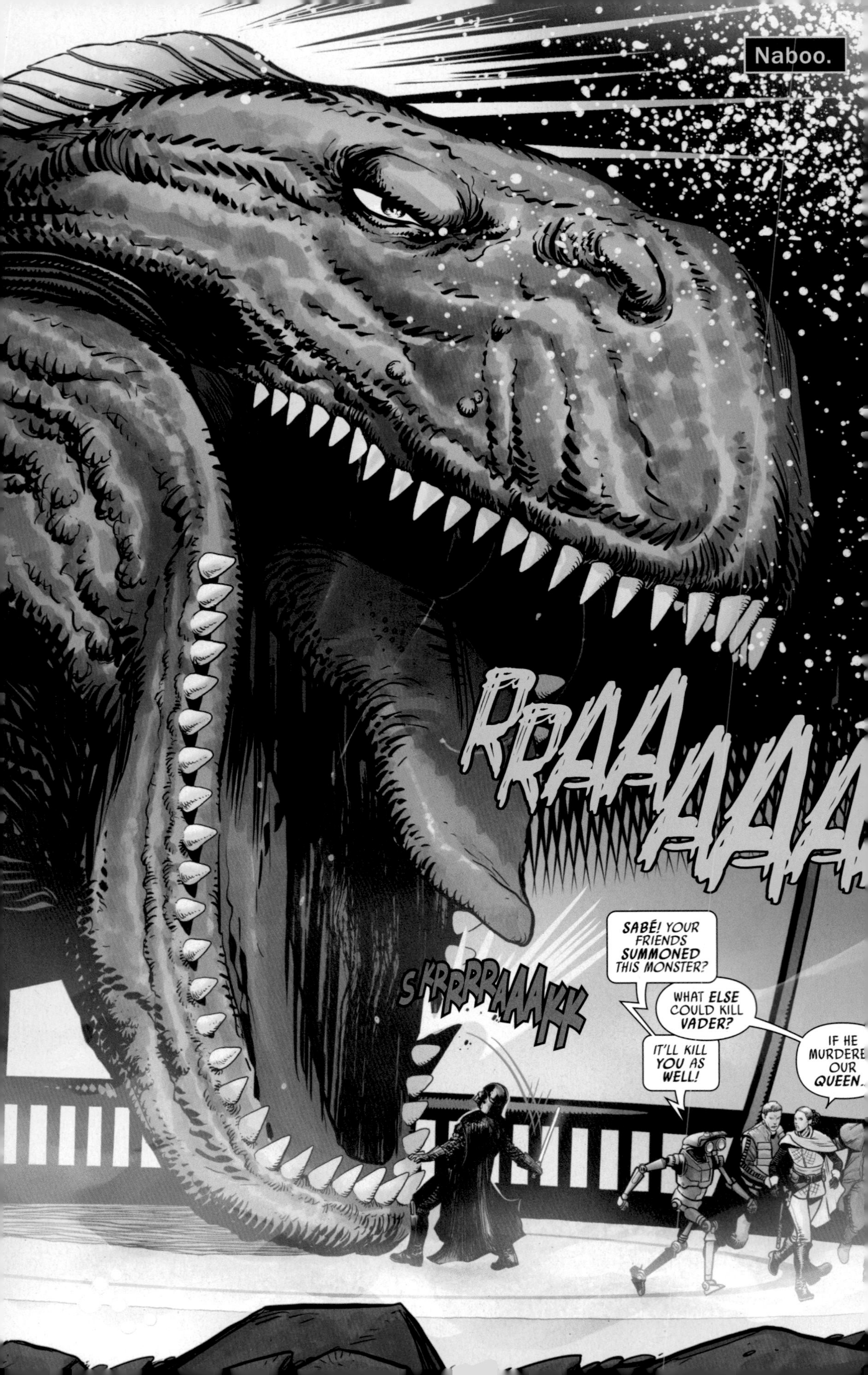
Naboo.
RRAAAAAA
SKRRRRAAAKK
SABÉ! YOUR FRIENDS SUMMONED THIS MONSTER?
WHAT ELSE COULD KILL VADER?
IT'LL KILL YOU AS WELL!
IF HE MURDERE OUR QUEEN...

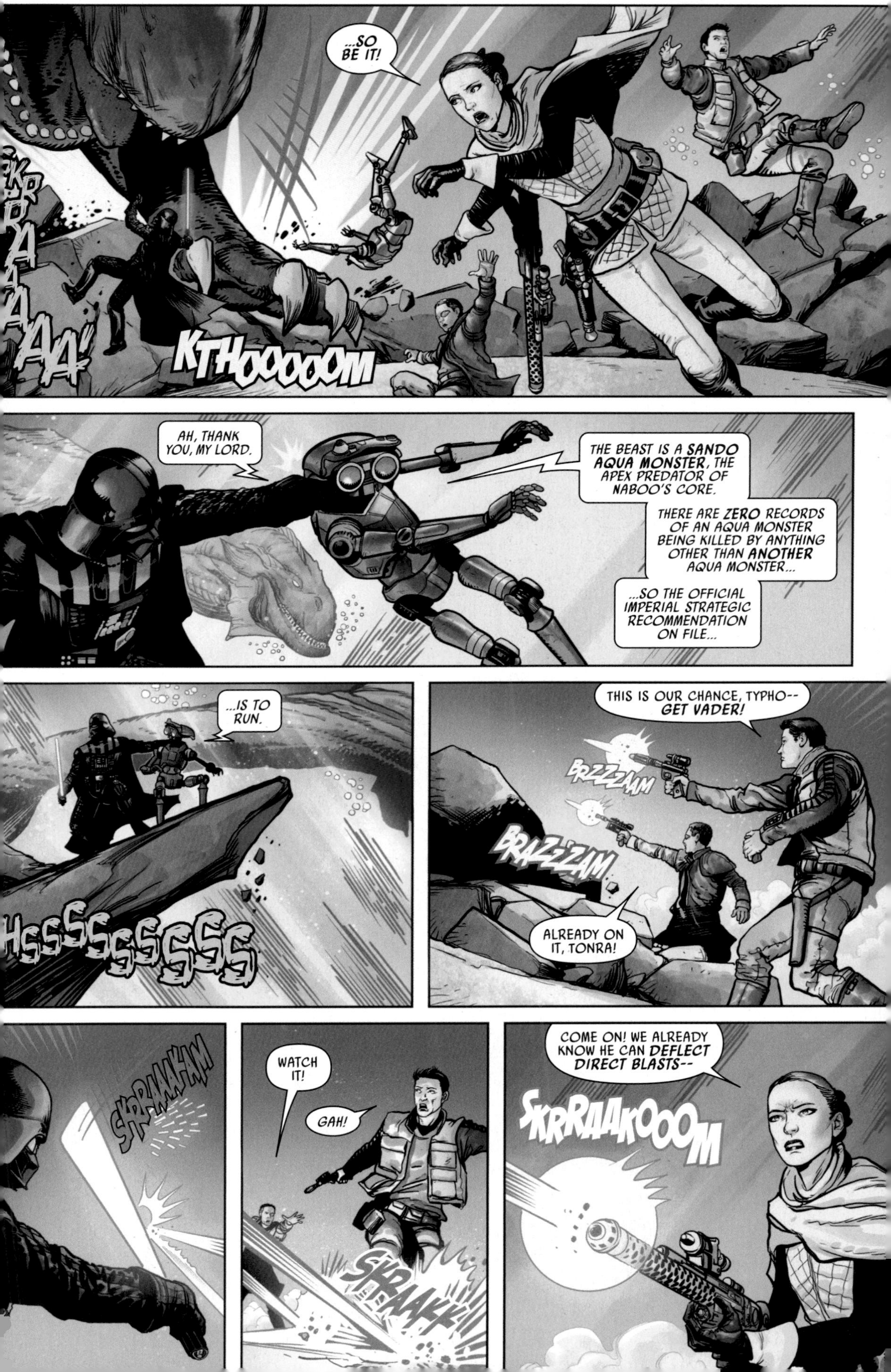
...SO BE IT!
SKRRAAAAAA!
KTHOOOOOOM
AH, THANK YOU, MY LORD.
THE BEAST IS A SANDO AQUA MONSTER, THE APEX PREDATOR OF NABOO'S CORE.
THERE ARE ZERO RECORDS OF AN AQUA MONSTER BEING KILLED BY ANYTHING OTHER THAN ANOTHER AQUA MONSTER...
...SO THE OFFICIAL IMPERIAL STRATEGIC RECOMMENDATION ON FILE...
...IS TO RUN.
HSSSSSSSSSS
THIS IS OUR CHANCE, TYPHO-- GET VADER!
BRZZZAAM
BRAZZZAM
ALREADY ON IT, TONRA!
SKRAAKAM
WATCH IT!
GAH!
SKRAAKK
COME ON! WE ALREADY KNOW HE CAN DEFLECT DIRECT BLASTS--
SKRRAAKOOOM

--IT'S TIME TO TRY SOMETHING DIFFERENT!

AH!

SKRRAKOOOM

KSSSHHH

IF FLEEING IS IMPOSSIBLE, IMPERIAL PROTOCOL RECOMMENDS HIDING.

IF HIDING IS IMPOSSIBLE--

RRRAAAAAAA!

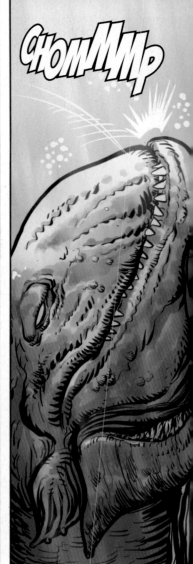

CHOMMMP

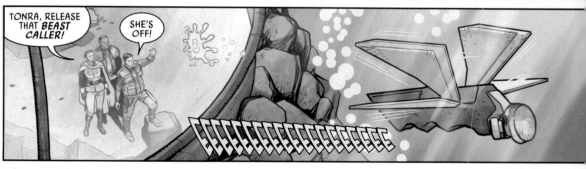

TONRA, RELEASE THAT *BEAST CALLER!*

SHE'S OFF!

EEEEEEEEEEEEEEEEEE

"THAT'S RIGHT, BEASTIE, GO ON!"

EEEEEEEEEEE

HRRRAANK?

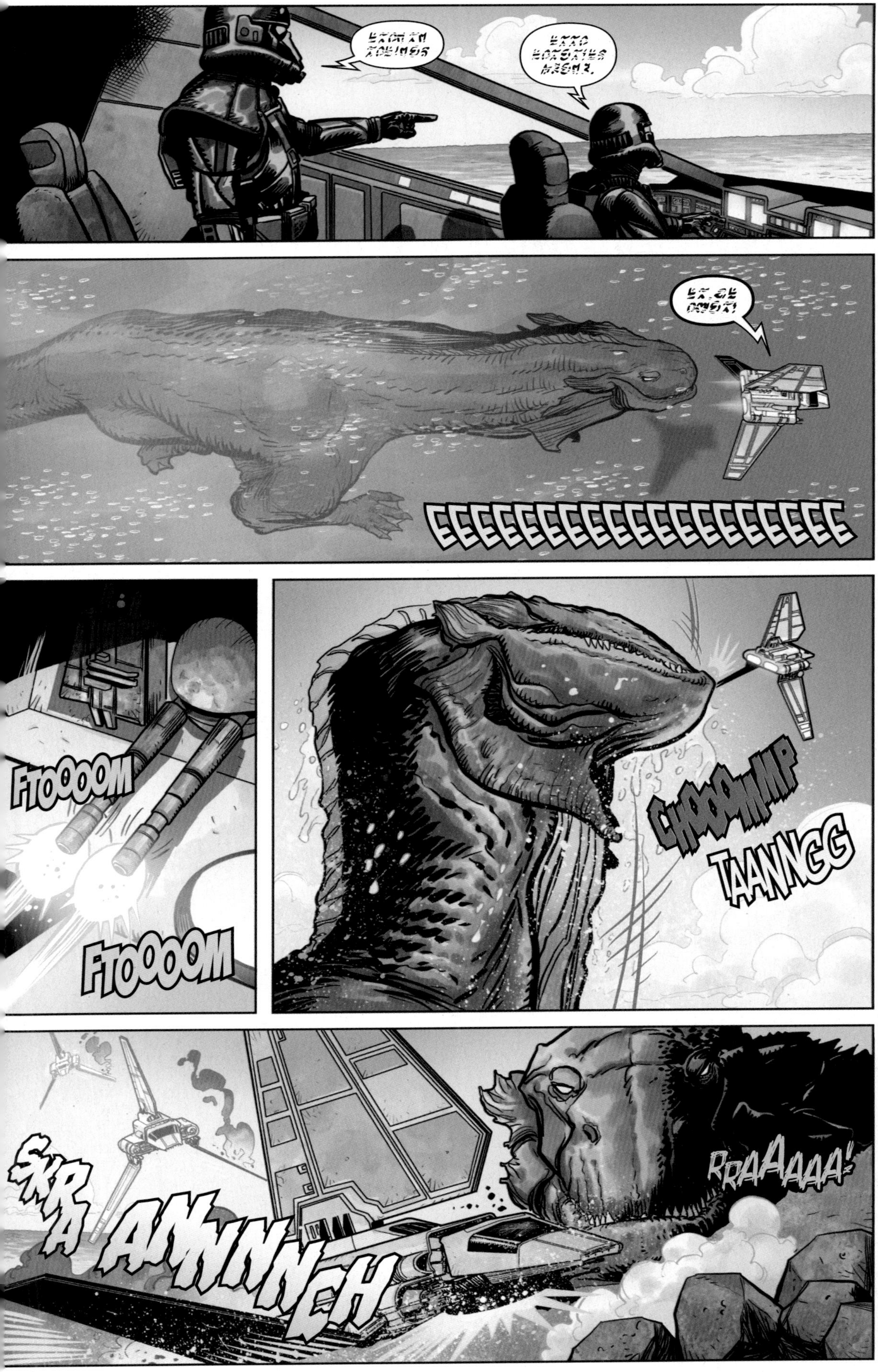
EEEEEEEEEEEEEEEEEEE
FTOOOOM
FTOOOOM
CHOOMMP
TAANNGG
SKRAANNNNCH
RRAAAAAA!

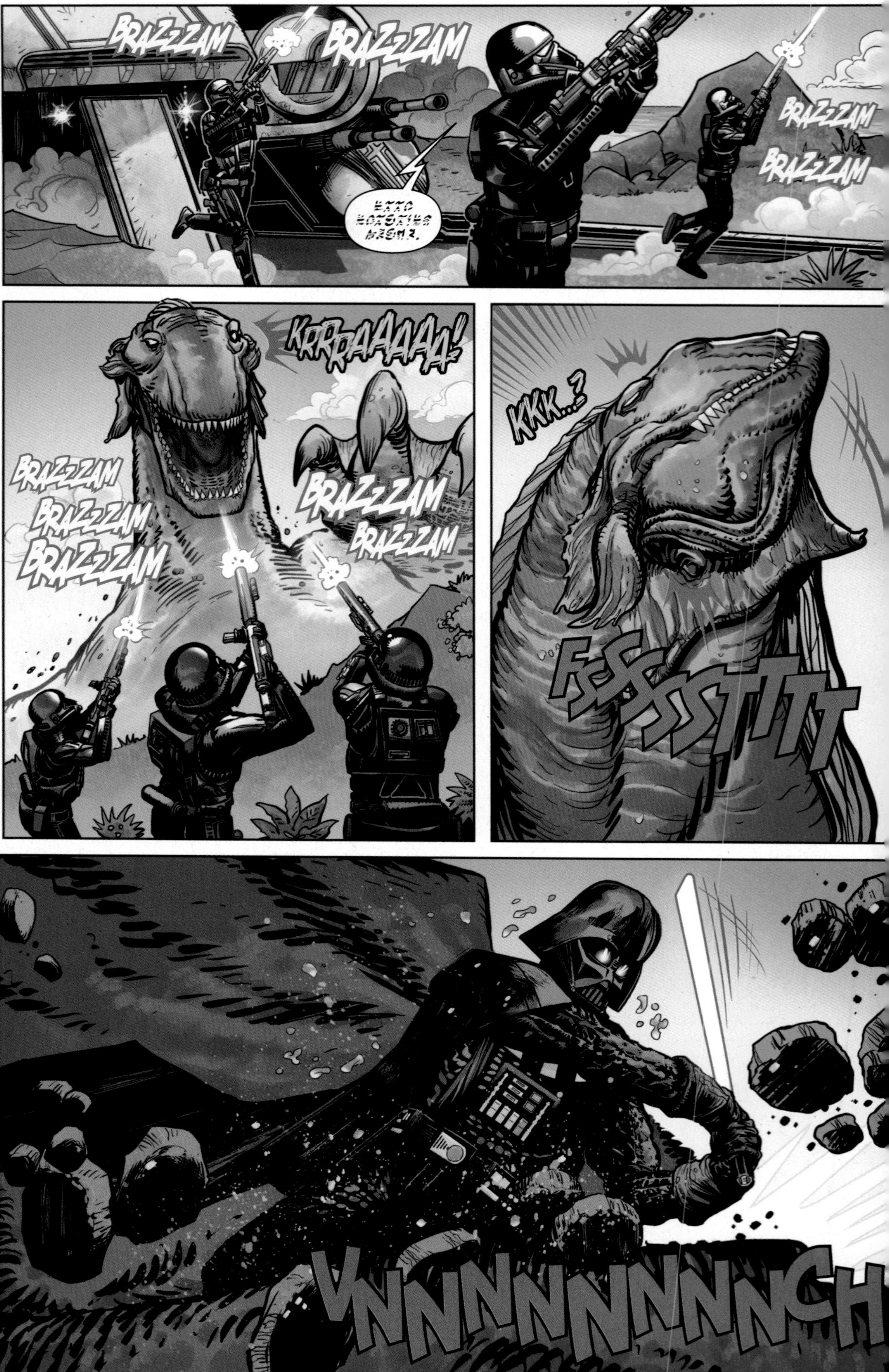
BRAZZZAM
BRAZZZAM
BRAZZZAM
BRAZZZAM
KRRRAAAAA!
BRAZZZAM
BRAZZZAM
BRAZZZAM
BRAZZZAM
BRAZZZAM
KKK...?
FSSSSTTTT
VNNNNNNNNNCH

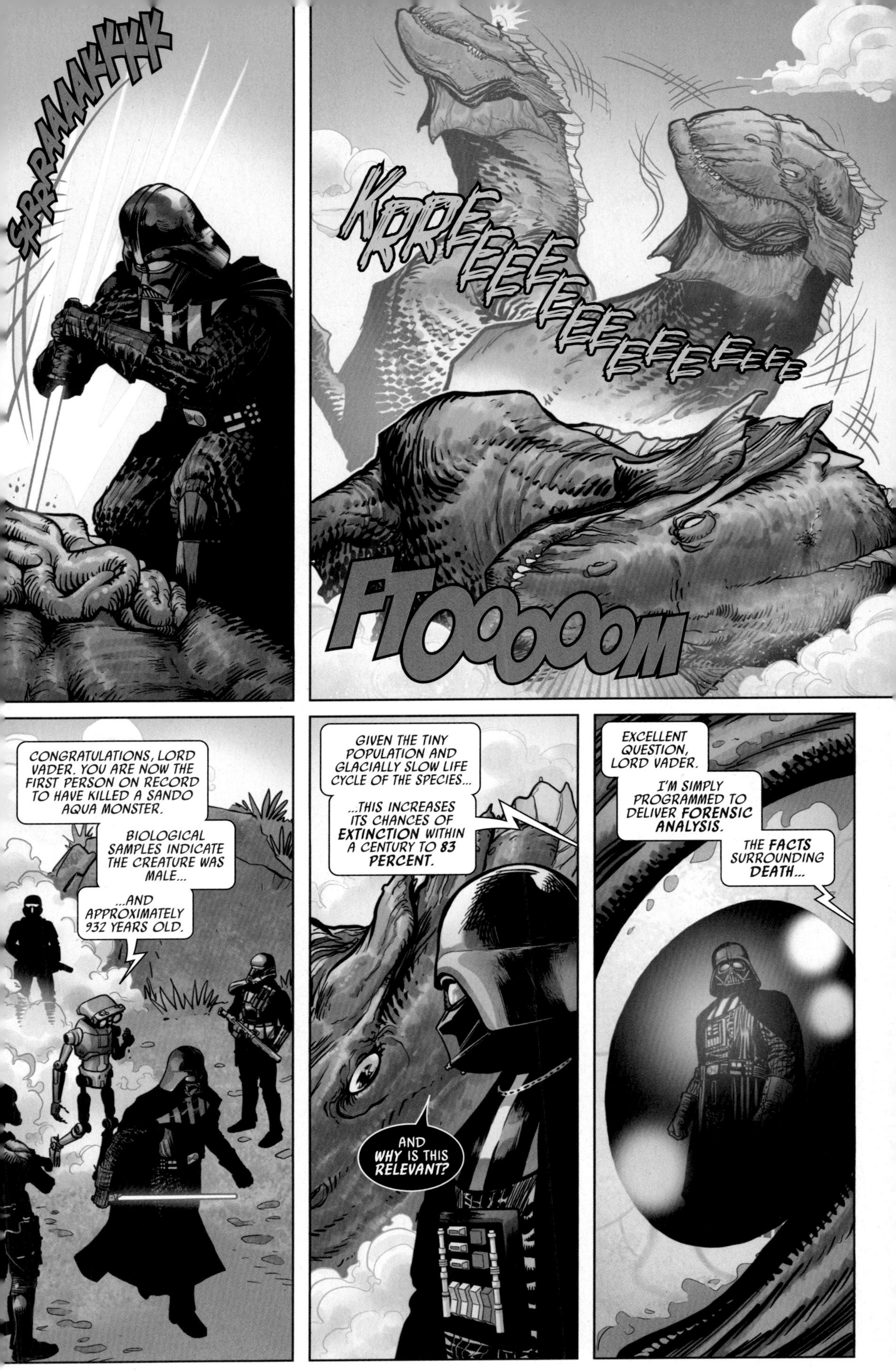
SKRRAAAAKKKK
KRREEEEEEEEEEEEEEEE
FTOOOOOOM
CONGRATULATIONS, LORD VADER. YOU ARE NOW THE FIRST PERSON ON RECORD TO HAVE KILLED A SANDO AQUA MONSTER.
BIOLOGICAL SAMPLES INDICATE THE CREATURE WAS MALE...
...AND APPROXIMATELY 932 YEARS OLD.
GIVEN THE TINY POPULATION AND GLACIALLY SLOW LIFE CYCLE OF THE SPECIES...
...THIS INCREASES ITS CHANCES OF EXTINCTION WITHIN A CENTURY TO 83 PERCENT.
AND WHY IS THIS RELEVANT?
EXCELLENT QUESTION, LORD VADER.
I'M SIMPLY PROGRAMMED TO DELIVER FORENSIC ANALYSIS.
THE FACTS SURROUNDING DEATH...

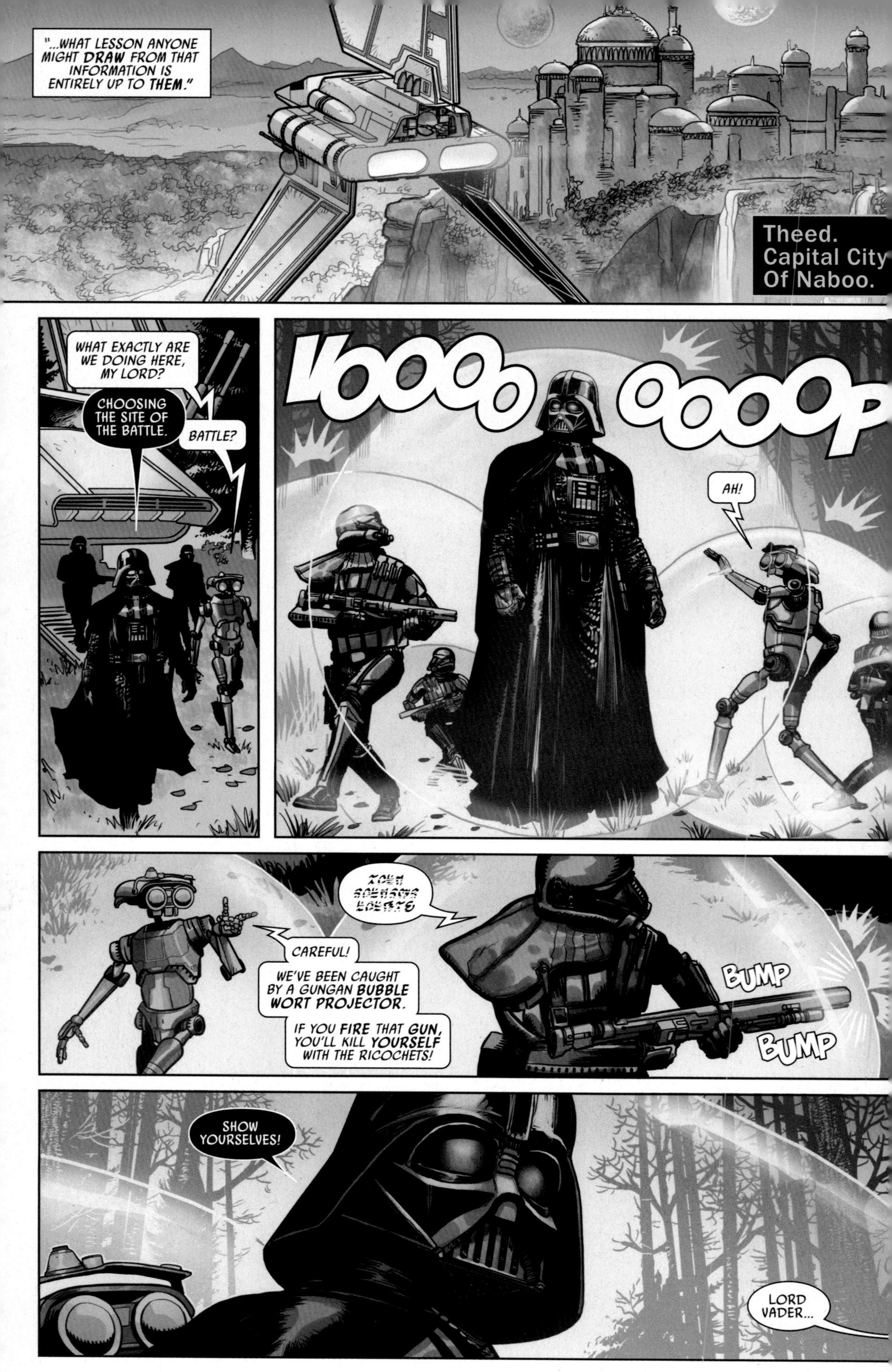
"...WHAT LESSON ANYONE MIGHT DRAW FROM THAT INFORMATION IS ENTIRELY UP TO THEM."
Theed. Capital City Of Naboo.
WHAT EXACTLY ARE WE DOING HERE, MY LORD?
CHOOSING THE SITE OF THE BATTLE.
BATTLE?
VOOOOO OOOOP
AH!
CAREFUL!
WE'VE BEEN CAUGHT BY A GUNGAN BUBBLE WORT PROJECTOR.
IF YOU FIRE THAT GUN, YOU'LL KILL YOURSELF WITH THE RICOCHETS!
BUMP
BUMP
SHOW YOURSELVES!
LORD VADER...

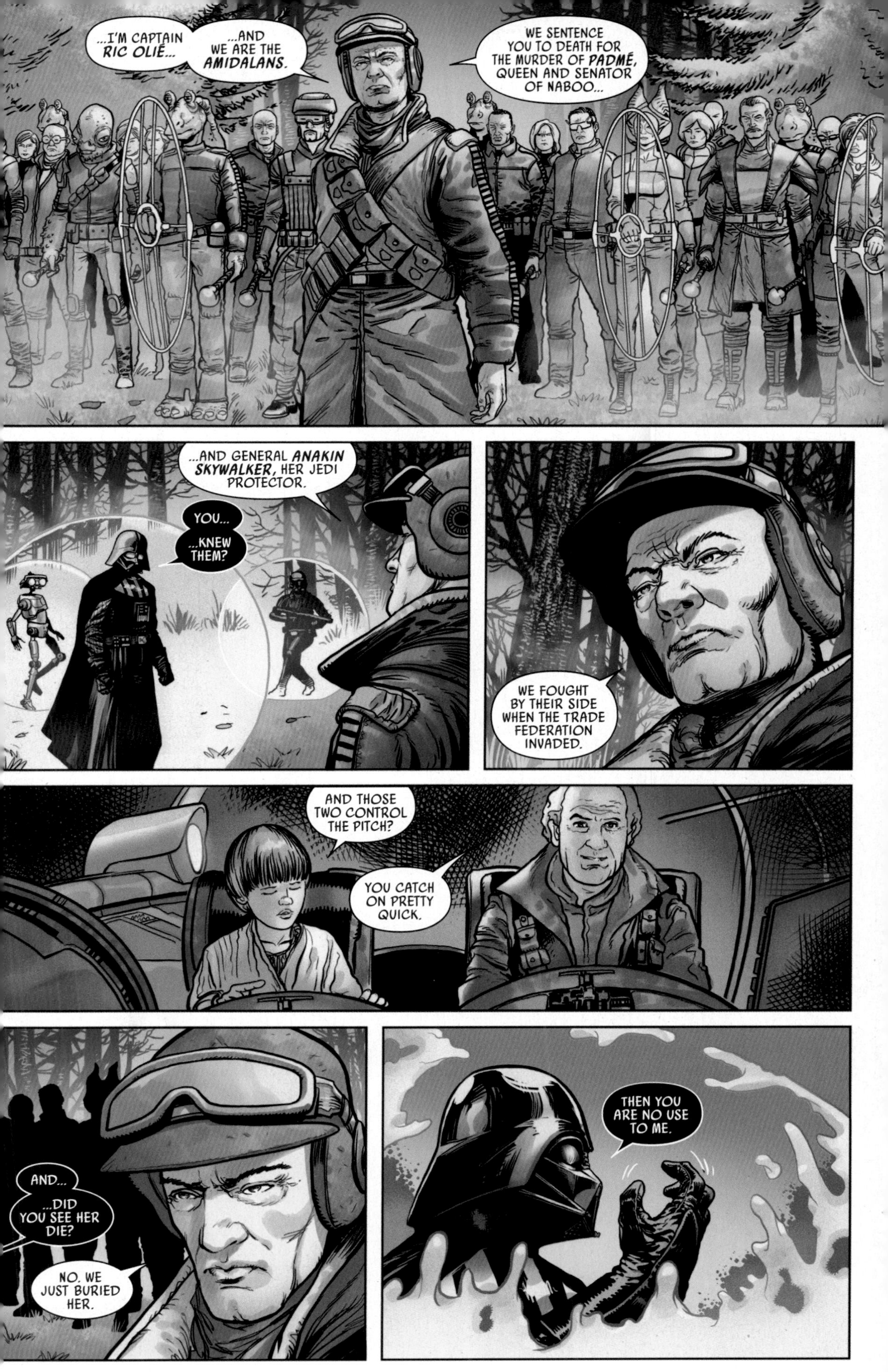

...I'M CAPTAIN RIC OLIÉ...
...AND WE ARE THE AMIDALANS.
WE SENTENCE YOU TO DEATH FOR THE MURDER OF PADMÉ, QUEEN AND SENATOR OF NABOO...
...AND GENERAL ANAKIN SKYWALKER, HER JEDI PROTECTOR.
YOU...
...KNEW THEM?
WE FOUGHT BY THEIR SIDE WHEN THE TRADE FEDERATION INVADED.
AND THOSE TWO CONTROL THE PITCH?
YOU CATCH ON PRETTY QUICK.
AND...
...DID YOU SEE HER DIE?
NO. WE JUST BURIED HER.
THEN YOU ARE NO USE TO ME.

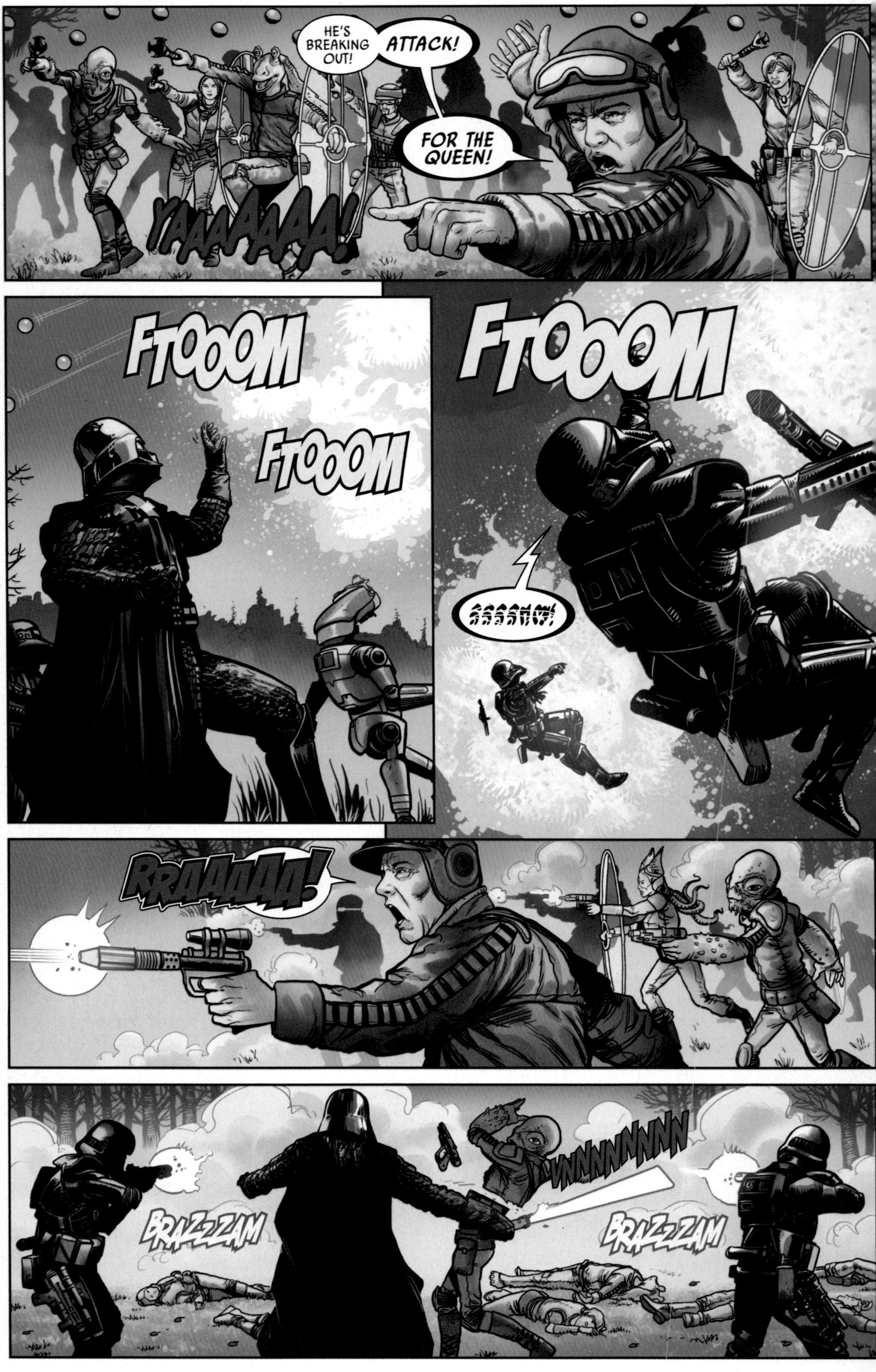
HE'S BREAKING OUT!
ATTACK!
FOR THE QUEEN!
YAAAAAAA!
FTOOOM
FTOOOM
FTOOOM
RRAAAAAA!
VNNNNNNNNN
BRAZZZAM
BRAZZZAM

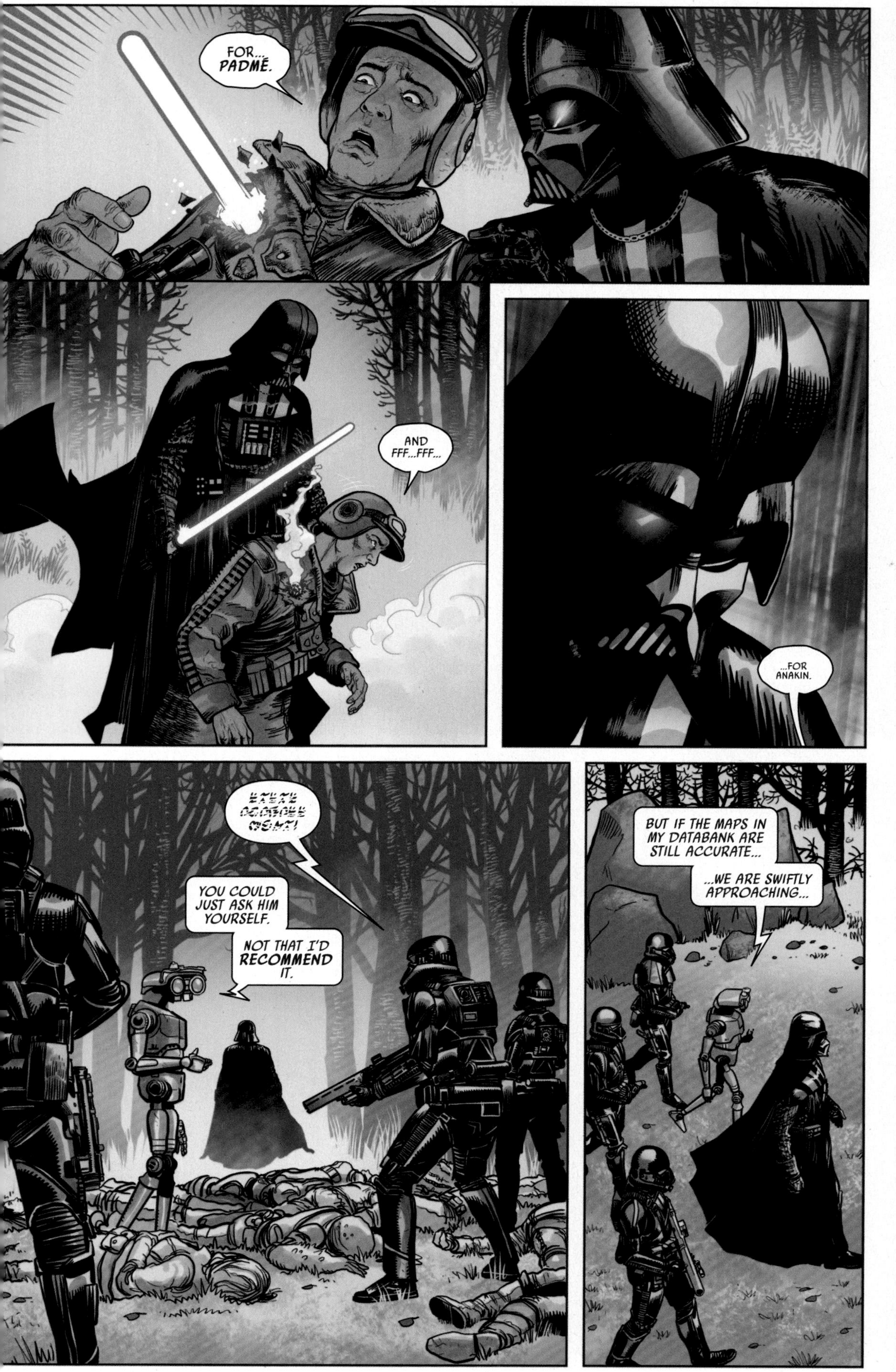
FOR... PADMÉ.
AND FFF...FFF...
...FOR ANAKIN.
YOU COULD JUST ASK HIM YOURSELF.
NOT THAT I'D RECOMMEND IT.
BUT IF THE MAPS IN MY DATABANK ARE STILL ACCURATE...
...WE ARE SWIFTLY APPROACHING...

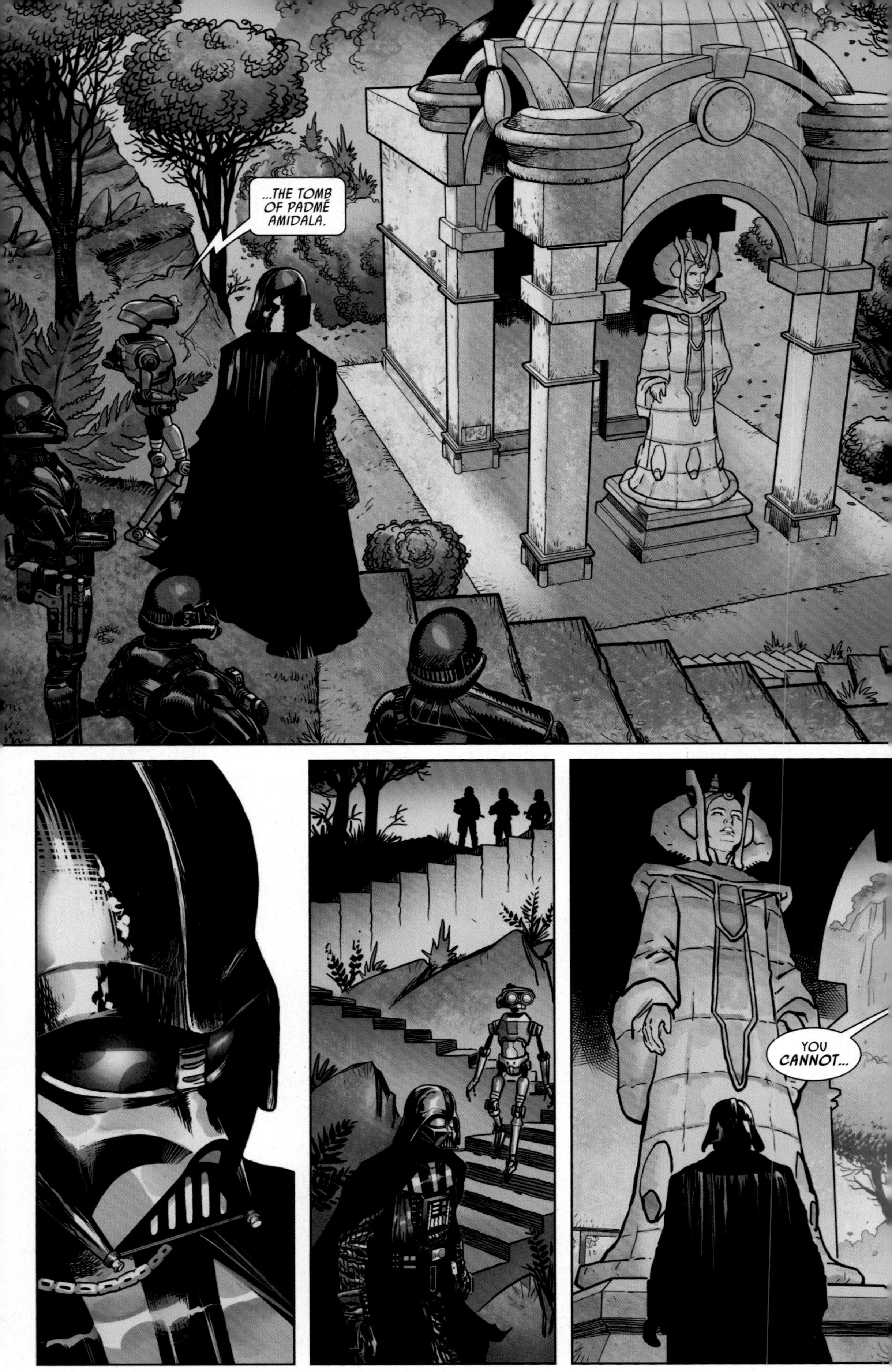
...THE TOMB OF PADMÉ AMIDALA.
YOU CANNOT...

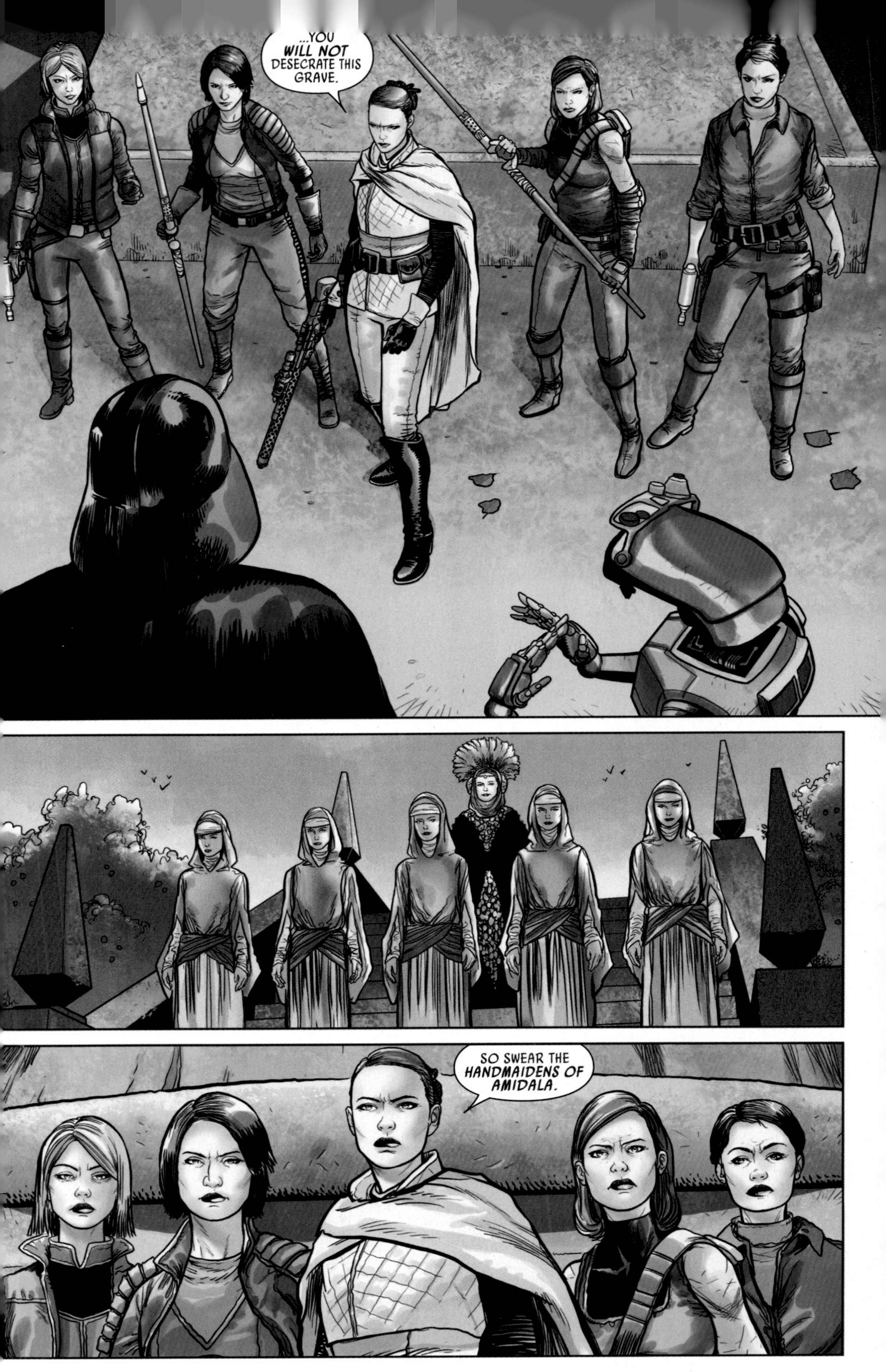
...YOU WILL NOT DESECRATE THIS GRAVE.
SO SWEAR THE HANDMAIDENS OF AMIDALA.

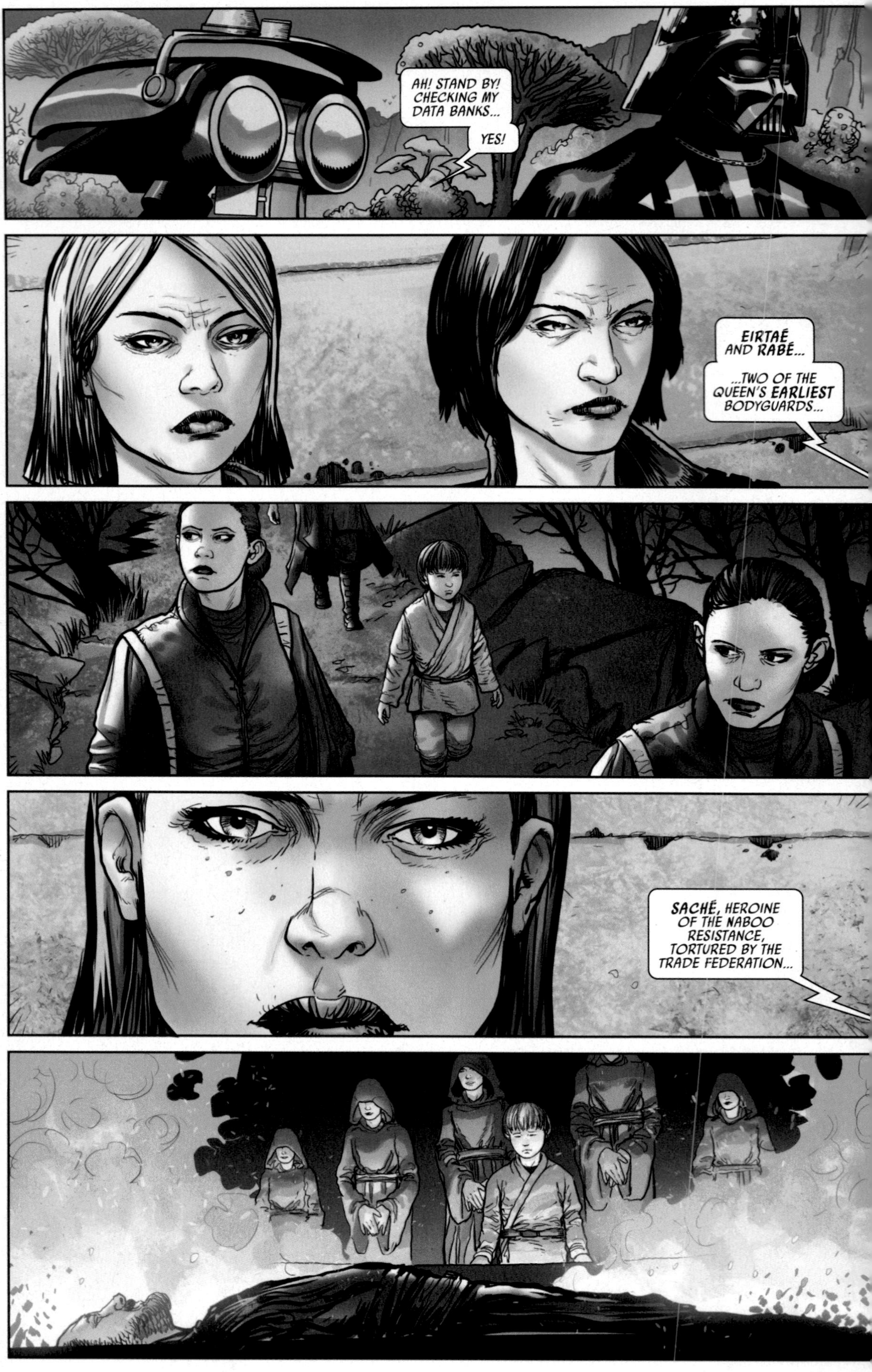
AH! STAND BY! CHECKING MY DATA BANKS...
YES!
EIRTAÉ AND RABÉ...
...TWO OF THE QUEEN'S EARLIEST BODYGUARDS...
SACHÉ, HEROINE OF THE NABOO RESISTANCE, TORTURED BY THE TRADE FEDERATION...

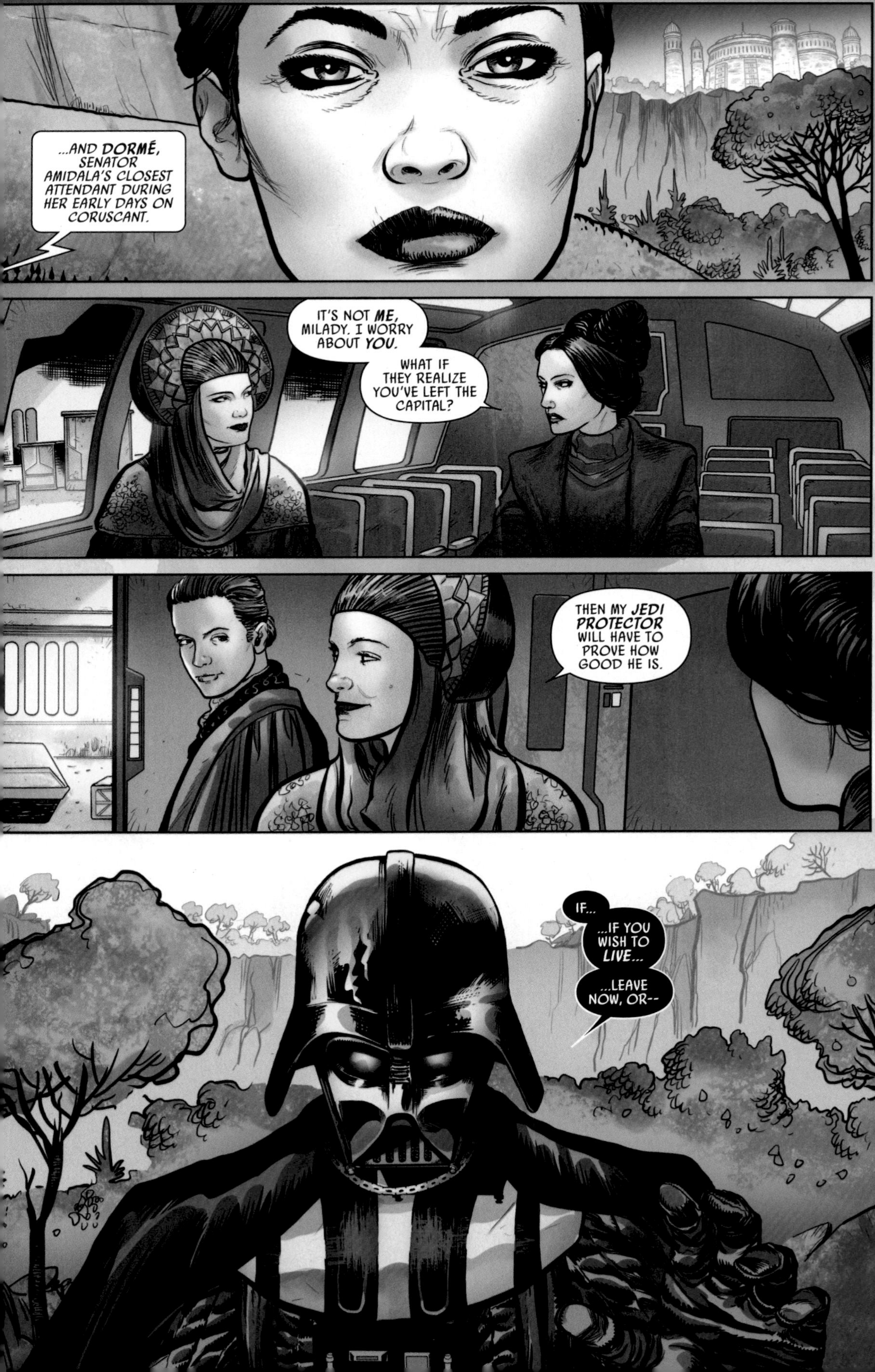
...AND DORMÉ, SENATOR AMIDALA'S CLOSEST ATTENDANT DURING HER EARLY DAYS ON CORUSCANT.
IT'S NOT ME, MILADY. I WORRY ABOUT YOU.
WHAT IF THEY REALIZE YOU'VE LEFT THE CAPITAL?
THEN MY JEDI PROTECTOR WILL HAVE TO PROVE HOW GOOD HE IS.
IF...
...IF YOU WISH TO LIVE...
...LEAVE NOW, OR--

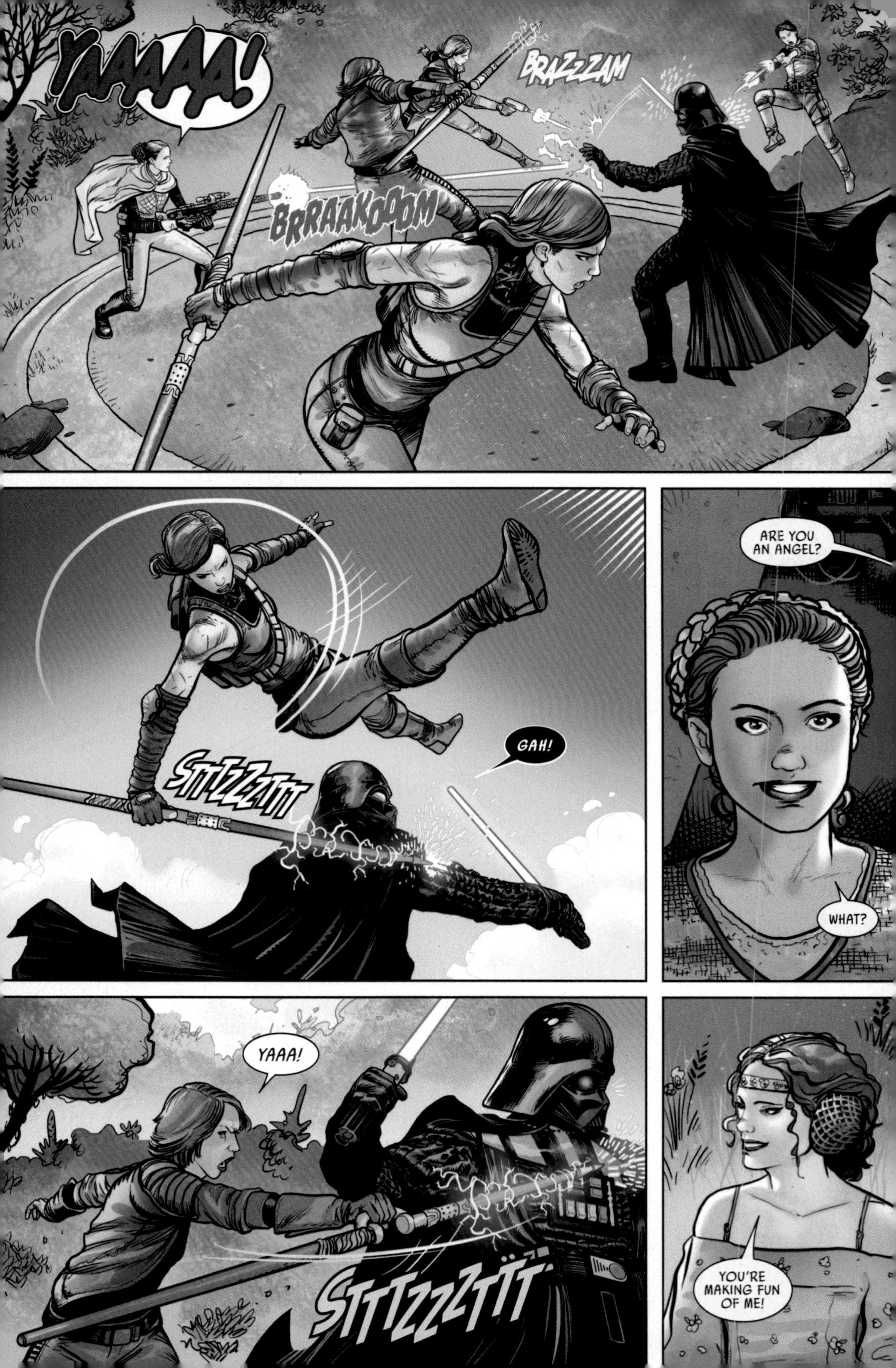
YAAAAA!
BRAZZZAM
BRRAAKOOOM
STTTZZZTTT
GAH!
ARE YOU AN ANGEL?
WHAT?
YAAA!
STTTZZZTTT
YOU'RE MAKING FUN OF ME!

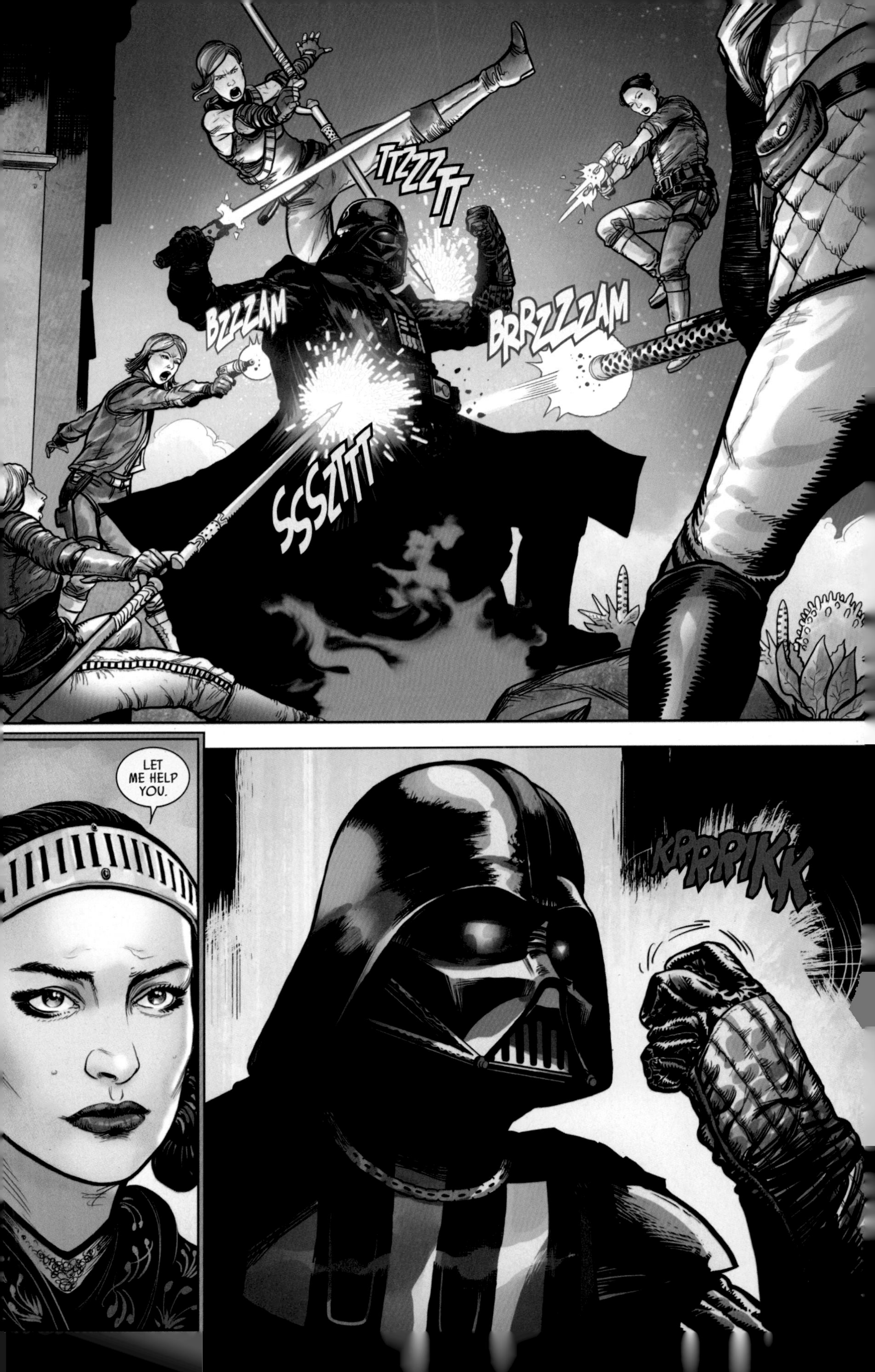
TTZZZTT
BZZZAM
BRRZZZAM
SSSZTTT
LET ME HELP YOU.
KRRRIKK

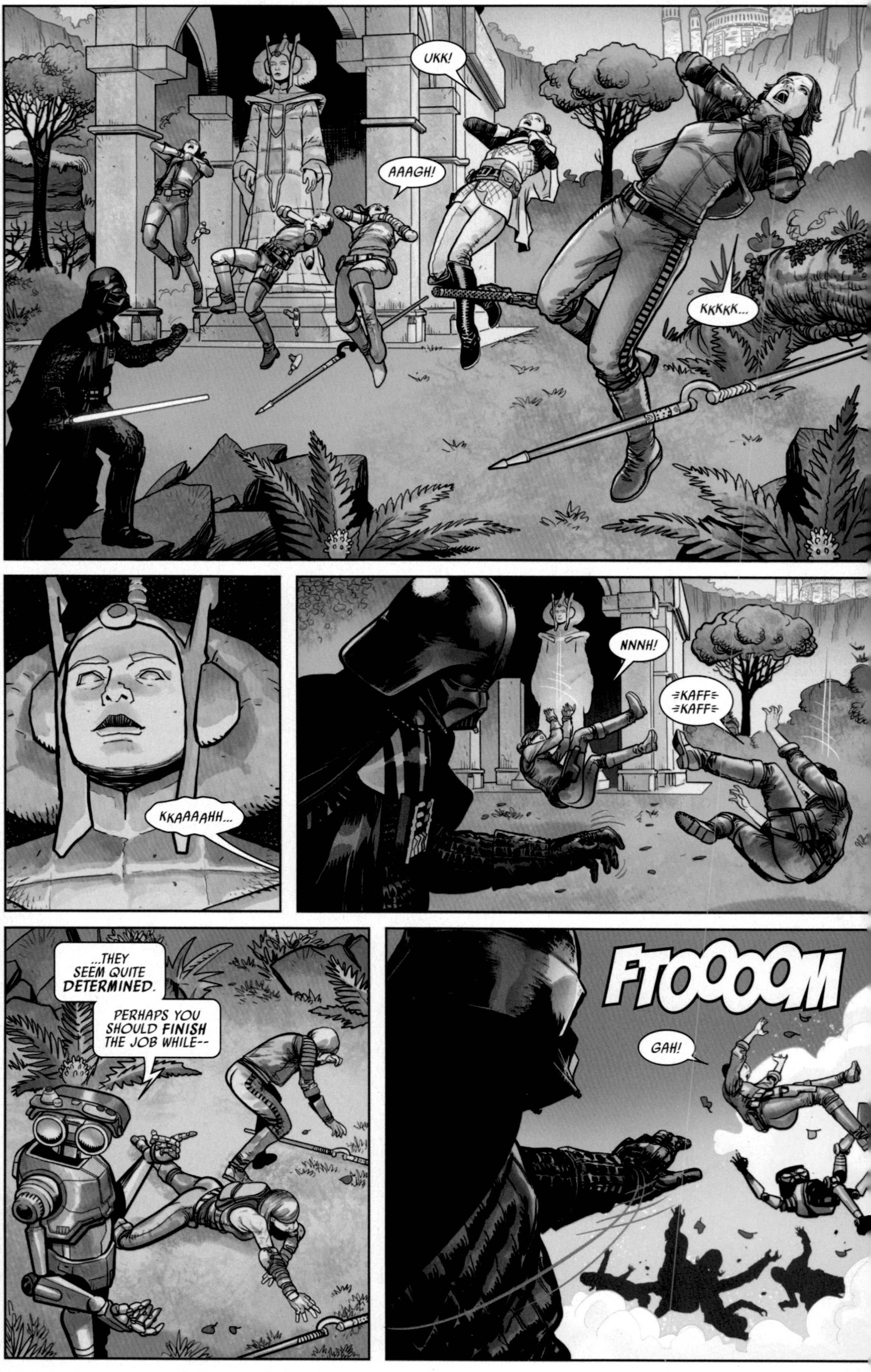
UKK!
AAAGH!
KKKKK...
KKAAAAHH...
NNNH!
KAFF KAFF
...THEY SEEM QUITE DETERMINED.
PERHAPS YOU SHOULD FINISH THE JOB WHILE--
FTOOOOM
GAH!

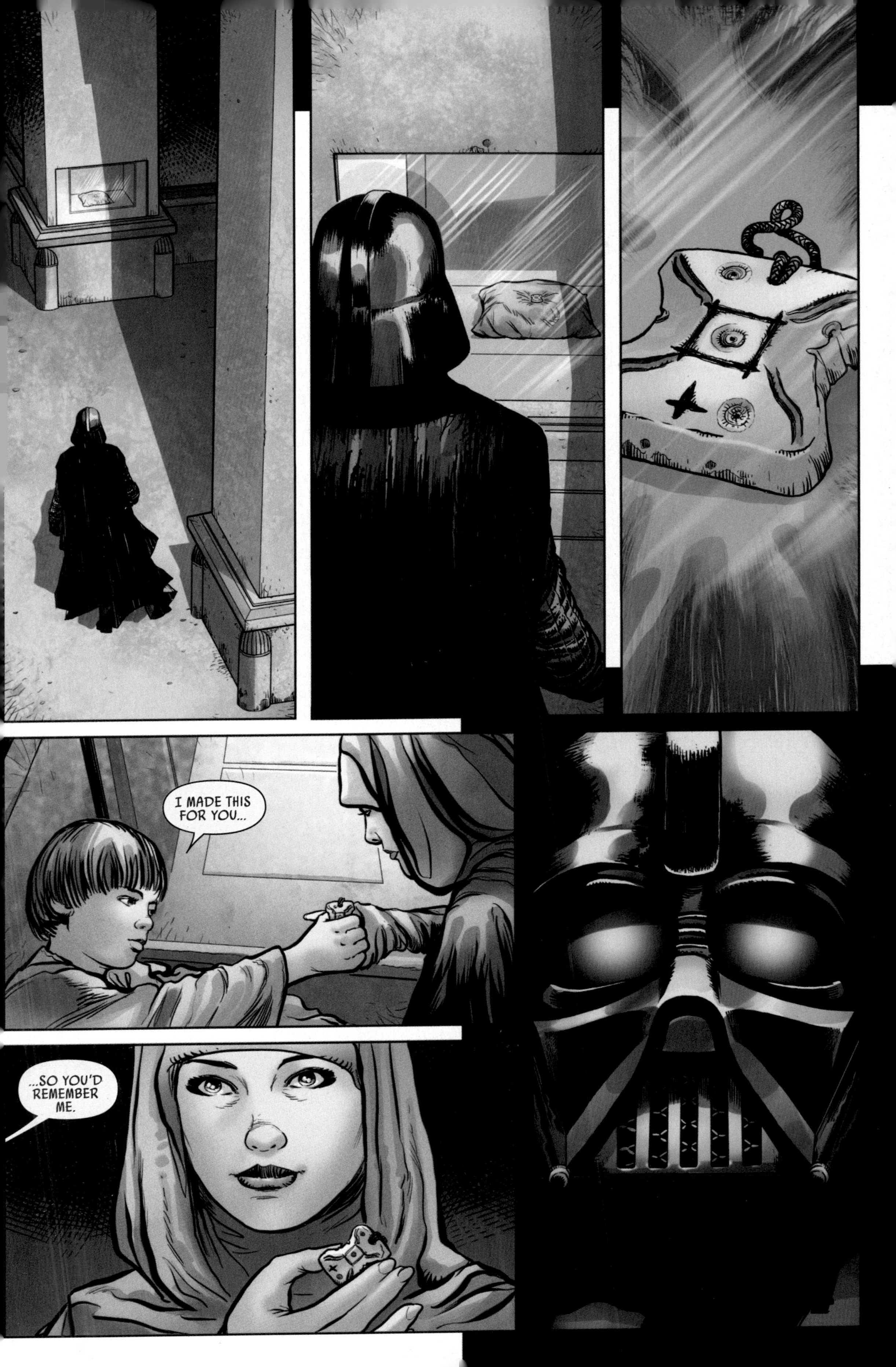
I MADE THIS FOR YOU...
...SO YOU'D REMEMBER ME.

I made this...

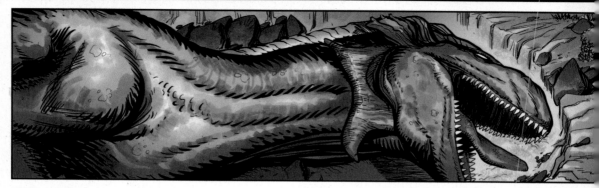

I'M S--SORRY, MY QUEEN...

PADMÉ...

...for you.

ARE... ARE YOU DONE?

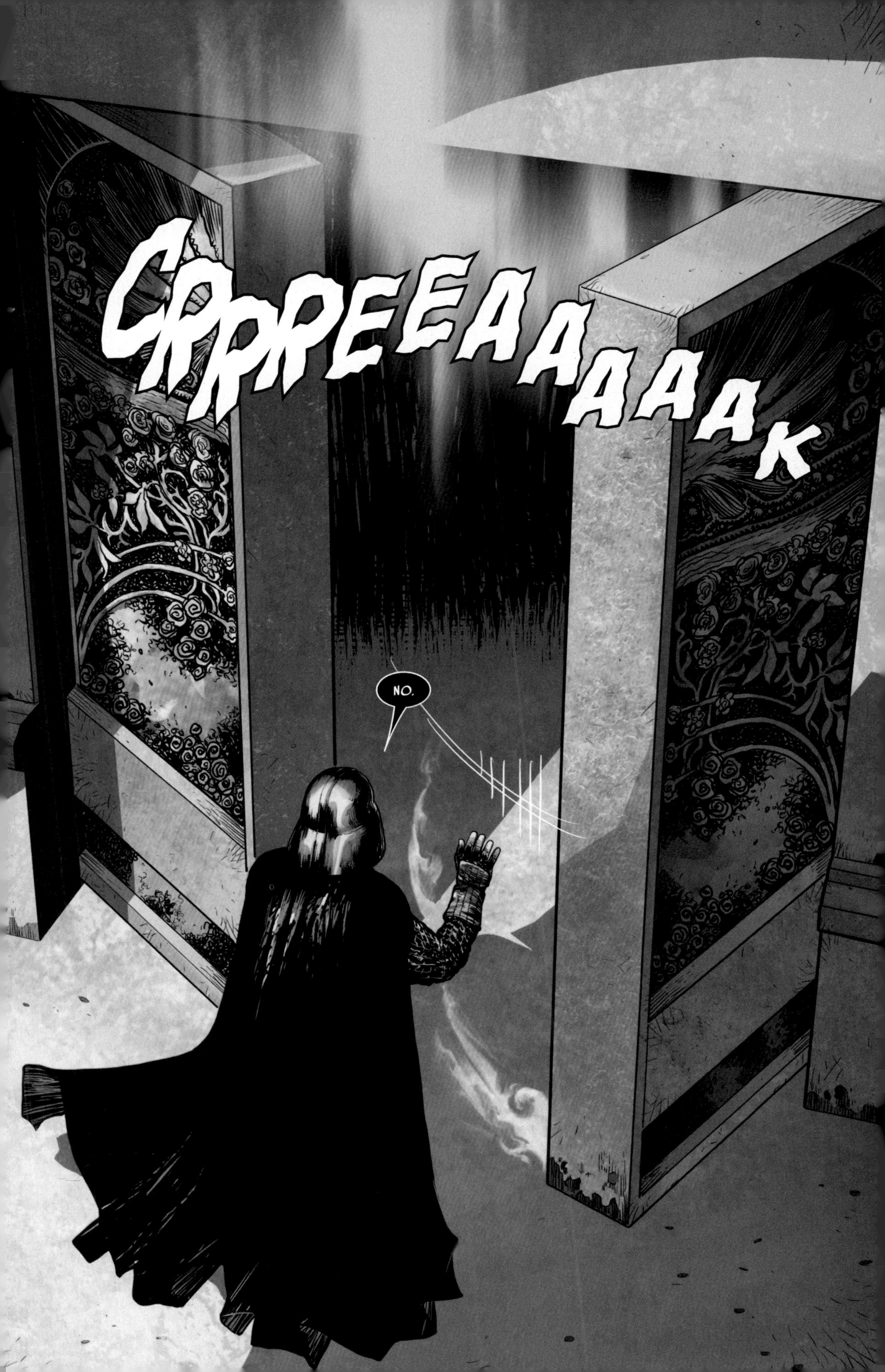
CRRREEAAAAAK
NO.

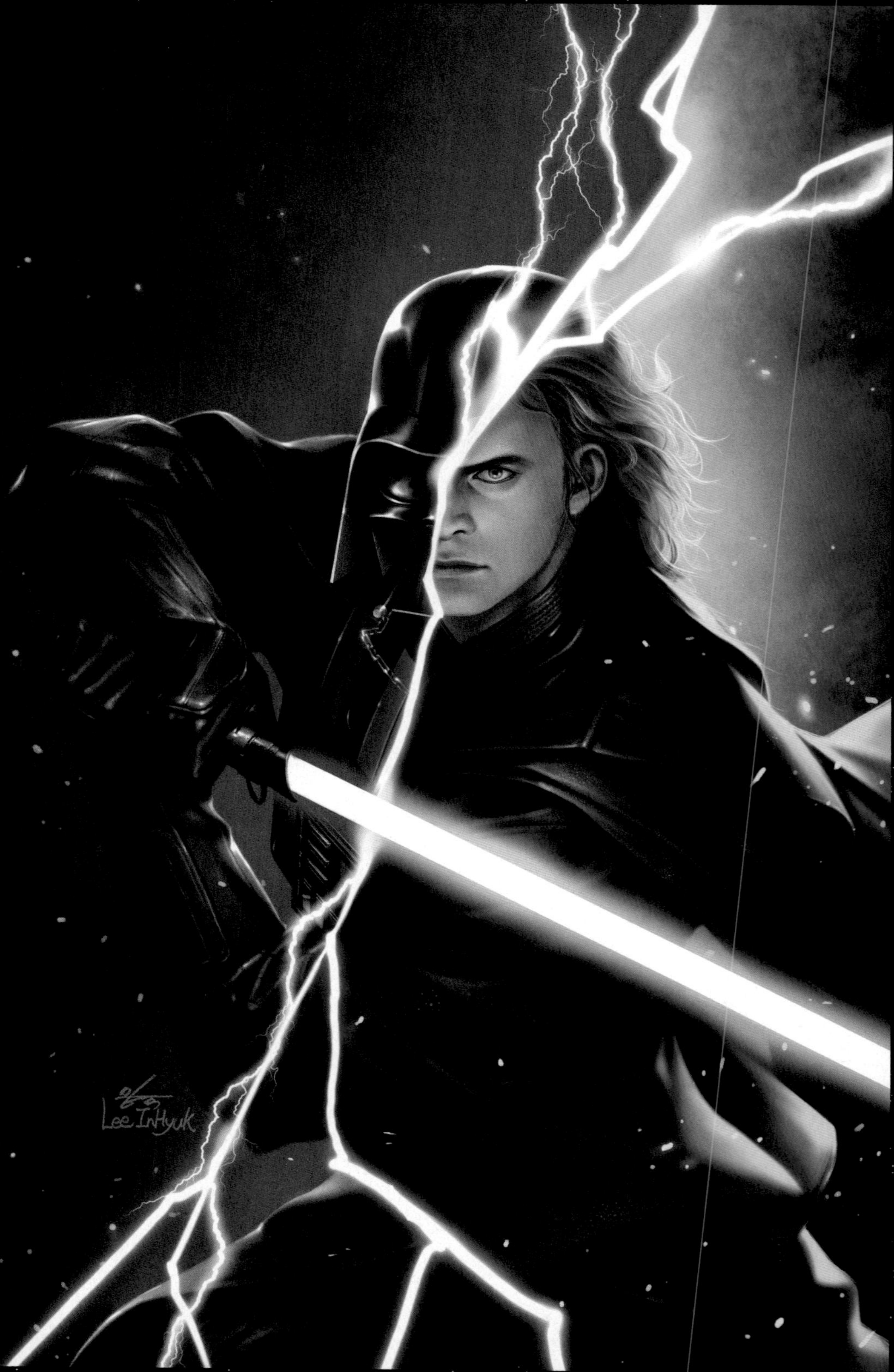
Lee InHyuk

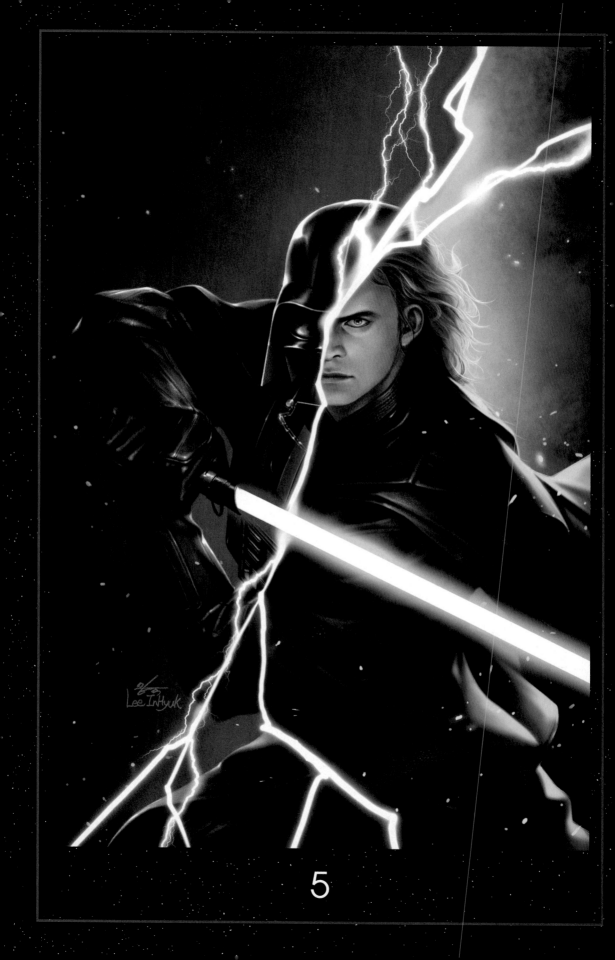

5

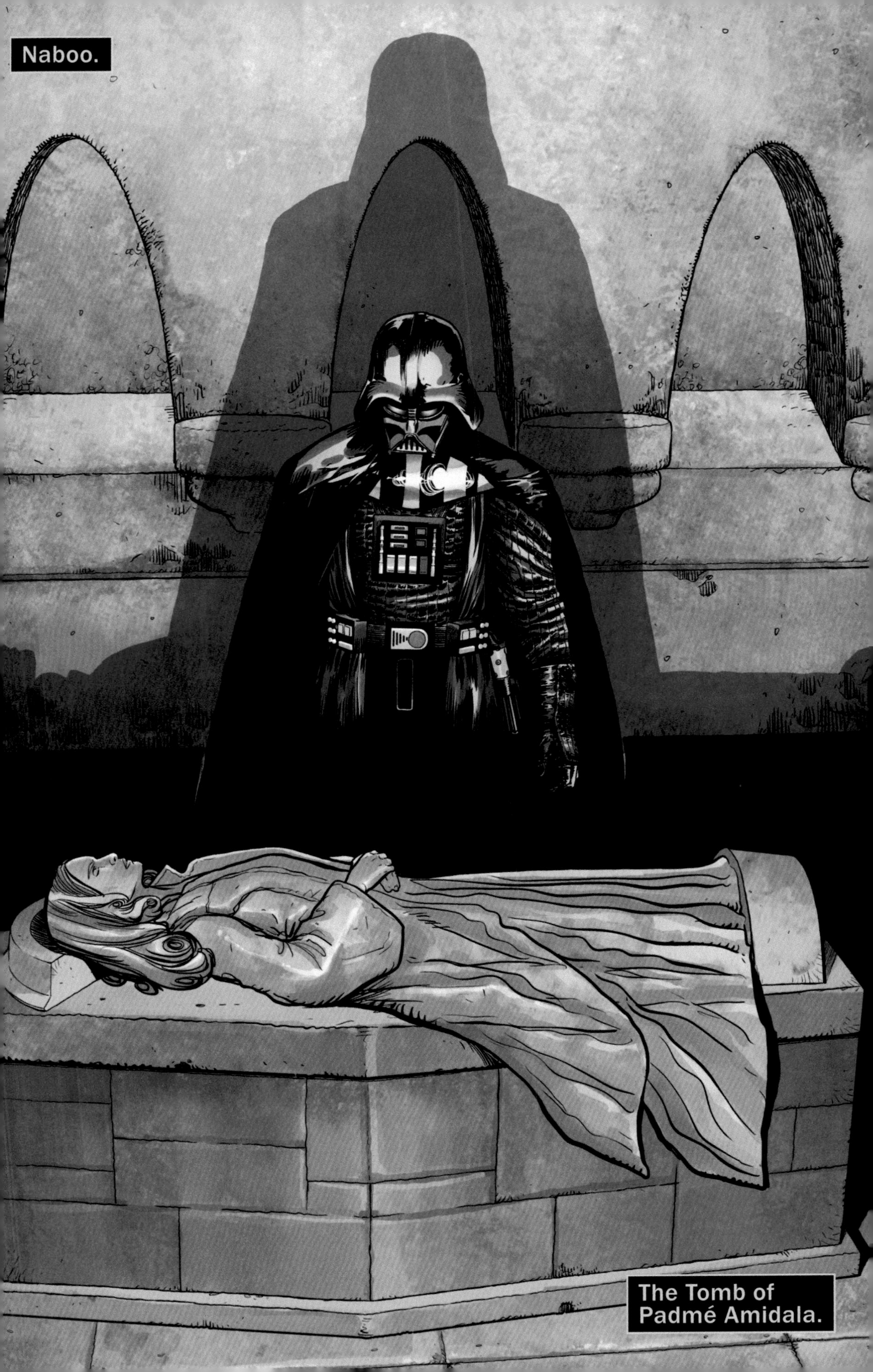
Naboo.
The Tomb of Padmé Amidala.

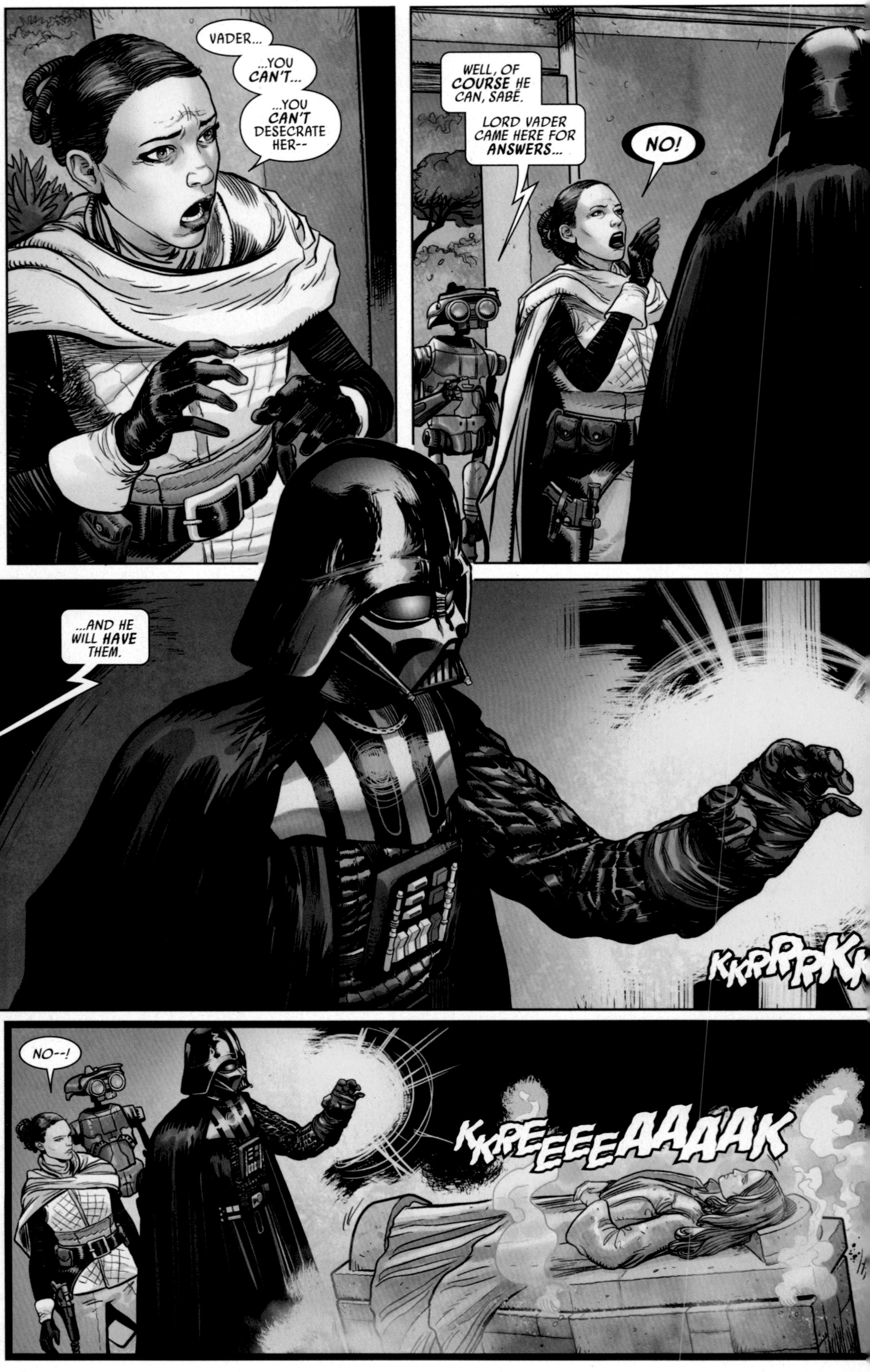
VADER...
...YOU CAN'T...
...YOU CAN'T DESECRATE HER--
WELL, OF COURSE HE CAN, SABÉ.
LORD VADER CAME HERE FOR ANSWERS...
NO!
...AND HE WILL HAVE THEM.
KKRRRRKK
NO--!
KKREEEEEAAAAK

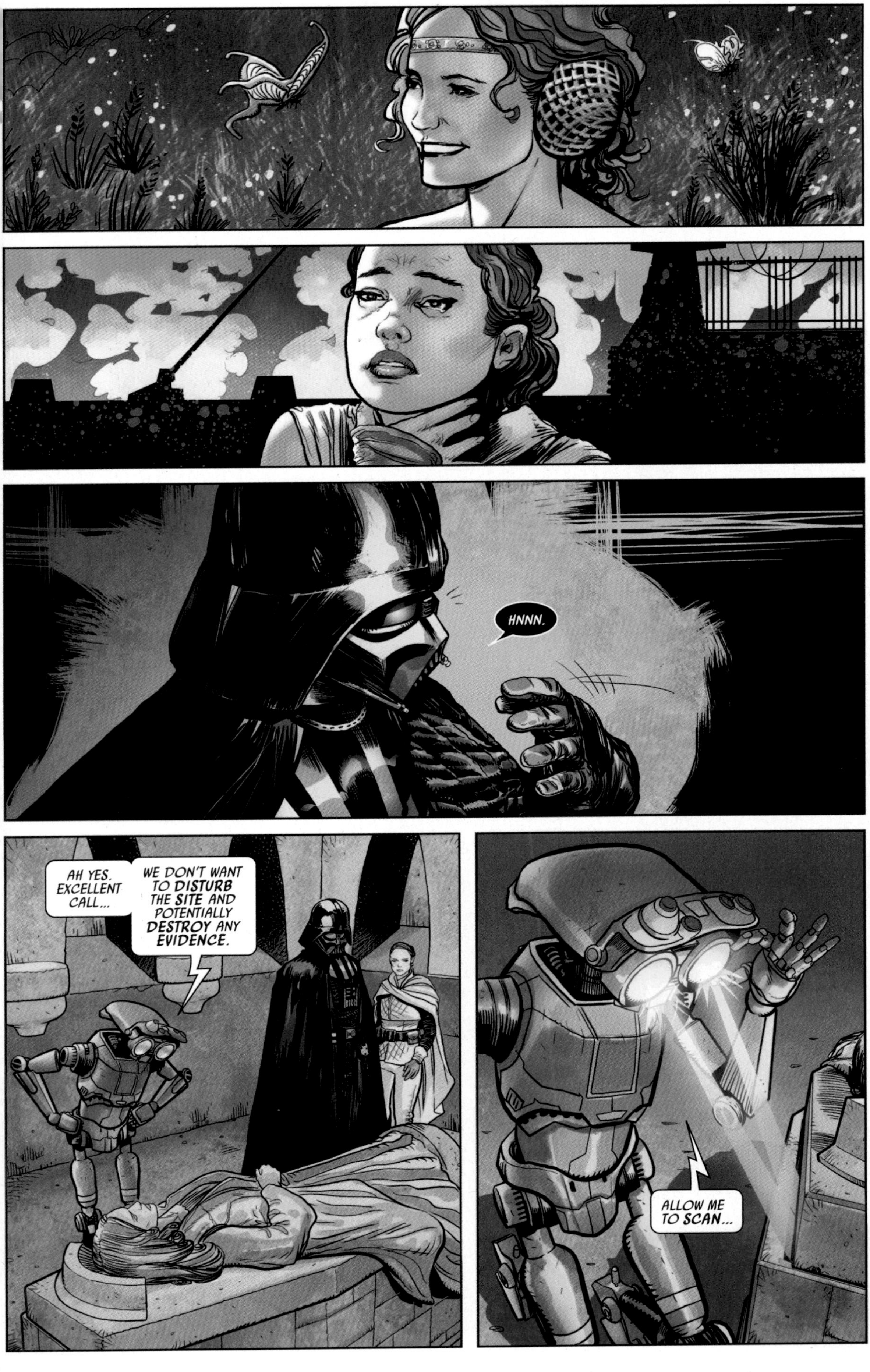
HNNN.
AH YES. EXCELLENT CALL...
WE DON'T WANT TO DISTURB THE SITE AND POTENTIALLY DESTROY ANY EVIDENCE.
ALLOW ME TO SCAN...

AHA!

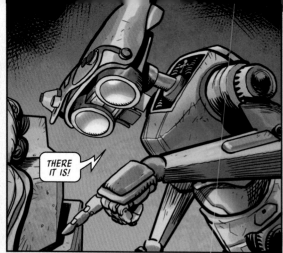

THERE IT IS!

A MED IMPLANT. STAMPED...

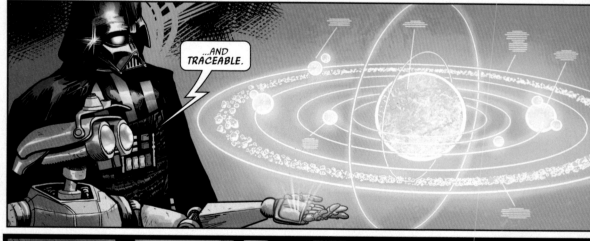

...AND TRACEABLE.

AH!

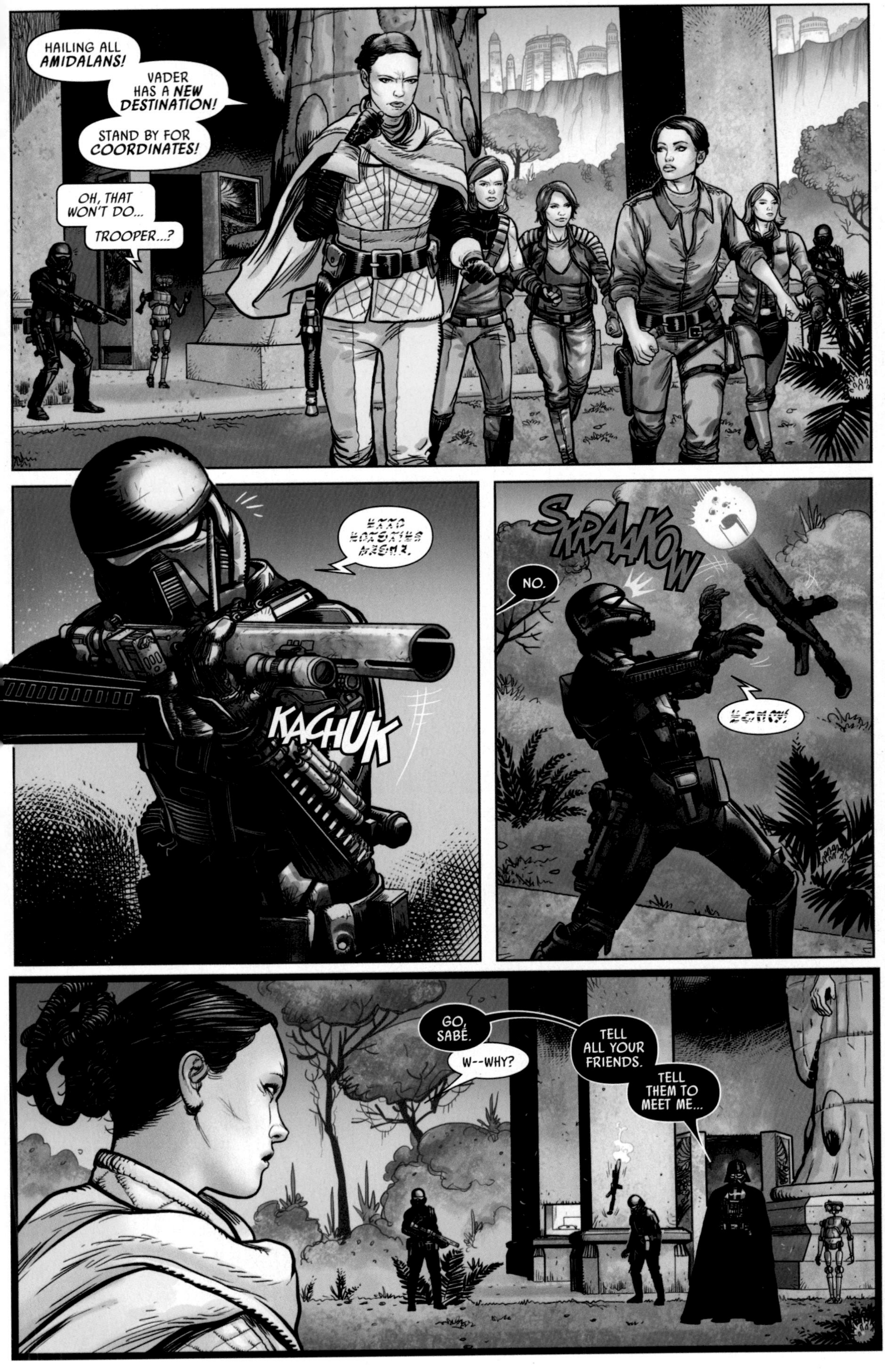
HAILING ALL AMIDALANS!
VADER HAS A NEW DESTINATION!
STAND BY FOR COORDINATES!
OH, THAT WON'T DO...
TROOPER...?
KACHUK
SKRAAKOW
NO.
GO, SABÉ.
W--WHY?
TELL ALL YOUR FRIENDS.
TELL THEM TO MEET ME...

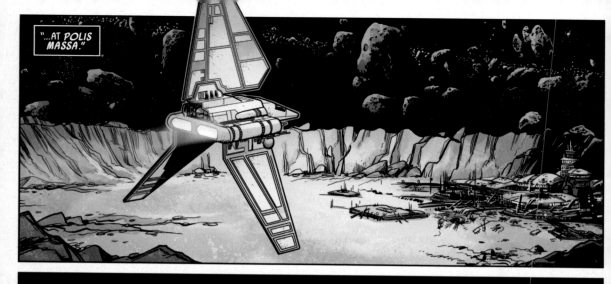

"...AT POLIS MASSA."

Where you hid her.

Where you hid my son.

Where I will make an end to this all.

A FORMER REBEL BASE.

DISCOVERED YEARS AGO AND BOMBARDED BY IMPERIAL TROOPS.

I DETECT NO SURVIVING ORGANIC LIFE-FORMS.

WHERE SHOULD WE--

AH. THE STARPORT CONTROL.

OF COURSE.

DAMAGED BUT NOT DESTROYED!

LET'S SEE WHAT'S WHAT...

THAT'S A GOOD SOUND!

SEARCHING FOR DATA ON ARRIVALS AND DEPARTURES DURING THE TIME PERIOD OF...

BLOOP

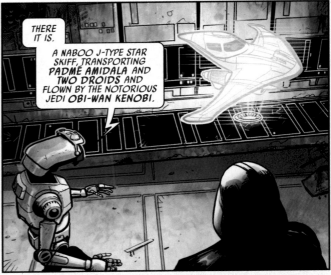

THERE IT IS.

A NABOO J-TYPE STAR SKIFF, TRANSPORTING PADMÉ AMIDALA AND TWO DROIDS AND FLOWN BY THE NOTORIOUS JEDI OBI-WAN KENOBI.

SHE WAS INJURED. HE APPARENTLY BROUGHT HER HERE TO TRY TO SAVE HER LIFE...

KENOBI...

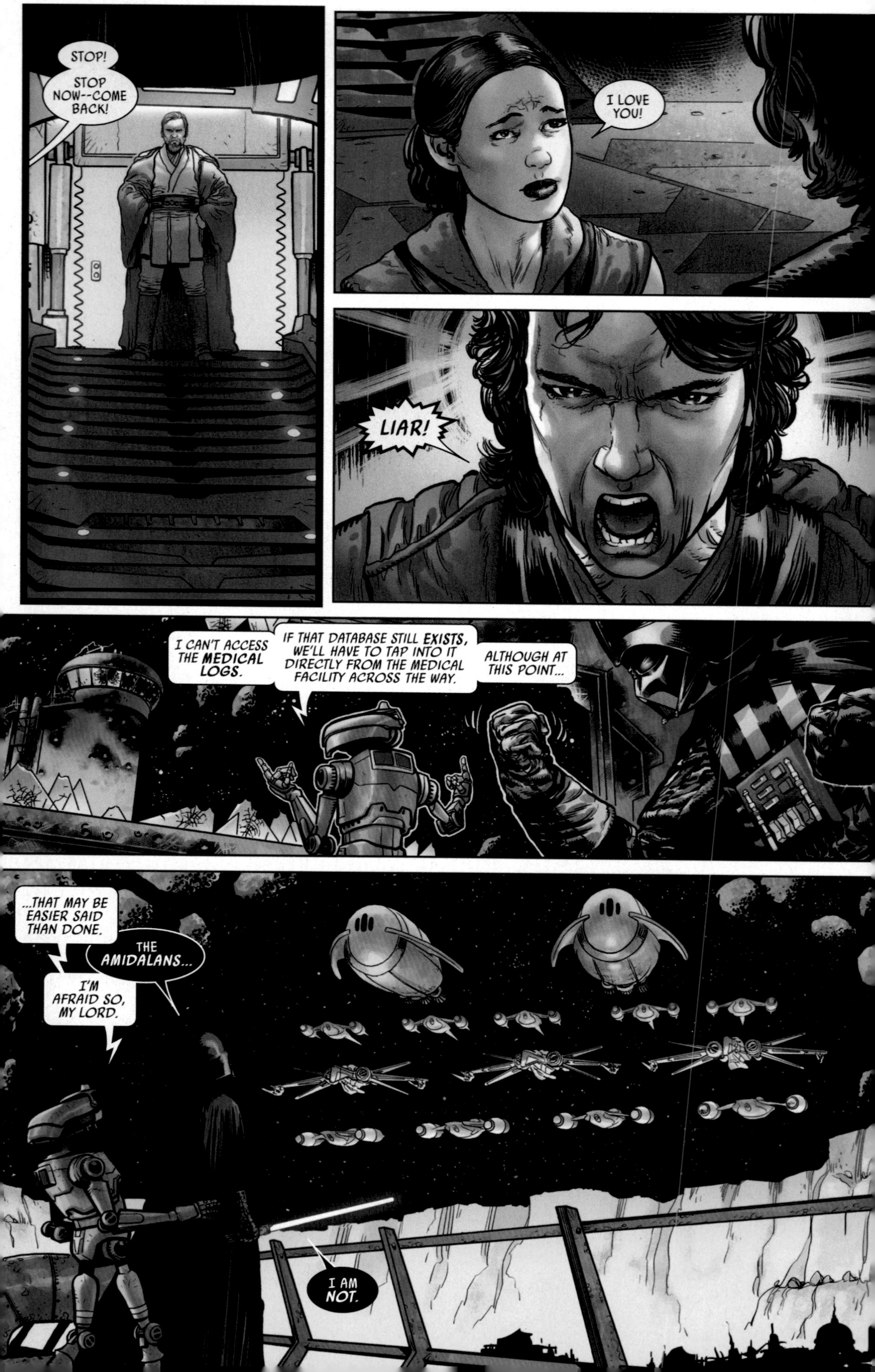
STOP!
STOP NOW--COME BACK!
I LOVE YOU!
LIAR!
I CAN'T ACCESS THE MEDICAL LOGS.
IF THAT DATABASE STILL EXISTS, WE'LL HAVE TO TAP INTO IT DIRECTLY FROM THE MEDICAL FACILITY ACROSS THE WAY.
ALTHOUGH AT THIS POINT...
...THAT MAY BE EASIER SAID THAN DONE.
THE AMIDALANS...
I'M AFRAID SO, MY LORD.
I AM NOT.

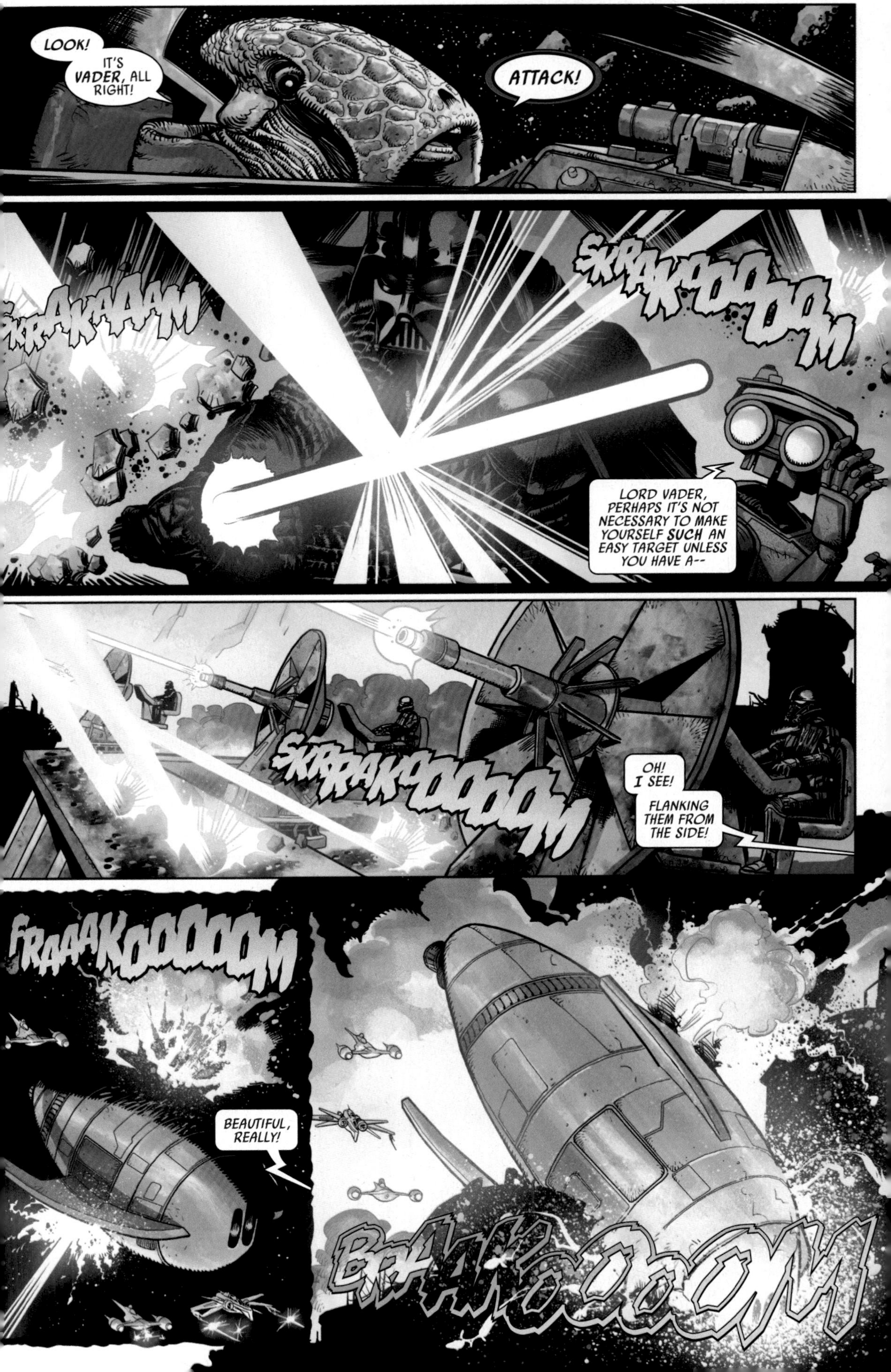
LOOK!
IT'S VADER, ALL RIGHT!
ATTACK!
SKRAKAAAM
SKRAKOOOOOM
LORD VADER, PERHAPS IT'S NOT NECESSARY TO MAKE YOURSELF SUCH AN EASY TARGET UNLESS YOU HAVE A--
SKRRAKOOOOOM
OH! I SEE!
FLANKING THEM FROM THE SIDE!
FRAAAKOOOOOM
BEAUTIFUL, REALLY!
BRAKOOOOM

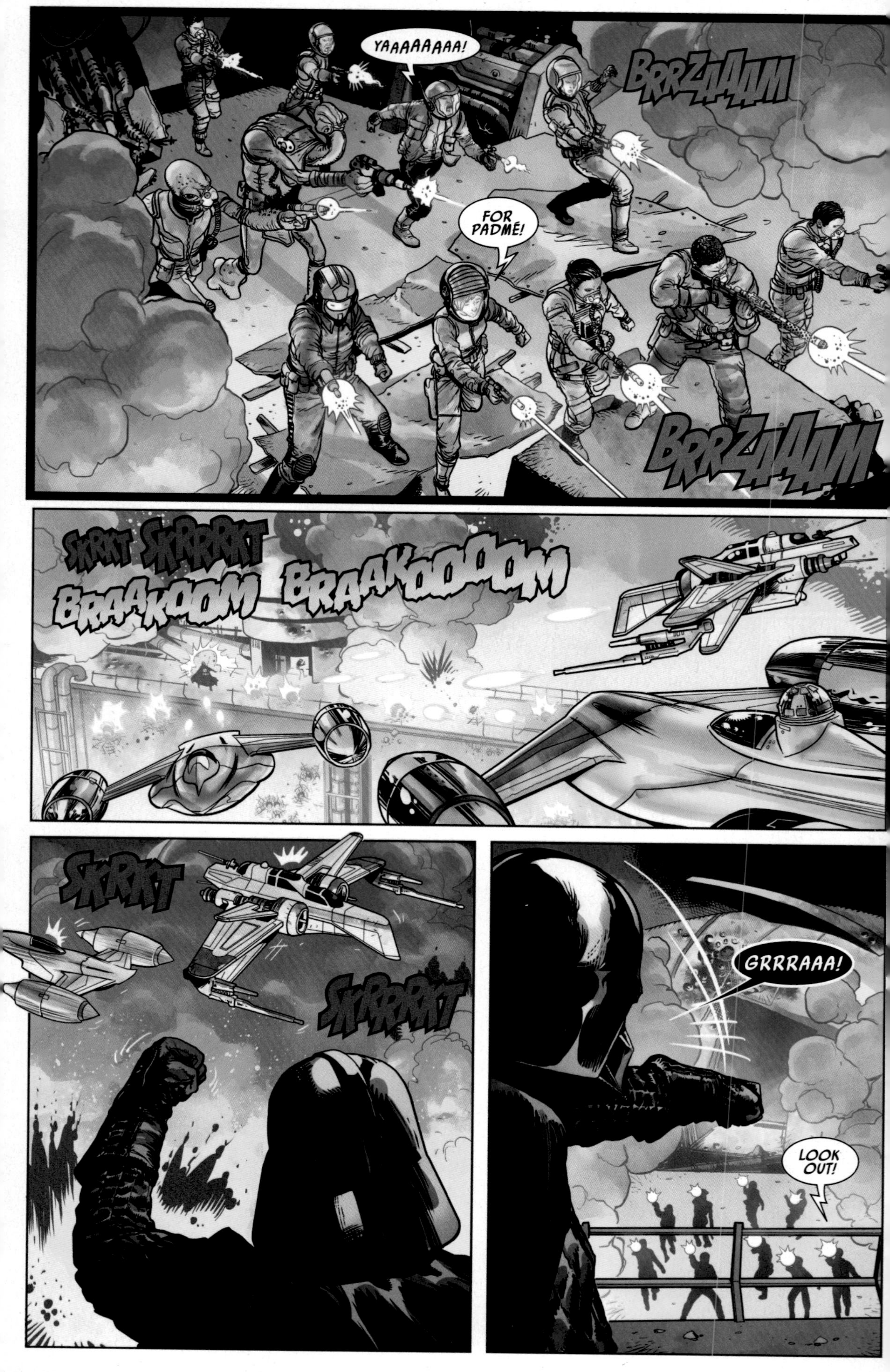
YAAAAAAAA!
BRRZAAAM
FOR PADMÉ!
BRRZAAAM
SKRKT SKRRRKT
BRAAKOOM
BRAAKOOOOM
SKRKT
SKRRRKT
GRRRAAA!
LOOK OUT!

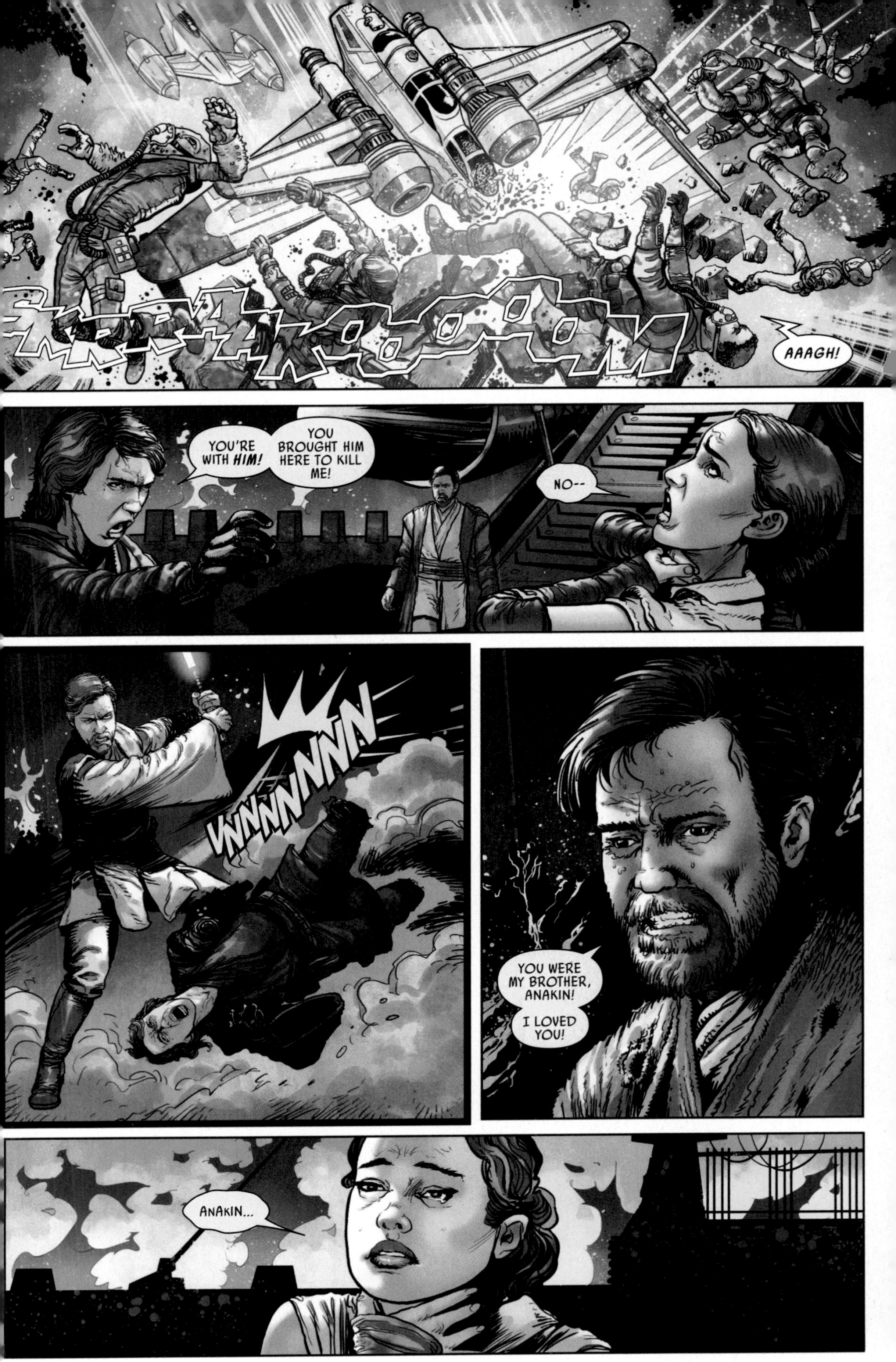
KRAKOOOOM
AAAGH!
YOU'RE WITH HIM!
YOU BROUGHT HIM HERE TO KILL ME!
NO--
VVNNNNNNN
YOU WERE MY BROTHER, ANAKIN!
I LOVED YOU!
ANAKIN...

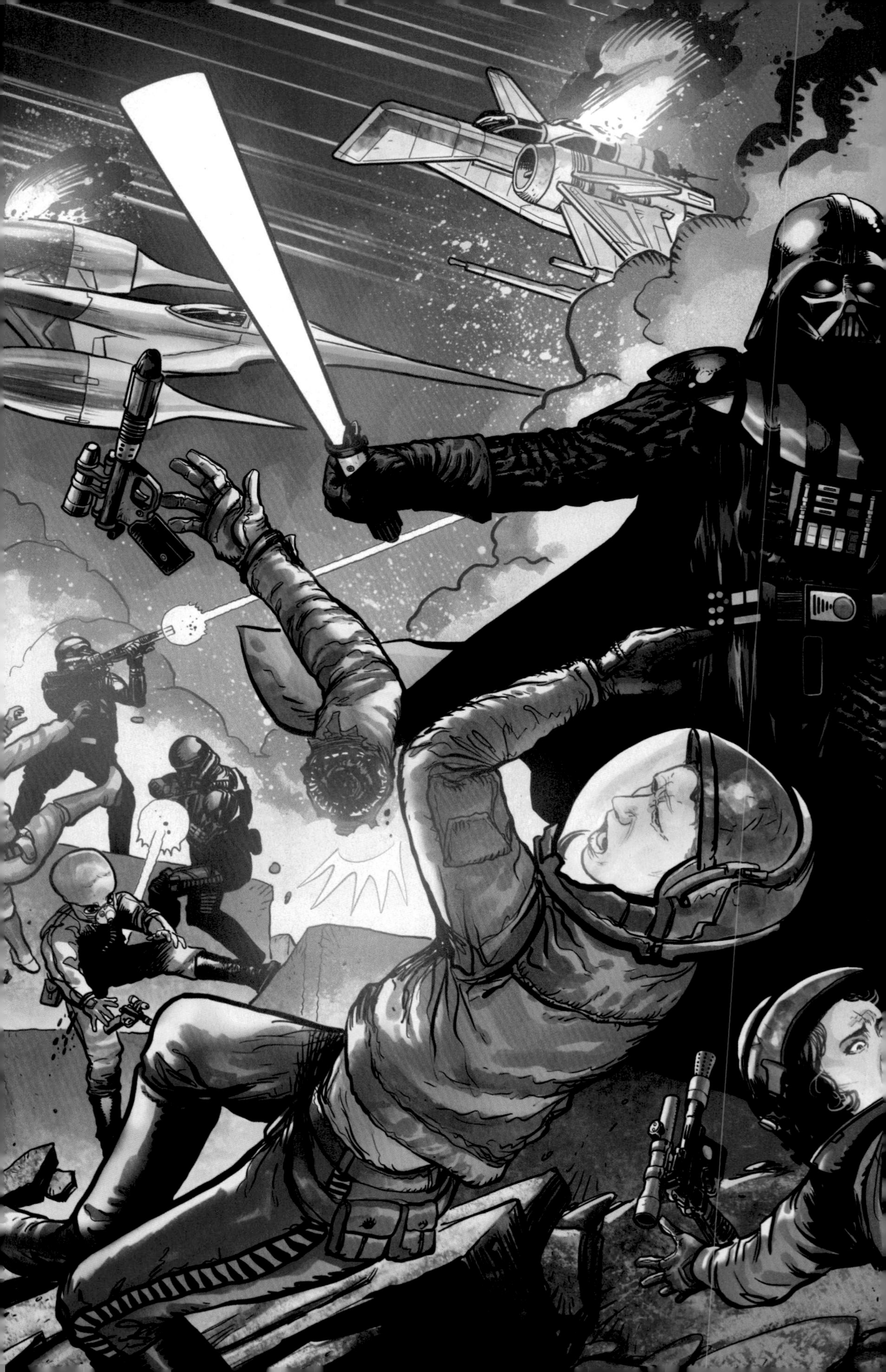

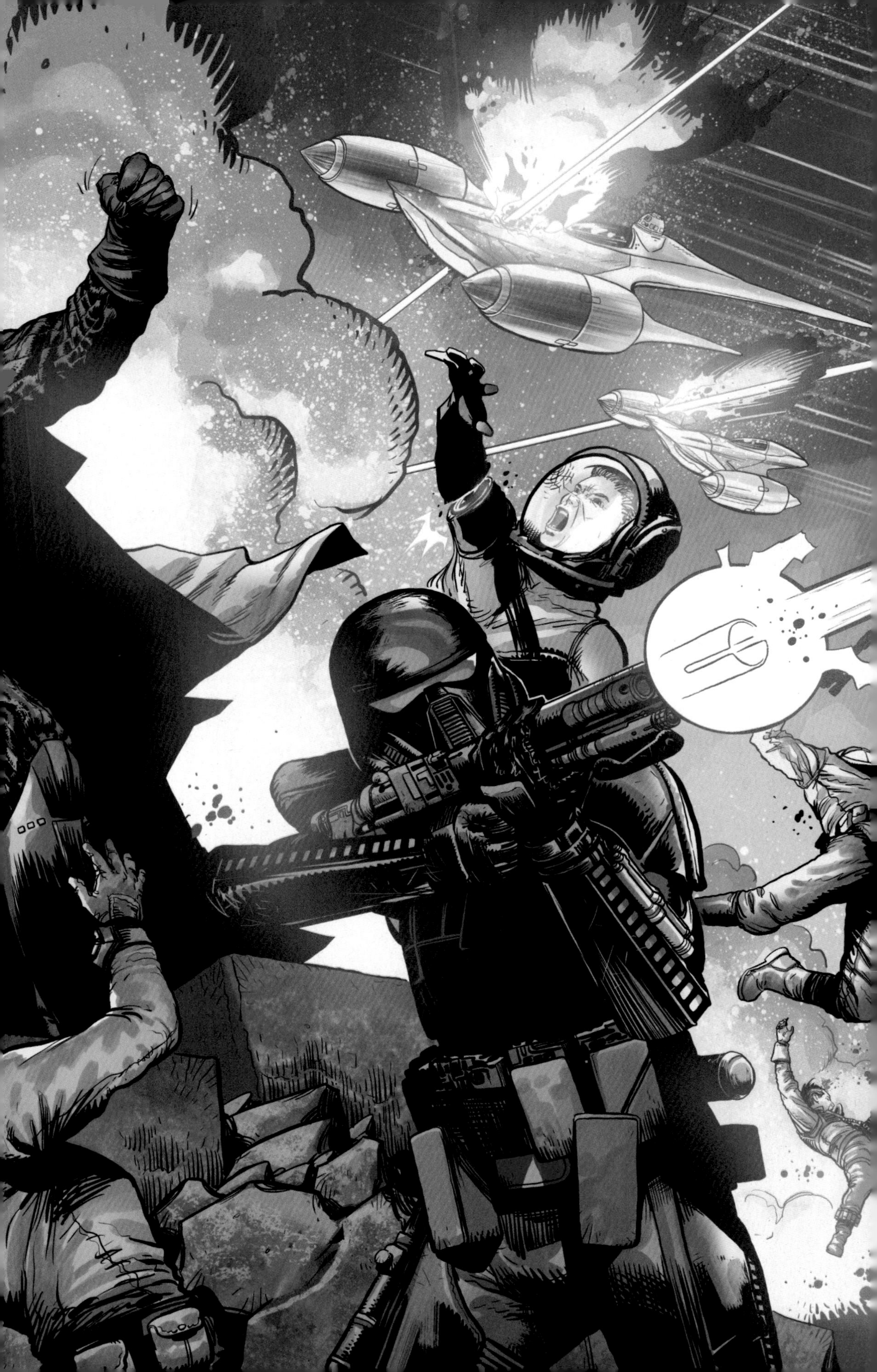

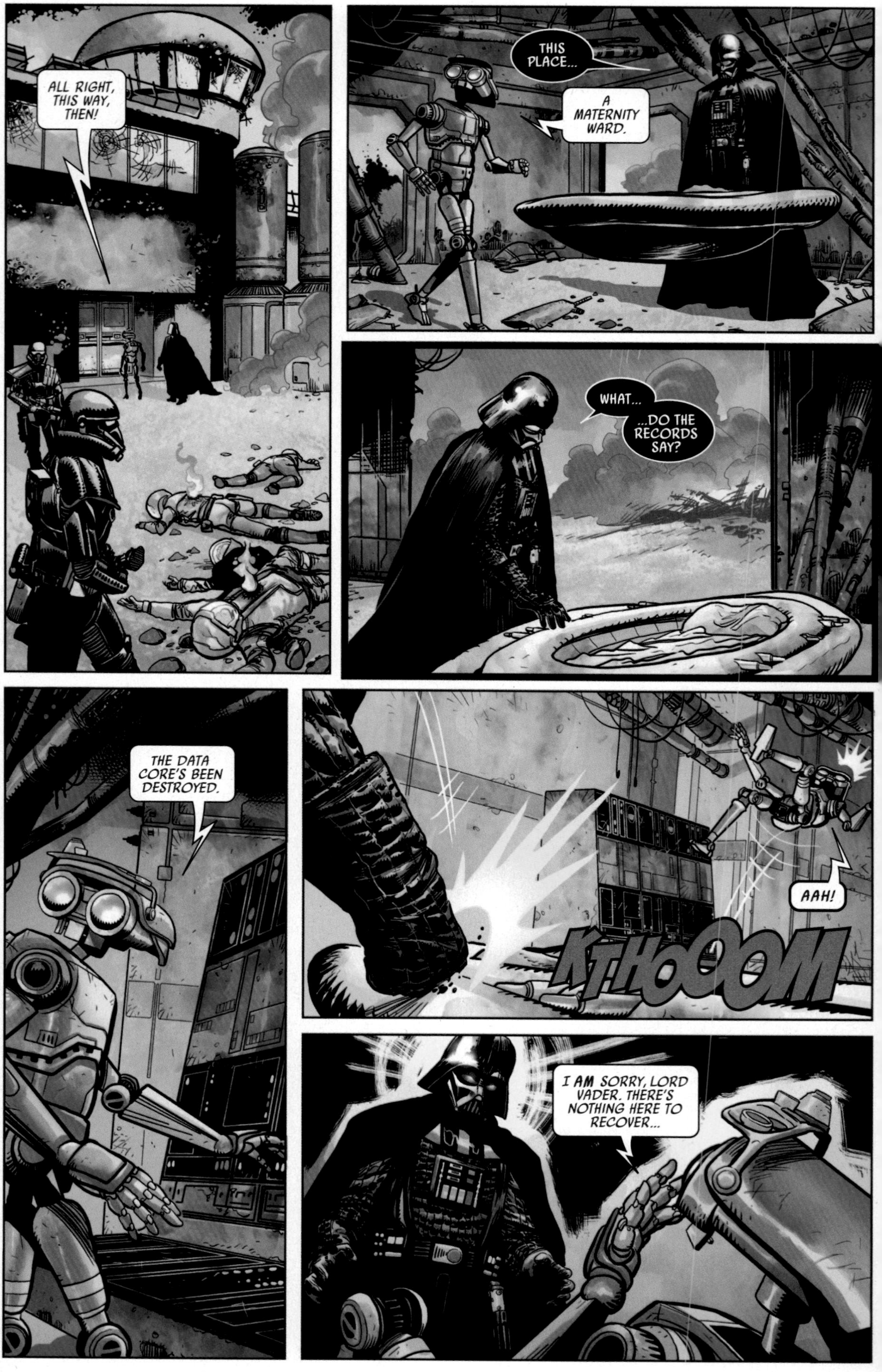
ALL RIGHT, THIS WAY, THEN!
THIS PLACE...
A MATERNITY WARD.
WHAT...
...DO THE RECORDS SAY?
THE DATA CORE'S BEEN DESTROYED.
AAH!
KTHOOOM
I AM SORRY, LORD VADER. THERE'S NOTHING HERE TO RECOVER...

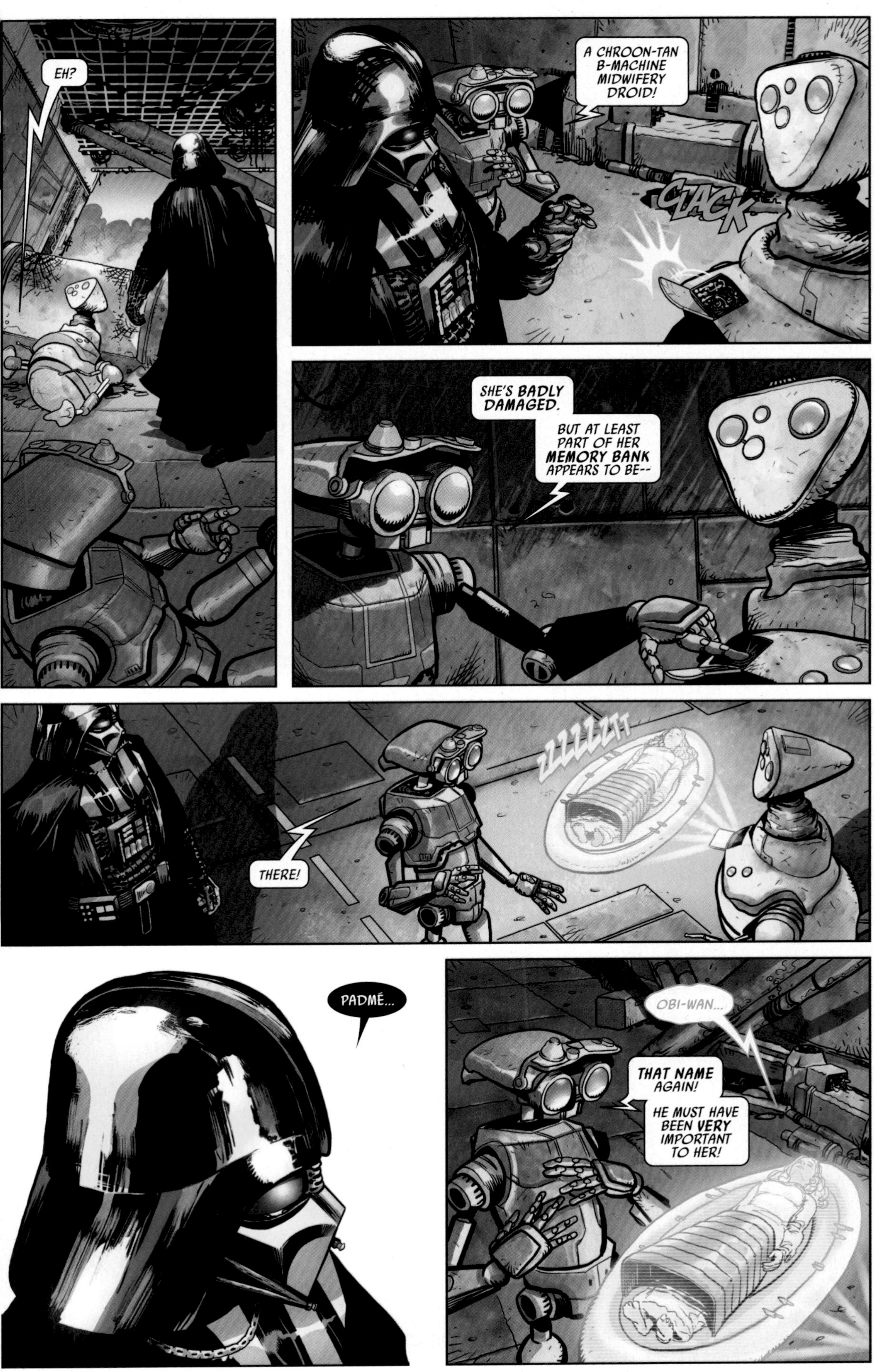
EH?
A CHROON-TAN B-MACHINE MIDWIFERY DROID!
CLACK
SHE'S BADLY DAMAGED.
BUT AT LEAST PART OF HER MEMORY BANK APPEARS TO BE--
ZZZZZZTT
THERE!
PADMÉ...
OBI-WAN...
THAT NAME AGAIN!
HE MUST HAVE BEEN VERY IMPORTANT TO HER!

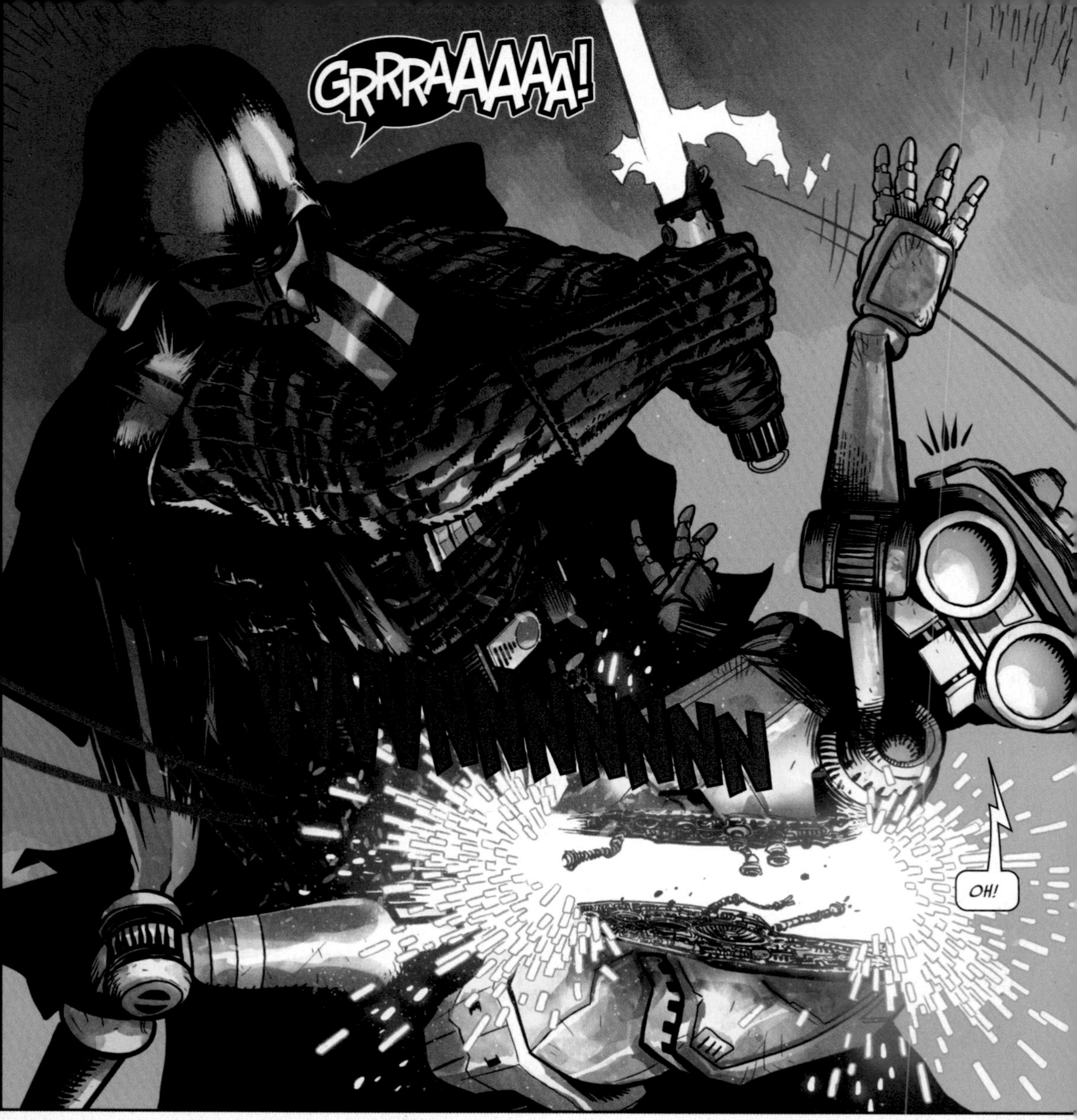
GRRRAAAAAA!
VVVMMMMNNNNNNN
OH!
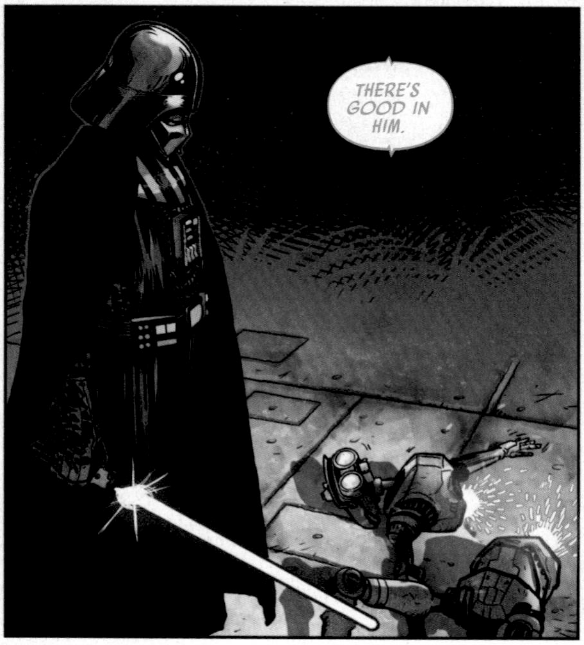
THERE'S GOOD IN HIM.
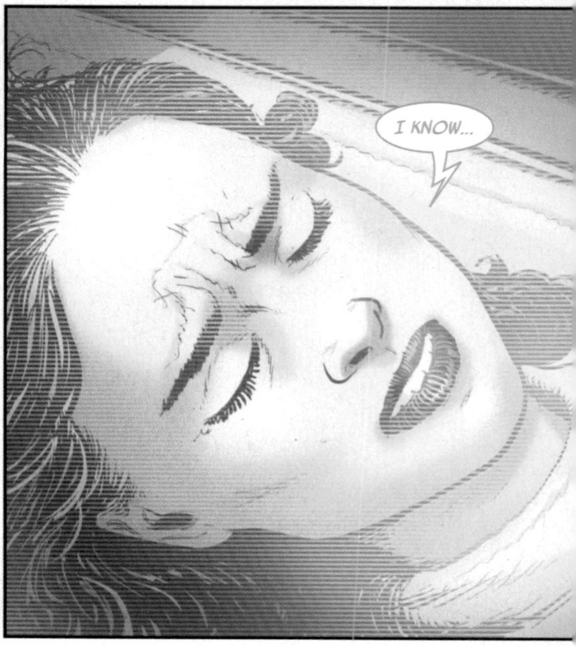
I KNOW...

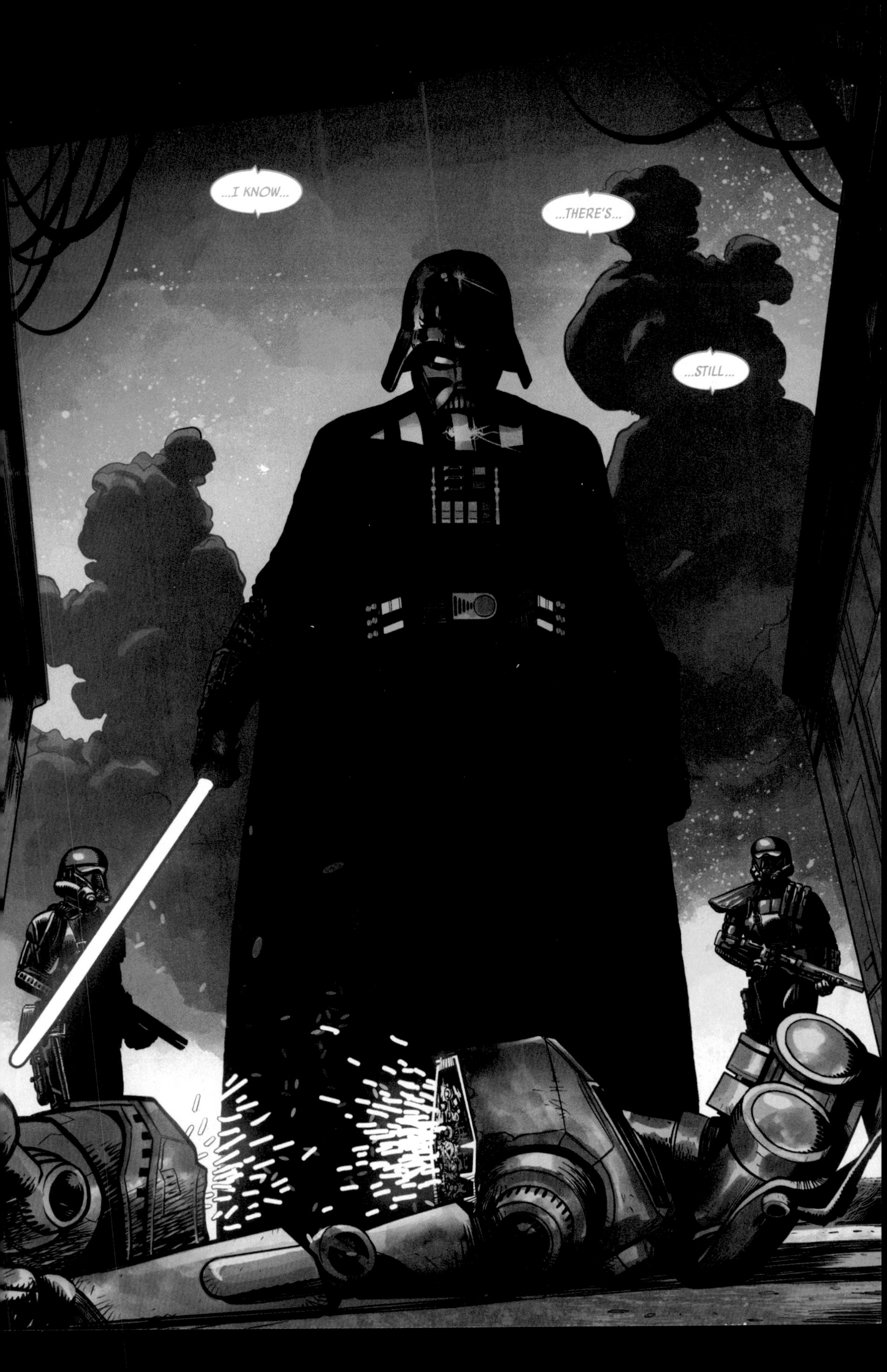
...I KNOW...
...THERE'S...
...STILL...

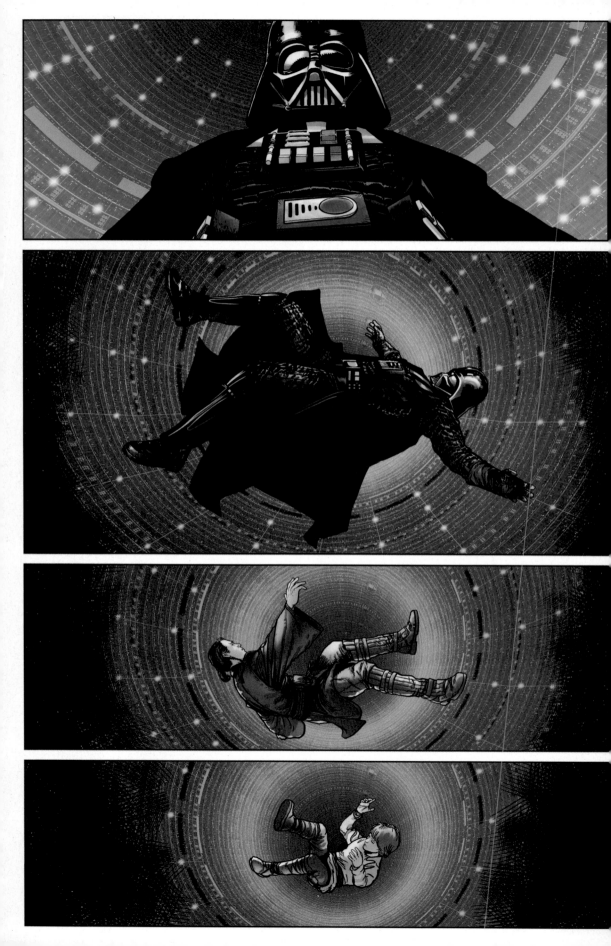

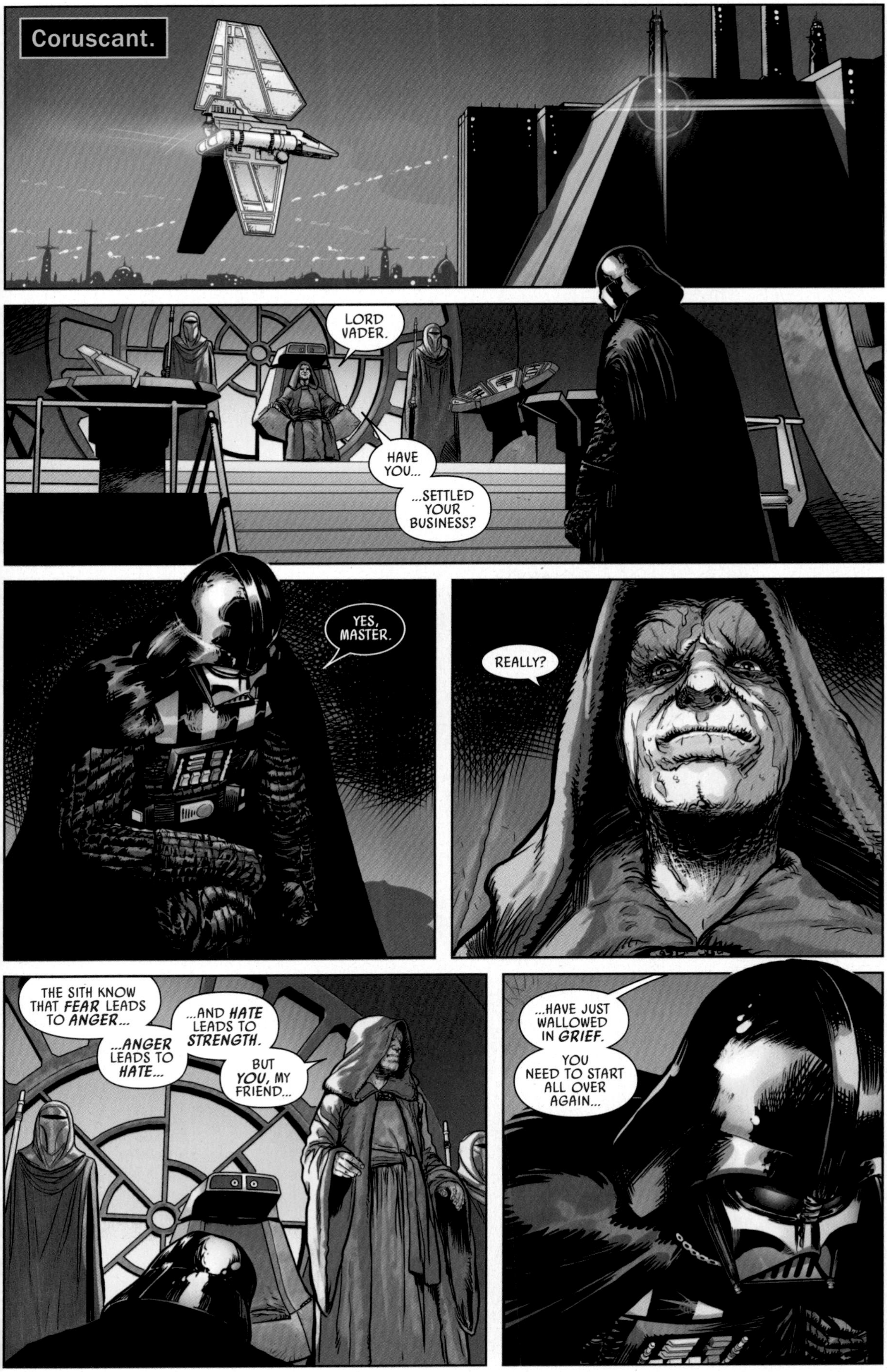
Coruscant.
LORD VADER.
HAVE YOU...
...SETTLED YOUR BUSINESS?
YES, MASTER.
REALLY?
THE SITH KNOW THAT FEAR LEADS TO ANGER...
...ANGER LEADS TO HATE...
...AND HATE LEADS TO STRENGTH.
BUT YOU, MY FRIEND...
...HAVE JUST WALLOWED IN GRIEF.
YOU NEED TO START ALL OVER AGAIN...

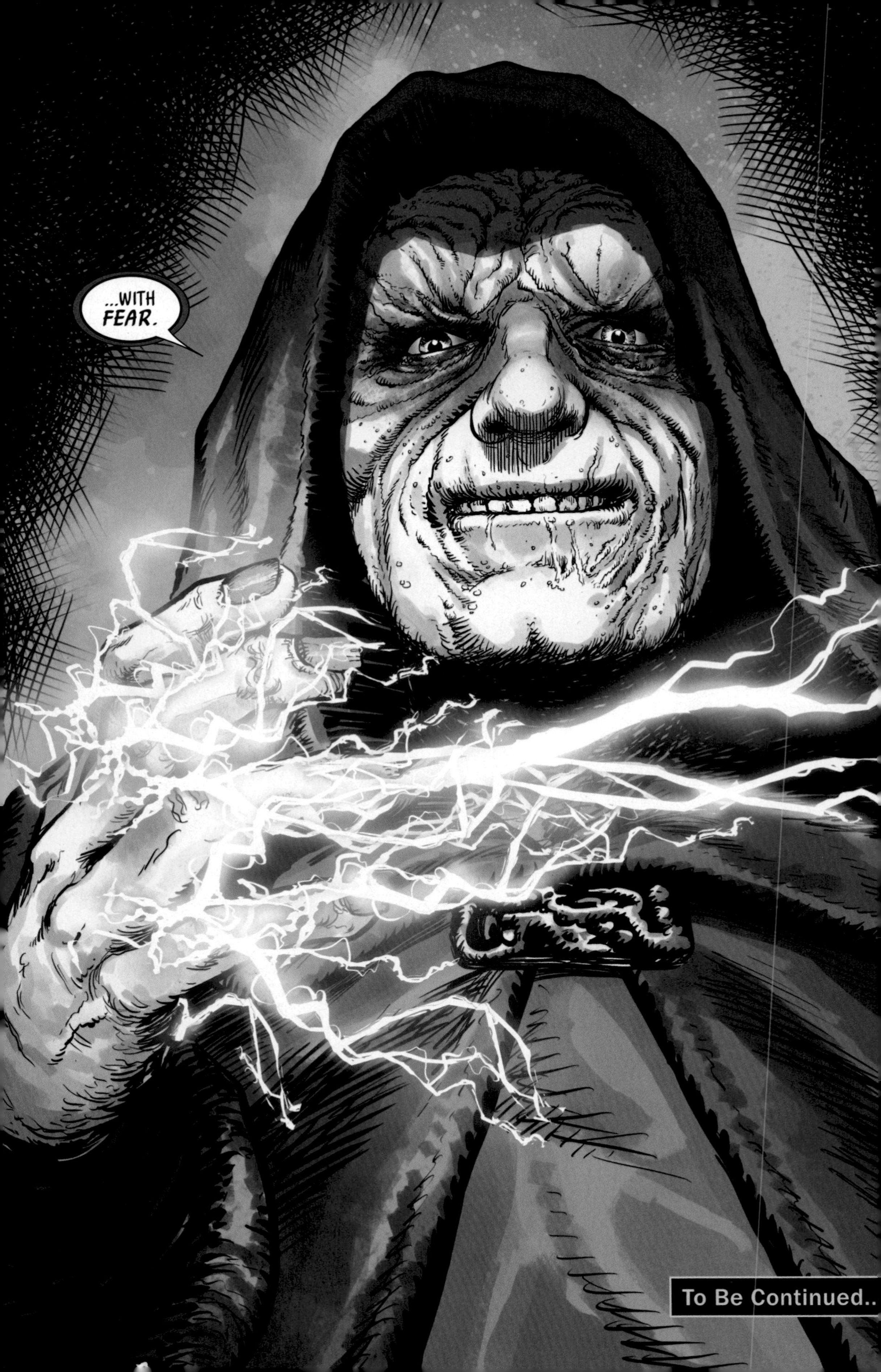
...WITH FEAR.
To Be Continued..

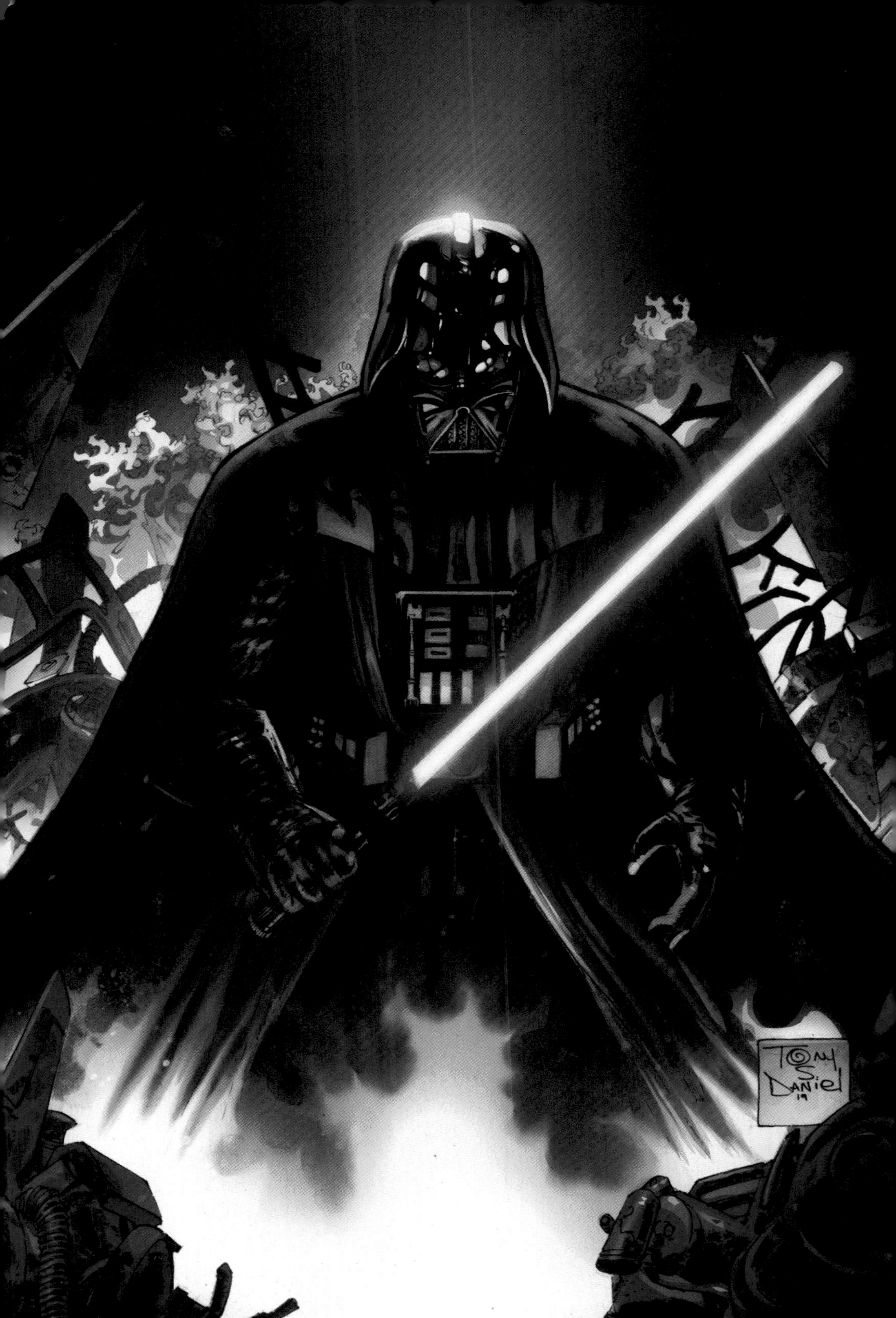
TONY S. DANIEL 19

#1 Variant by
TONY DANIEL & DAVID CURIEL

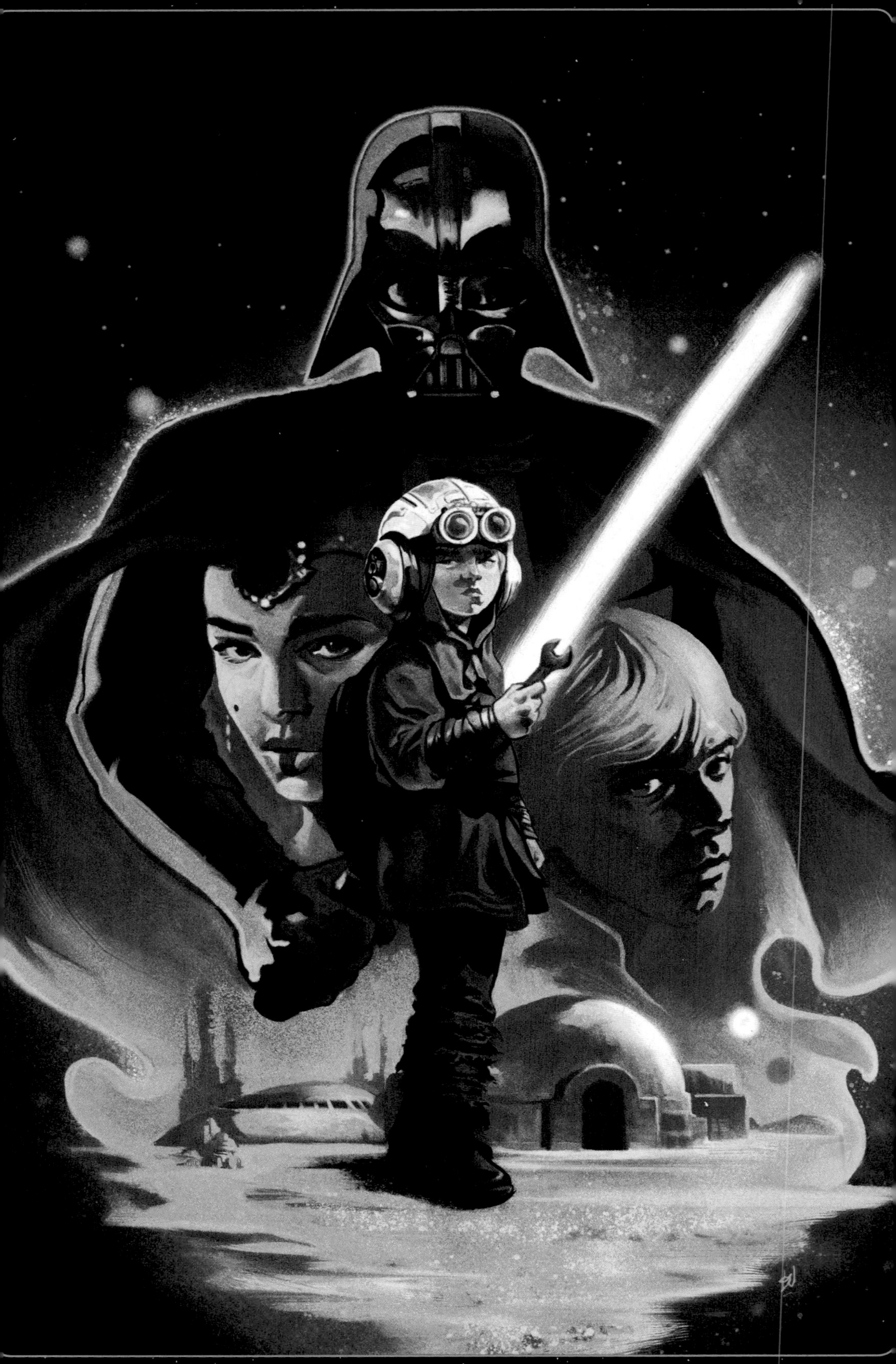

#1 Variant by
MIKE DEL MUNDO

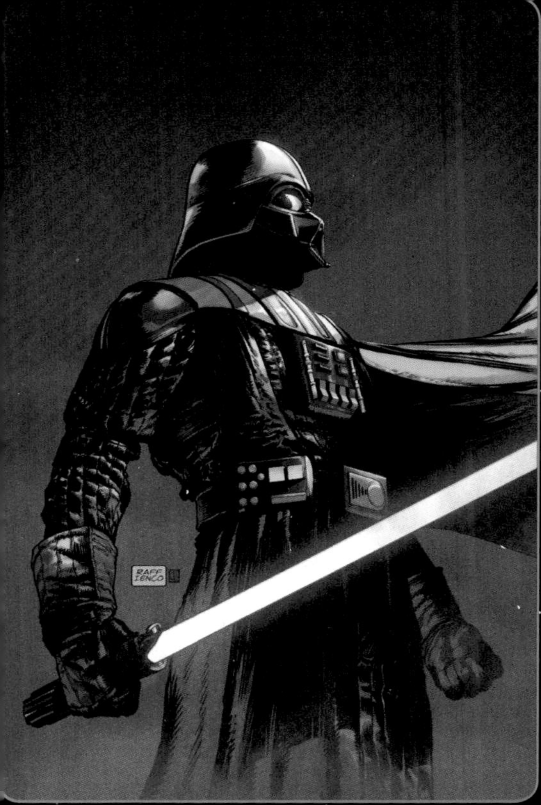
RAFF IENCO

#1 Variant by
RAFFAELE IENCO & NEERAJ MENON

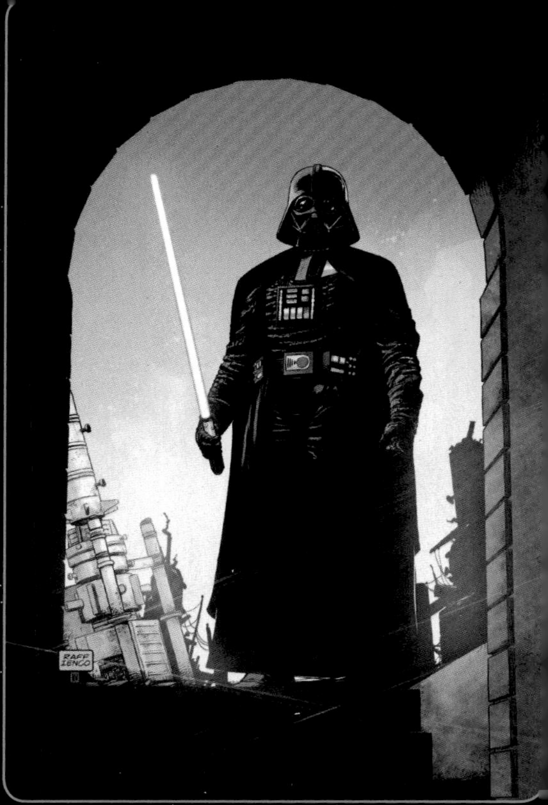
RAFF IENCO

#2 Variant by
RAFFAELE IENCO & NEERAJ MENON

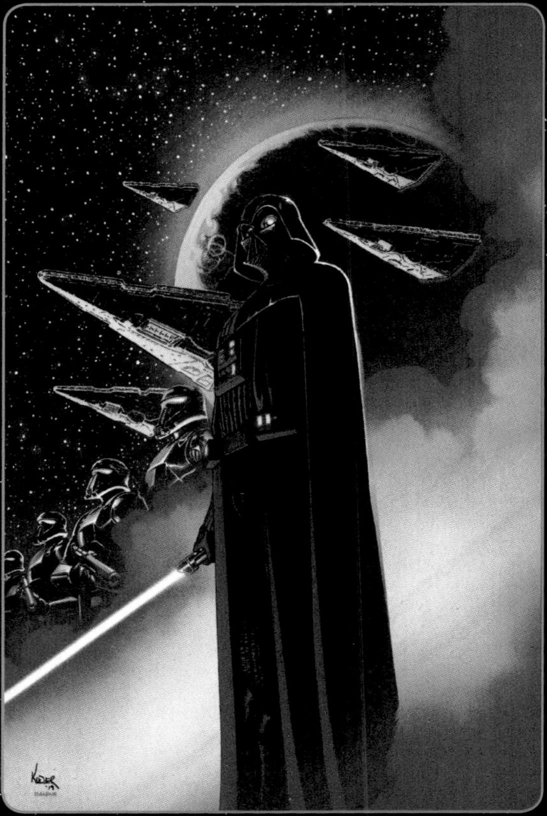

#1 Variant by

THIS GUIDE WILL SHOW YOU WHERE TO BEGIN!

FOLLOW THE ADVENTURES OF LUKE, HAN AND LEIA IN THESE

STAR WARS™

COLLECTED EDITIONS!

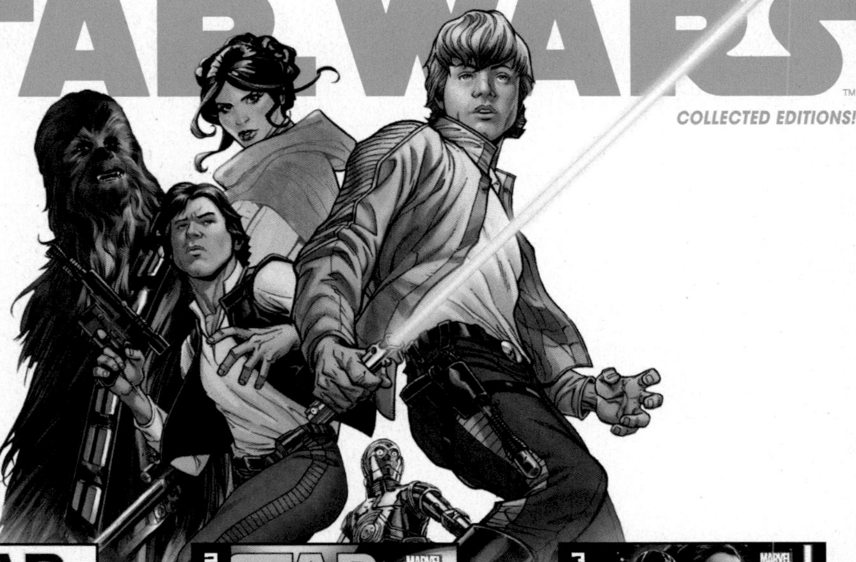

START HERE

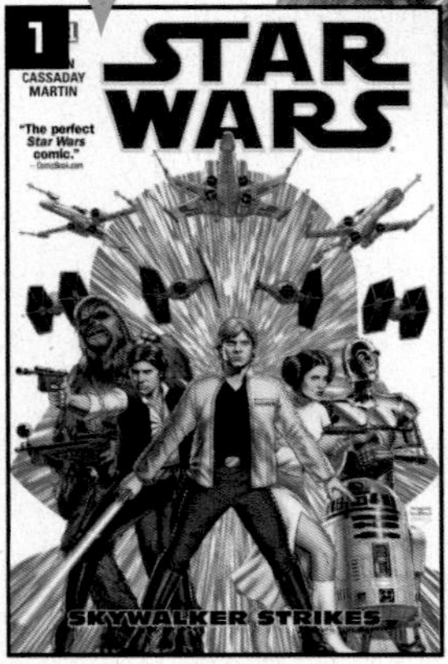
1
STAR WARS
CASSADAY
MARTIN
"The perfect Star Wars comic."
SKYWALKER STRIKES

Star Wars Vol. 1:
Skywalker Strikes

ISBN 978-0-7851-9213-8

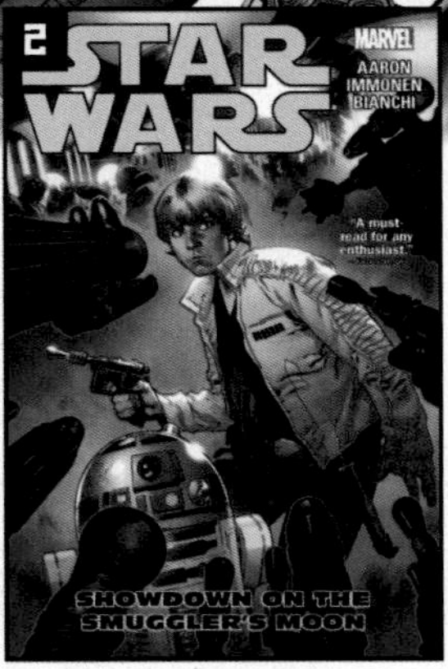
2
STAR WARS
MARVEL
AARON
IMMONEN
BIANCHI
"A must-read for any enthusiast."
SHOWDOWN ON THE SMUGGLER'S MOON

Star Wars Vol. 2:
Showdown on the Smuggler's Moon

ISBN 978-0-7851-9214-5

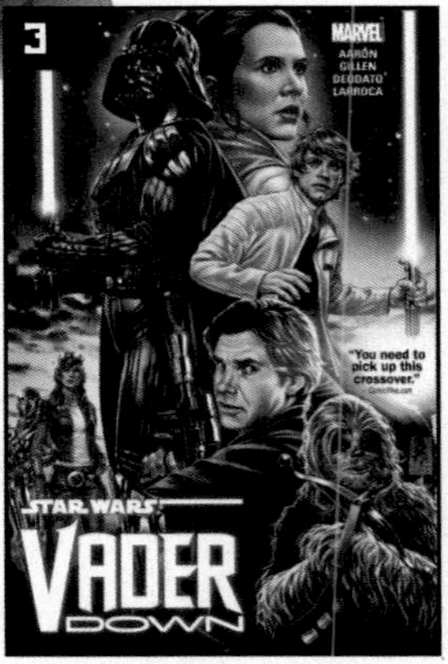
3
MARVEL
AARON
GILLEN
DEODATO
LARROCA
"You need to pick up this crossover."
STAR WARS
VADER DOWN

Star Wars:
Vader Down

ISBN 978-0-7851-9789-8

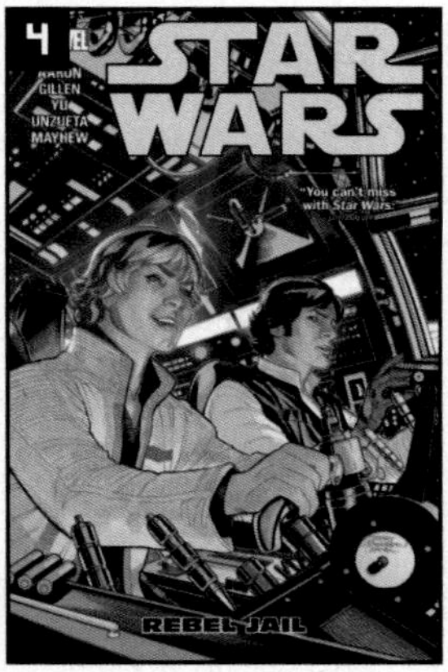
4
STAR WARS
GILLEN
YU
UNZUETA
MAYHEW
"You can't miss with Star Wars."
REBEL JAIL

Star Wars Vol. 3:
Rebel Jail

ISBN 978-0-7851-9983-0

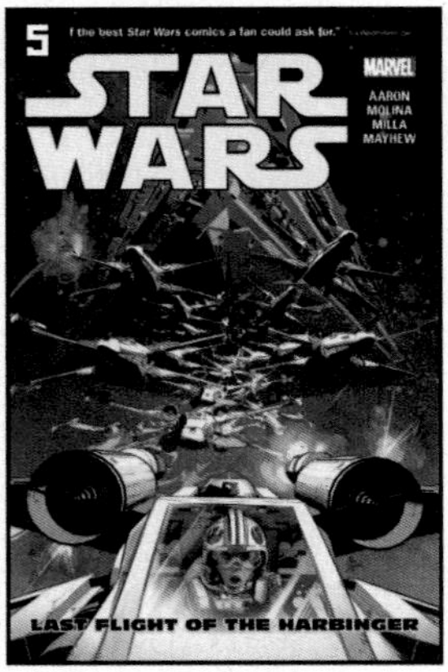
5
STAR WARS
MARVEL
AARON
MOLINA
MILLA
MAYHEW
LAST FLIGHT OF THE HARBINGER

Star Wars Vol. 4:
Last Flight of the Harbinger

ISBN 978-0-7851-9984-7

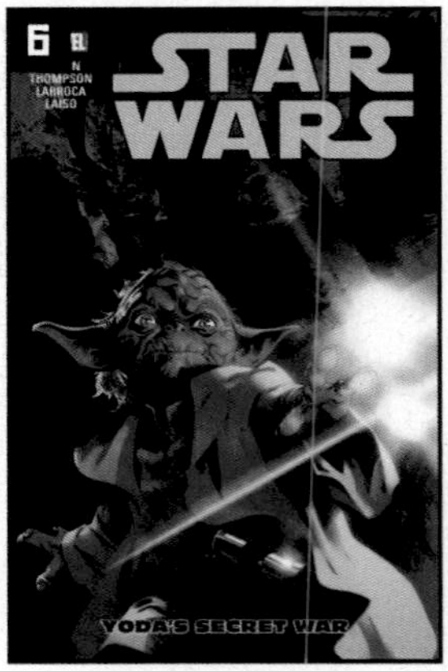
6
STAR WARS
THOMPSON
LARROCA
LAISO
YODA'S SECRET WAR

Star Wars Vol. 5:
Yoda's Secret War

ISBN 978-1-302-90265-0

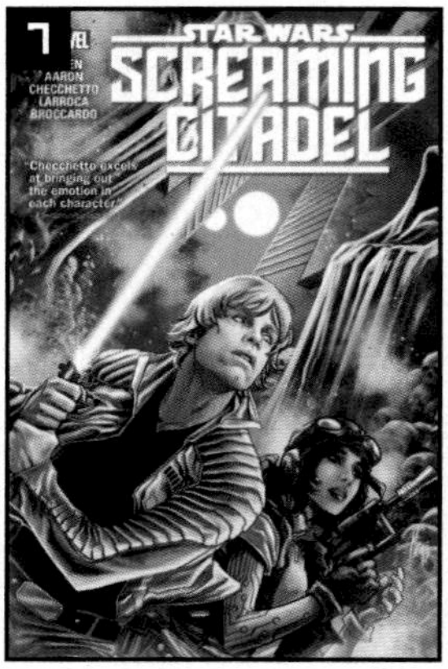
7
STAR WARS
SCREAMING CITADEL

Star Wars:
The Screaming Citadel
ISBN 978-1-302-90678-8

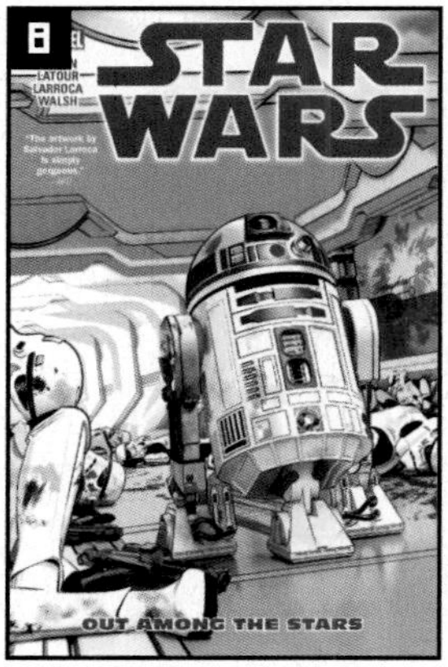
8
STAR WARS
OUT AMONG THE STARS

Star Wars Vol. 6:
Out Among the Stars
ISBN 978-1-302-90553-8

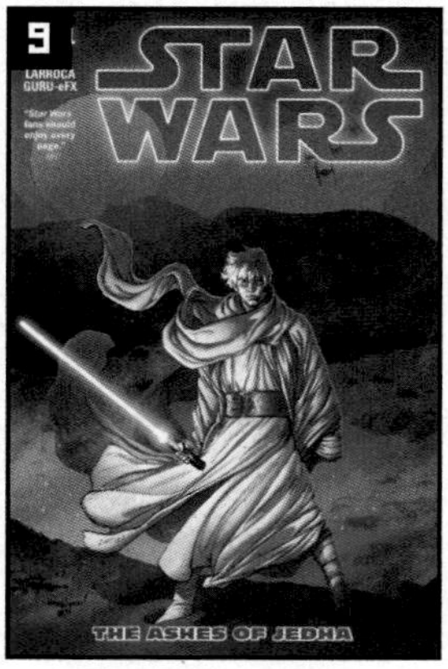
9
STAR WARS
THE ASHES OF JEDHA

Star Wars Vol. 7:
The Ashes of Jedha
ISBN 978-1-302-91052-5

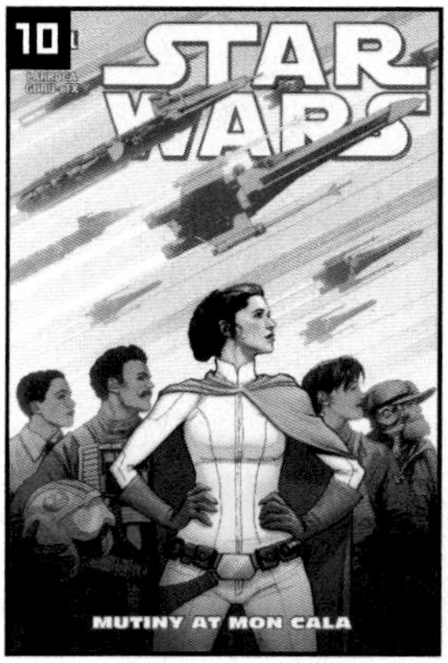
10
STAR WARS
MUTINY AT MON CALA

Star Wars Vol. 8:
Mutiny at Mon Cala
ISBN 978-1-302-91053-2

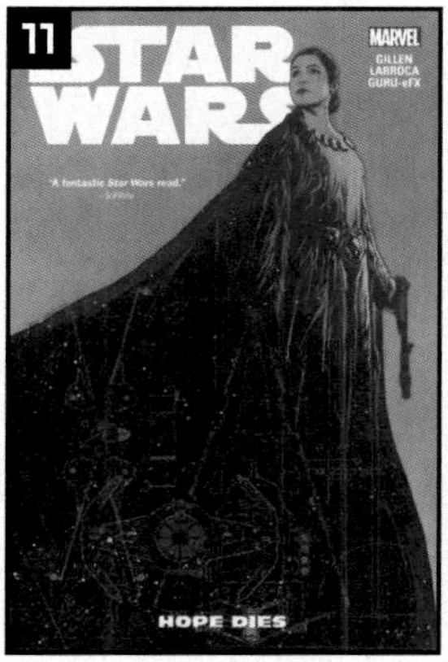
11
STAR WARS
MARVEL
GILLEN
LARROCA
GURU-eFX
HOPE DIES

Star Wars Vol. 9:
Hope Dies
ISBN 978-1-302-91054-9

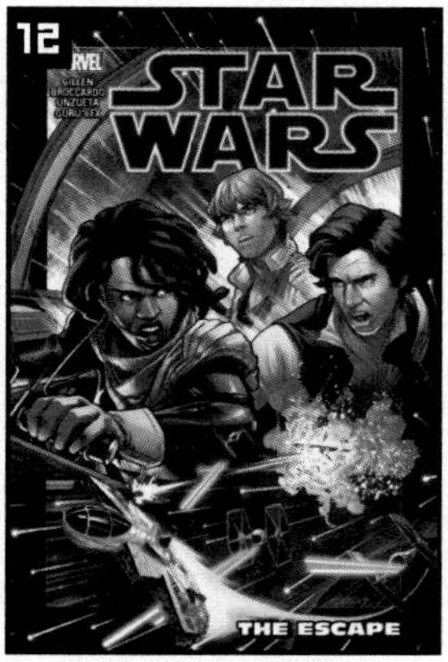
12
STAR WARS
THE ESCAPE

Star Wars Vol. 10:
The Escape
ISBN 978-1-302-91449-3

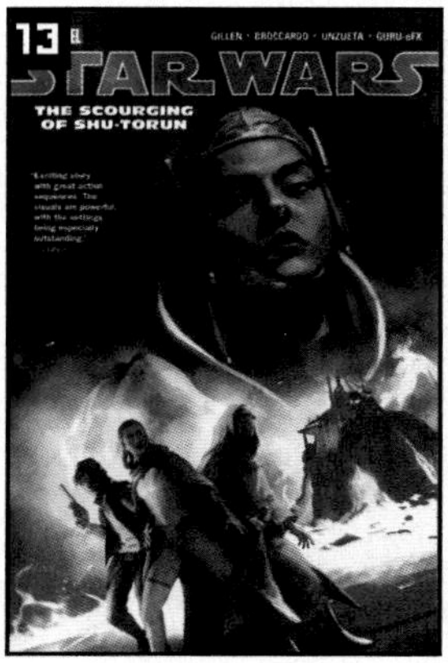
13
GILLEN · BROCCARDO · UNZUETA · GURU-eFX
STAR WARS
THE SCOURGING OF SHU-TORUN

Star Wars Vol. 11:
The Scourging of Shu-Torun
ISBN 978-1-302-91450-9

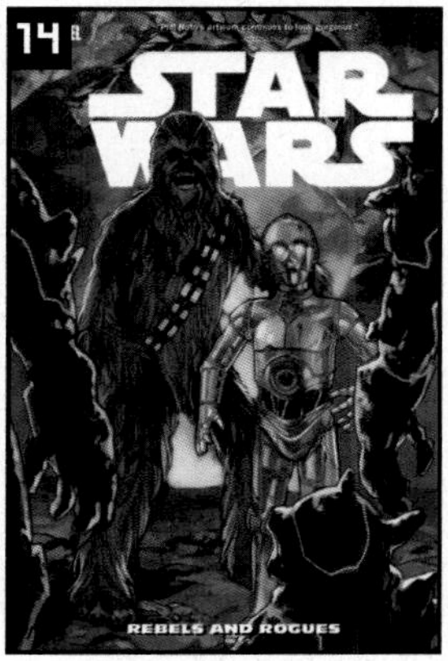
14
STAR WARS
REBELS AND ROGUES

Star Wars Vol. 12:
Rebels and Rogues
ISBN 978-1-302-91451-6

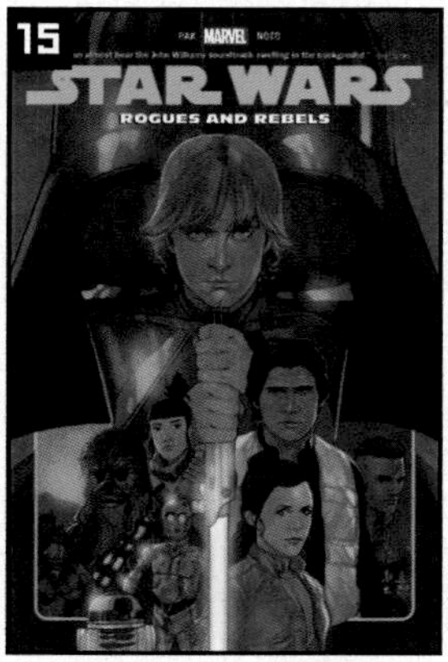
15
PAK
MARVEL
NOTO
STAR WARS
ROGUES AND REBELS

Star Wars Vol. 13:
Rogues and Rebels
ISBN 978-1-302-91450-9

WAY ACROSS THE GALAXY!

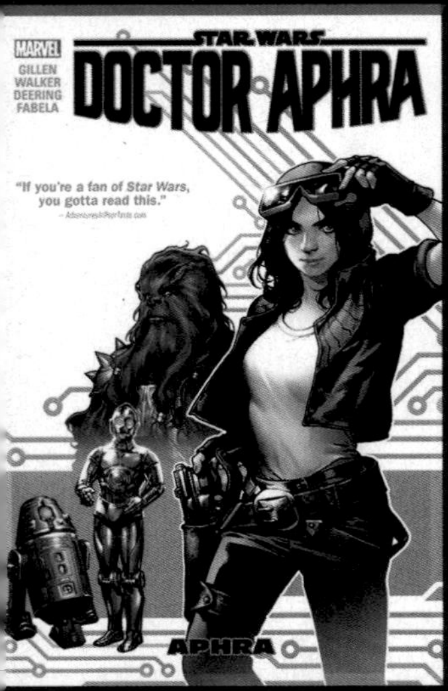

MARVEL
GILLEN
WALKER
DEERING
FABELA
STAR WARS
DOCTOR APHRA
"If you're a fan of Star Wars, you gotta read this."
APHRA

STAR WARS:
DOCTOR APHRA VOL. 1 –
APHRA TPB

ISBN: 978-1302913212

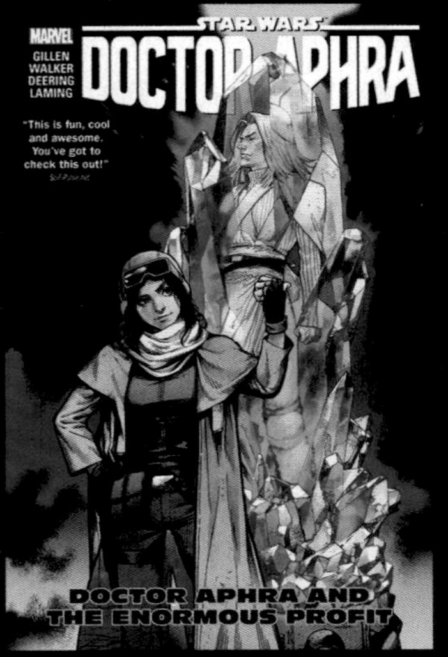

MARVEL
GILLEN
WALKER
DEERING
LAMING
STAR WARS
DOCTOR APHRA
"This is fun, cool and awesome. You've got to check this out!"
DOCTOR APHRA AND THE ENORMOUS PROFIT

STAR WARS:
DOCTOR APHRA VOL. 2 –
DOCTOR APHRA AND
THE ENORMOUS PROFIT TPB

ISBN: 978-1302907631

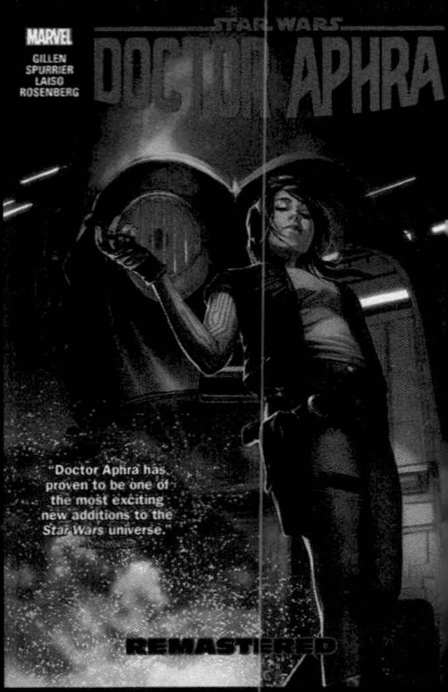

MARVEL
GILLEN
SPURRIER
LAISO
ROSENBERG
STAR WARS
DOCTOR APHRA
"Doctor Aphra has proven to be one of the most exciting new additions to the Star Wars universe."
REMASTERED

STAR WARS:
DOCTOR APHRA VOL. 3
REMASTERED TPB

ISBN: 978-1302911522

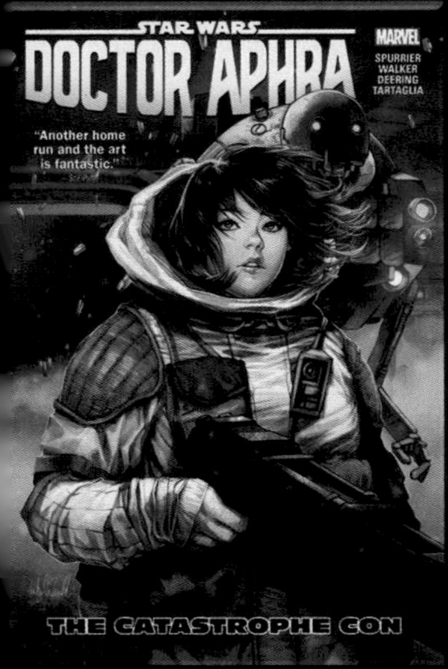

STAR WARS
DOCTOR APHRA
MARVEL
SPURRIER
WALKER
DEERING
TARTAGLIA
"Another home run and the art is fantastic."
THE CATASTROPHE CON

STAR WARS:
DOCTOR APHRA VOL. 4 –
THE CATASTROPHE
CON TPB

ISBN: 978-1302911539

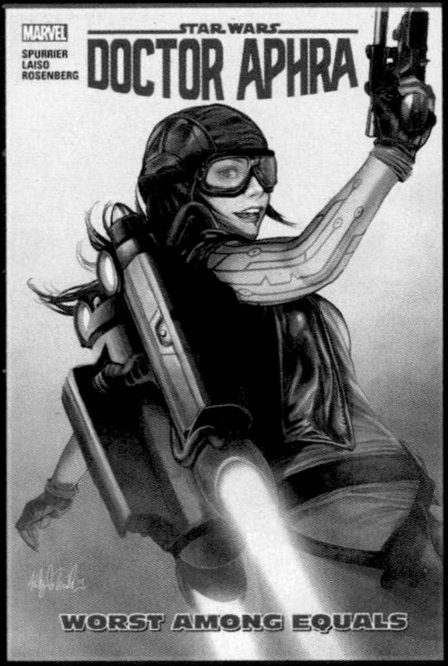

MARVEL
SPURRIER
LAISO
ROSENBERG
STAR WARS
DOCTOR APHRA
WORST AMONG EQUALS

STAR WARS:
DOCTOR APHRA VOL. 5 –
WORST AMONG
EQUALS TPB

ISBN: 978-1302914875

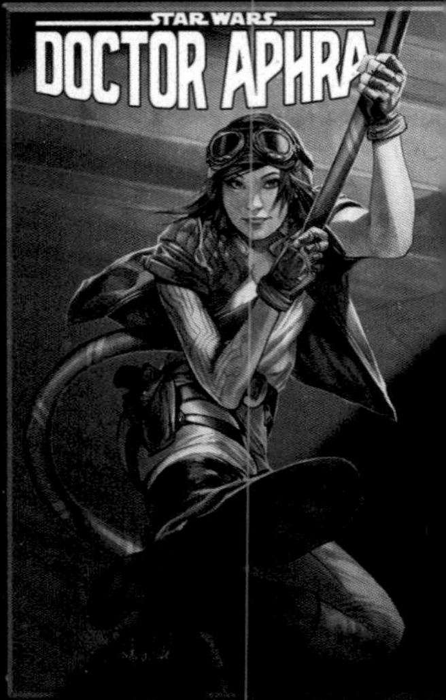

STAR WARS
DOCTOR APHRA

STAR WARS:
DOCTOR APHRA VOL. 6
UNSPEAKABLE REBEL
SUPERWEAPON TPB

ISBN: 978-1302914882